OPEN ROAD'S BEST OF

Honduras

by Charlie Morris

Open Road Travel Guides – designed for the amount of time you *really* have for your trip!

Open Road Publishing

Open Road's new travel guides.
Designed to cut to the chase.

You don't need a huge travel encyclopedia - you need a *selective guide* to steer you right. If you're going on vacation for a few weeks or less, get a guide that brings you the *best* of any destination for the amount of time you *really* have for your trip!

Open Road - the guide you need for the trip you want.

The New Open Road *Best Of* Travel Guides.
Right to the point.
Uncluttered.
Easy.

Open Road Publishing
P.O. Box 284, Cold Spring Harbor, NY 11724
www.openroadguides.com

ISBN 1-59360-069-0
Library of Congress Control No. 2006929778

About the Author

Charlie Morris is also the author of *Open Road's Best of Costa Rica, Open Road's Best of Belize,* and *Switzerland Guide.*

CONTENTS

Your Passport to the **Perfect Trip!**

Maps

PHOTO CREDITS

Front cover photo©Corbis. Back cover photo and top photo p. 1 januszl@flickr.com. The following photos are from Charlie Morris: pp. 9, 19, 67, 73, 129, 136, 138, 141, 142, 145, 147, 172 bottom, 227, 241, 242. The following photos are from Bruce Morris: pp. 20, 24, 25, 28, 47, 59, 137. The following photos are from flickr.com: p. 7: fatal Cleopatra; pp. 39, 41, 50 Kevin Reid; p. 43 DrewAndMerissa; p. 46 Aindrila; p. 72: Corinne; pp. 77, 85: Salvatore88; p. 80: Ardyiii ; p. 88: Tom-Riddle; pp. 89, 183, 222: Marcio Barrios; p. 92: Sprandall ; p. 94: mode; p. 95: lightpainter; p. 111, 114, 116, 164, 178: alodavicho; pp. 98, 235, 261: Blipem; p. 100: asorsz; p. 101: NG71; p. 104, 107: Ryan Henderson; p. 117: jcwrenn; p. 121: midnightinmoscow; p. 123: teerlinck; p. 144: MCMartinez84; p. 148: Pixel Drip; p. 150: The G's; p. 155: jgump 2; p. 156: aaronernestoortizlopez; pp. 149, 159, 170, 171: MacAllenBrothers; pp. 3 bottom, 163: Rebekah Travis; p. 166: Lyori; p. 167: Saira!; p. 168: wild8yam; p. 172 top, dweekly; p. 173, 195: chrishay; p. 174: hikarenchang; p. 176: Zoe Mosh; p. 177: gracias lempira; p. 182: bleuet/Anne-Marie; p. 184, 187: cjaxx; p. 191: Maryann...; p. 194: colleenjbarry; p. 200: arturotreminio; p. 206: Mr. Cavin; p. 221: ndbutter; p. 223: Justin Lee; p. 224: popularpatty; pp. 228, 229: Simon Marsh; pp. 3 top, 231: e_lepple; p. 234: danielandrewclem; p. 239, 240: endoftheworldresort; p. 247: egmb757lover; p. 251: mynameischance; p. 252: osmaster; p. 269: Eyvi. Note: the use of these photos does not represent an endorsement of this book or any services listed within by any of the photographers listed above.

1. INTRODUCTION

Honduras is an undiscovered tropical paradise. All the wonders of Central America are here: chalk-white Caribbean beaches, azure seas, vast tracts of untouched rain forest inhabited by colorful flowers and birds, mysterious Mayan ruins and colonial architecture slowly decaying in the steaming jungle.

Compared to well-trodden nearby tourist destinations such as Belize and Costa Rica, much of Honduras is **a new travel frontier**. Outside of the Bay Islands and the Mayan ruins of Copán, the country receives a mere trickle of North American visitors. Honduras came late to the ecotourism game, but the country is catching up quickly.

You won't find many five-star resorts, championship golf courses or big-bucks health spas here. But if you don't mind a little adventure, you'll be rewarded with the experience of visiting some of the largest remaining expanses of primary rain forest and mangrove wetlands in the Americas, unsullied by hordes of trampling, t-shirt-wearing tourists.

The greatest asset of this peaceful country is her people. The *Catrachos* are some of the friendliest folks you'll meet anywhere. Don't be surprised to be invited into a Honduran home to share a meal of beans and rice and maybe a sip of fiery local *guaro*. The people of Honduras are **a fascinating mix of cultures**, from the proud and independent Mestizos to the Garífuna of the Caribbean coast, with their lively *punta* music, to the Miskito and Pech in their remote jungles.

The activities are endless. The Bay Islands offer **diving and snorkeling** on coral walls that plummet thousands of feet into the abyss. **Fishing** is spectacular, with bonefish on the flats, tarpon and snook in the lagoons and billfish offshore. The rivers offer everything from world-class whitewater rafting to peaceful wildlife-observation trips through the jungle. The **beautiful mountain landscapes** are perfect for hiking, horseback riding and mountain biking.

Of course, many travelers also enjoy more sedate pursuits, such as sipping a cool drink while basking on a beautiful beach, and the opportunities for doing that in Honduras are second to none.

2. OVERVIEW

Honduras has a huge variety of landscapes and scenery for such a small country. You can explore the cloud forest-clad mountains and relax on pristine Caribbean beaches, all on the same trip. Cultural monuments range from ancient Mayan temples to Spanish forts and ornate colonial churches. There are fun activities for all interests and all levels of strenuousness. If you want to get deep in the jungle and be an ecotourist, or if your tastes run to action sports such as diving, fishing or whitewater rafting, you can find the trip of a lifetime here. Along the way, you'll find attractive and comfortable accommodations, exotic cuisine and charming local crafts.

The Bay Islands

These three small islands off the north coast – **Roatan, Guanaja** and **Utila** – seem more like a small Caribbean country in their own right than like a part of Honduras. The locals speak English with a Creole lilt, and the lobster and fresh fish taste great at a late-night cookout on the beach.

The coral reef that fringes the islands is one of the top diving destinations in the world, a fact that makes the Bay Islands by far Honduras's most visited region. Here you'll find luxury dive lodges as well as charming budget lodgings, and a fascinating mix of people grooving to some of the country's liveliest nightlife.

The North Coast

The Caribbean coastline alternates between lovely sand beaches and vast mangrove wetlands. This is the place to find your perfect tropical beach, with clear blue waters, fine white sand and swaying palm trees.

Some of the country's finest national parks are in this region. **Pico Bonito National Park** has wide expanses of primary rain forest among rugged peaks. The **Cangrejal River** offers rafting and kayaking on Class II-V rapids. **Jeanette Kawas** and **Cuero y Salado National Parks** show an entirely different ecosystem – mangrove wetlands teeming with birds, fish and animals.

Don't miss visiting one of the beachfront villages of the Garífuna people – their unique and colorful culture welcomes visitors. Locals and tourists alike love the lively party scenes in **La Ceiba** and **Tela**.

Copán & the West

The Mayan ruins of **Copán** are one of the largest and most interesting pre-Columbian sites in Central America. The city was a Mayan cultural capital, and the ruins are rich with sculpture and hieroglyphics. The many visitors find plenty to do in the region.

The area around Copán is a landscape of rugged hills, seldom visited by the tourist legions who troop through the ruins. Along the **Lenca Trail**, you'll find some of the country's most picturesque colonial villages.

The national park of **Celaque** features a mile-high cloud forest. Other splendid wilderness areas include easy-to-visit **Cusuco** and remote **Azul Meambar** and **Santa Bárbara**.

La Moskitia

Honduras's eastern region isn't just off the beaten path – there's no path at all! No roads lead to this vast wilderness, a lowland area where several rivers wind to the sea through huge tracts of mangrove-lined waterways. Indigenous groups such as the Miskito, Pech and Tawahka live out in the jungles with few concessions to the modern world.

Tegucigalpa & the South

The capital city offers the best urban experience in Honduras. Here you'll find impressive colonial architecture and the country's finest art museums.

Observing the Animals

The greatest thrill in Honduras is the chance to see wild animals going about their daily business in the forest. If you spend some time in one or more of the parks and preserves, your chances of seeing some critters are good. However, some animals are much more easily seen than others, and some visitors have unrealistic expectations.

White-nosed **coatis** (locally known as *pizotes*) are frequently seen, and they are friendly and fun. Monkeys are everyone's favorites, and they are pretty common (a little too common, say the owners of stolen sunglasses and hats). Honduras has three species of **monkeys**: spider monkeys, white-faced capuchins, and howler monkeys, whose cries boom through the forest.

We'd all love to see a **wild cat**, and Honduras has five species: pumas, jaguars, ocelots, margays and jaguarundis. Outside of a zoo or rehabilitation center, however, you're unlikely to spot one of these secretive, nocturnal predators.

If you really want to see some of the rarer forest denizens, visit one of the more remote parks, walk quietly, and take your hikes in the early morning or just before dusk. **I highly recommend hiring a local guide**, who can show you animals (and plants) that you would never see on your own.

At **La Tigra National Park**, you can enjoy the cloud forest and a 60-meter waterfall, just a short ride from the city. The surrounding mountain region has several nicely preserved colonial villages with delightful local handicrafts on offer.

Off the south coast, you can climb a volcano on the **Isla del Tigre**, and stroll black-sand beaches in a region that sees almost no foreign tourists.

Wildlife

Long protected simply by isolation and a lack of human inhabitants, Honduras's amazing wilderness areas are coming under pressure from increasing population and the demands of a modern economy. The government has begun to see the value of protecting these areas, and has created an impressive system of **national parks and nature reserves** throughout the country. Honduras has a wide variety of different climates and ecosystems, and the parks have been planned to preserve at least a sample of each one.

Visitors can expect to see lovely flowers, butterflies, hummingbirds, colorful parrots and macaws, coatis, monkeys, sloths, agoutis, crocodiles and iguanas. The lucky may see anteaters, peccaries, tapirs, ocelots, manatees or whales.

Bird Watching

With over 730 (and counting) bird species available for viewing, it's impossible for even the most hard-core birder to visit Honduras without adding significantly to their life list. Multicolored **scarlet macaws** and **toucans**, along with a wide assortment of Little Brown Birds (LBBs), flit through the forest, and vast flocks of **shore birds** patrol the coasts. If the birding gods smile on you, you may even see a **quetzal**, **trogon**, or **ferruginous pygmy owl**. Some lodges and tour companies cater specifically to birders.

Tropical River Cruises

One of the very best ways to get close to wildlife (without getting out of breath) is to take a **jungle cruise** along the spectacular mangrove canals along the North Coast, or through the lagoons

BELIZE
Bay Islands
Utila
Roatan
Guanaja
CARIBBEAN SEA
Puerto Cortés
Omoa
Tela
La Ceiba
Trujillo
LA MOSKITIA
Puerto Lempira
GUATEMALA
San Pedro Sula
Yoro
Copán Ruinas
Santa Rosa de Copán
Catacamas
Juticalpa
Gracias
Nueva Ocotepeque
Comayagua
Tegucigalpa
Danlí
Yuscarán
EL SALVADOR
Isla del Tigre
Gulf of Fonseca
Choluteca
NICARAGUA
PACIFIC OCEAN

and rivers of La Moskitia. Monkeys and crocodiles are close enough to touch (but don't).

Diving & Snorkeling

The **Bay Islands** are a world-class diving destination, with mile after mile of fringing reefs and spectacular walls. A rainbow of coral and tropical fish awaits you. A very well developed dive industry makes it easy to plan the dive vacation of a lifetime. **Utila** is famous as one of the cheapest places in the world to get your certification.

Because many of the reefs are located just a short way off shore, the wonders of the undersea world are easily accessible to **snorkelers** too. Even if you've never snorkeled before, you simply must give it a try before you leave Honduras.

Fishing

Honduras has a huge variety of fishing opportunities. In the **Bay Islands**, you can fish the flats for bonefish, permit, tarpon and barracuda. The reefs hold snapper, grouper and jacks - you might bring home a couple of yellowtail snapper for the grill. Offshore anglers battle with blue and white marlin, sailfish, wahoo, dorado, tuna, kingfish and shark.

In the deserted lagoons of **La Moskitia**, lucky anglers enjoy fantastic fishing for four different species of snook. **Brus Laguna** has some of the best tarpon fishing in the world. Silver kings that average 40-80 pounds will trash your tackle with astonishing leaps into the air.

Whitewater Rafting

A top global destination for whitewater rafting and kayaking, Honduras offers several rivers suitable for all skill levels. The **Cangrejal River**, on the boundary of the Pico Bonito Cloud forest park, offers class III and IV rapids. Racing through the lush green jungle is an unforgettable experience.

Mayan Ruins

The city of **Copán** was one of the major cultural sites of the ancient Mayan world. It's richer in sculptures, hieroglyphics and art treasures than any other known Mayan site. Its wonders include the Hieroglyphic Staircase with 1,500 intricate glyphs, the many carved stelae of the Forest of the Kings, the Ball Court with its macaw carvings, the rose-painted Temple of the Sun, and Altar Q with bas-reliefs of Copán's 16 rulers.

Other Mayan sites are scattered around the country, some of them as yet unexcavated. According to legend, an undiscovered White City lies somewhere out in the unexplored vastness of La Moskitia.

Colonial Architecture

The Spanish left a legacy of beautiful architecture. On the North Coast, you can visit two forts that they built to defend the young colony from British pirates. In **Tegucigalpa** and other cities, you can see some grand and imposing cathedrals. In the highlands, you can wander through delightful villages of tile roofs and cobblestone streets, with spectacular views and a perfect tropical mountain climate.

Garífuna Villages

The **Garífuna** of the North Coast are a unique culture, descended from a mix of Africans and Native American Caribs. Many of their picturesque villages, with thatched-roof huts and wooden fishing boats pulled up on the beach, welcome visitors. Beachfront open-air restaurants called *champas* serve fresh grilled fish.

The Garífuna's distinctive, rhythmic *punta* music is a staple at the North Coast's lively clubs and discos.

Taking the Kids

Hondurans love kids. Kids love the beach and anything to do with monkeys. In the Bay Islands and Copán, you'll find attractions specially aimed at kids, and most tourist areas of the country have organized tours and activities appropriate for the whole family.

Many lodging places have larger rooms available for family groups. Burgers, chicken, fried potatoes and other kid-friendly food is not hard to find. **Tropical fruits** are a special treat!

Catracho Cuisine

Typical Honduran cuisine features beans and rice, tortillas, cheese and other Latin American staples. Try a *baleada* (the local version of a burrito) or *anafre* (a sort of hot bean dip). Excellent fresh **seafood** is available all along the coast, especially in the Bay Islands, where the local fare has more of a Caribbean flavor. Ripe **tropical fruits** and locally-grown **coffee** are not to be missed.

Honduras By the Numbers

Location:	Central America, with Guatemala and El Salvador to the west, Nicaragua to the southeast
Land Area:	112,090 sq km
Highest Point:	Cerro Las Minas, 2,870 m
Coastline:	820 km
Biodiversity:	215 mammal species, 730 bird species, 250 reptile and amphibian species
Population:	7,300,000
Languages:	Spanish, English (in Caribbean region), indigenous languages
Life Expectancy:	69 years
Literacy:	76%
Poverty rate:	53%
Government:	Democratic republic
Independence:	1821 (from Spain)
Economy:	Agriculture: 14%; Industry: 31%; Services: 55%

3. WILDLIFE

If you're looking for a place to observe tropical animals and plants in their natural habitat, then Honduras is one of the best choices you could make. Because of its location and geography, Honduras has an astounding variety of wildlife. While Honduras's wilderness areas are under threat from several quarters, the country still has vast areas where the animals roam free, undisturbed by human contact.

Within the borders of this small nation are 215 mammal species, 730 bird species, 250 reptile and amphibian species, and countless thousands of plant species (and this is just what's been described so far: when it comes to plants and small invertebrates, there are thought to be thousands more that scientists haven't gotten around to classifying yet).

With **over 40 national parks, refuges and reserves** of various kinds, the critters have plenty of space to roam around, and you are welcome to pay them a visit. Much of the tourist industry is built around showing off the country's natural wonders. Plenty of lodgings and tour operators are at your disposal to help you get a glimpse of those exotic animals and plants.

Honduras has **many different habitats**, including rain forest, cloud forest, dry broadleaf forest, pine savannah, marshes and mangrove swamps. Each has its own unique ecosystem, and its own set of inhabitants.

Only a few parks have much in the way of tourist facilities. Your best bet is usually to make arrangements with a local guide or tour company. With a guide, you'll learn much more about the local ecosystem, and probably see animals you would never have seen on your own. **Sloths**, for example, are hard to spot unless you know what you're looking for – to you or me, they tend to look like a lump of moss on a branch. At some parks, going with a guide is your only option: some of the best are accessible only by boat, and the most remote have no trails at all, and require hacking a path with a machete.

Here are some of the wild creatures you may hope to see, starting with the most common.

Mammals

The **white-nosed coati** (*nasua narica*), which locals call a *pizote* (pronounced pee-SOH-tay), is a cute and gregarious creature with a long tail and a prehensile nose, which it uses to snuffle among the leaf litter on the forest floor for bugs, small lizards and frogs.

You're almost certain to see at least a few *pizotes*, as they are quite common, diurnal (active during the day), and not particularly shy. *Al contrario*, at some of the more frequented parks, where people have been feeding them, you may be accosted by bands of them begging for goodies. Their antics can be amusing, but you really shouldn't feed them or any other wild animals.

Honduras also has **raccoons** (*procyon lotor*), the same as the familiar North American variety. They occupy much the same niche as the *pizotes*, but are active at night. Another commonly seen forest dweller is the **agouti**, which looks something like a large brown guinea pig.

Honduras has three species of monkeys. The most common is the playful **spider monkey** (*ateles geoffroyi*). You may also see the **white-faced capuchin** (*cebus capucinus*). The large black **howler monkeys** (*alouatta palliate*) make a loud noise that sounds less like howling than like the barking of a large dog. Even if you don't see them, you're sure to hear them far off in the forest.

Sloths are not rare, but are tough to spot in the wild, at least without a local guide. There are two varieties, the two-toed (*choloepus hoffmanni*) and the three-toed (*bradypus variegatus*). Sloths spend most of their time in trees snoozing, inching along branches at a snail's pace, and eating leaves. Ironically, their slow and sedentary ways protect them from predators. Apparently, it's not only humans who tend to mistake a sloth for a lump of moss on a branch.

The very patient may catch a glimpse of some of the rarer mammals, including **anteaters**, **coyotes**, **foxes**, and the **tayra**, a sleek weasel-like carnivore. Herds of **peccaries**, like small wild pigs, root around on the forest floor. You may well see the signs of their depredations. **River otters** are especially fascinating to watch. Small forest mammals range from exotic ones such as the **kinkajou** (*potos flavus*) to more mundane species such as **porcupines, armadillos, skunks** and dozens of species of rodents.

There are eight species of **opossum** and over 100 species of **bats**! The country's largest animal is **Baird's tapir**, a pachyderm that looks something like a rhinoceros without any horns. The tapir (locally called *danto*) is nowadays very rare because of over-hunting.

Honduras has no less than five wild cats. The kings

of the jungle are the magnificent spotted **jaguar** (*panthera onca*) and the **puma** (*puma concolor*), a tawny relative of the North American cougar and Florida panther. Smaller felines are the beautiful little spotted **ocelot** (*leopardus pardalis*) and **margay** (*leopardus wiedii*). The slightly larger **jaguarundi** (*herpailurus yaguarondi*) looks like a strange cross between a bear and a cat.

The puddy-tats are fairly rare, mostly nocturnal, and very shy of people. Your chances of seeing one in the wild are almost nil, unless you spend a good bit of time in one of the more remote reserves. There are a few small zoos and rehabilitation centers where you can see captive cats.

Don't Overlook the Small Stuff

We all want to see something really cool, such as a large mammal or a particularly exotic bird. But this isn't a TV show, and the critters don't always perform on a schedule that's convenient for us. **Don't obsess about trophy sightings** so much that you miss the less glamorous, but fascinating, beauty all around. Trees, flowers, lush tropical greenery, fruits and spices, butterflies and all kinds of interesting bugs (take a night hike to see some really exotic creepy-crawlies) are easy to see, going about their daily business unnoticed by humans who rush by, searching for the elusive quetzal.

Reptiles & Amphibians

Snappy saurians may make you think twice about swimming in the rivers. The lagoons of the Moskitia and around Tela Bay are stiff with **crocodiles** and the smaller **caimans**. You'll see a few on almost any river boat ride.

There's a huge variety of snakes (100 species), including the **boa constrictor**, the bright yellow **eyelash palm pit viper**, the **fer-de-lance** (or *terciópelo*), one of the world's deadliest snakes, and the **bushmaster**, the world's largest pit viper, which can grow to 10 feet long and is locally called *matabuey* (ox-killer)! Watch your step in the forest, but don't worry – snakebites are rare. There's a variety of brightly-colored frogs, called **poison-arrow frogs** because the local Indians make poison arrows from them. According to legend, if you lick one you'll get high, but I'd stick to rum if I were you. Notable lizards include enormous **green iguanas**, and the **Jesus Christ lizard**, named for its ability to "walk on water" by skipping quickly across the surface.

Birds

The variety of birds is simply amazing. As this small country has more bird species than most continents, birders (or *twitchers*, as the English call them) have plenty of opportunities to add species to their *life lists*. Only a true birder can understand the excitement of seeing the endemic **honduran emerald**, or the rare **red-throated parakeet**, **green-breasted mountain-gem** or **vitelline warbler**.

Everyone, however, loves such flamboyant fliers as **toucans** and **toucanets**, **hummingbirds** (16 varieties, each more brightly colored than the last) and Honduras's iconic bird, the **scarlet macaw**. These very large members of the parrot family are, despite the name, arrayed in all the colors of the rainbow. You'll see them throughout the country, munching out in the almond trees (their images you'll see everywhere, on t-shirts, refrigerator magnets, and the like).

Some birds have attained mythic status, like the **trogon**, the **resplendent quetzal**, the **harpy eagle** and the **curassow**, a ground bird that looks something like a well-dressed turkey. At night, you may see one of the many stately species of **owls**. Coastal regions teem with majestic **herons** (including the rufescent tiger heron), **egrets**, **limpkins**, **ibises**, **jabirú storks**, **spoonbills**, **cormorants**, **ducks** and other shore birds.

Birders will find some action almost anywhere in the country. To maximize your sightings, visit both mountain forests and coastal wetlands. For example, a North Coast trip that includes **Pico**

Birding Checklist

With the help of one of the field guides or websites listed below and on the next page, you should be able to see a number of these birds on your trip!

Water Birds

Muscovy Duck ___
Cormorant ___
Anhinga ___
Frigatebird ___
Tiger Heron ___
Snowy Egret ___
Blue Heron ___
Night Heron ___
Ibis ___
Jabirú ___
Wood Stork ___
Purple Gallinule ___
Sandpiper ___
Kingfisher ___
Waterthrush ___

Forest Birds

Vulture ___
Osprey ___
Hawk ___
Caracara ___
Chachalaca ___
Parrot ___
Parakeet ___
Hummingbird ___
Trogon ___
Toucan ___
Woodpecker ___
Flycatcher ___
Kiskadee ___
Swallow ___
Catbird ___
Warbler ___
Tanager ___
Grackle ___
Oriole ___
Oropéndola ___

Bonito and **Punta Sal** or **Punto Izopo** will give you the birds of both worlds. Yes, your chances of seeing something really rare are better in one of the very remote areas such as **La Moskitia** or one of the almost-inaccessible parks of the interior. However, don't overlook more mundane locations. Tourist attractions such as shade-grown coffee farms and archaeological sites can have a surprisingly large number of birds, which may be easier to see at such partially-cleared sites than they are in the deep forest.

Honduras's most famous bird man is **Robert Gallardo**. His web site at www.birdsofhonduras.com has lots of material about the country's birds, as well as information on guided tours focused on birding. Tom Jenner's site at tomjenner.com/mayanbirding is another valuable resource.

Bird books include *A Guide to the Birds of Mexico and Northern Central America* by Howell and Webb, and the more recent *Birding Honduras: A Checklist and Guide* by Mark Bonta and David Anderson (see www.birdinghonduras.com).

Flora

Plant lovers will likewise be in Heaven. Here are thousands of exotic plant species. Visitors from subtropical climes will find familiar plants gone wild – have you ever seen a palm tree with a 10-foot diameter trunk and 30-foot-long fronds?

The tropical rain forest has many more species of trees than its temperate counterpart. Whereas a typical North American forest is dominated by only a few species of trees, Honduran forests have thousands. Many produce edible fruits or other useful products. A few are dangerous, like the manzanillo tree, locally called *el hinchador,* which has a caustic latex sap. Flowering trees such as the jacaranda add seasonal splashes of color.

Epiphytes (plants that grow on other plants) such as **orchids** (*orquídeas* [or-KEE-day-oss] in Spanish) and **bromeliads** occupy every available square inch in the dripping, humid cloud forest. There are hundreds of species of orchids here, and the country is a major supplier to the garden trade.

Orchids are not so easy to view in the wild, as most grow high up in trees. Fortunately, you can visit the National Collection of Orchids at **Lancetilla Botanical**

Garden (see Chapter 5). In fact, Lancetilla is a must-visit for any plant lover. The species are all neatly labeled, and you'll learn a lot about fruit trees and other cultivated plants that you aren't likely to see in the rain forest. Hummingbirds and butterflies are frequent visitors.

Dozens of wild and crazy **fruits** are available, both whole and fresh-squeezed. Whether familiar fruits such as mangos, papayas and pineapples (which are much sweeter and juicier here than the mass-shipped varieties you find at the supermarket in Des Moines) or exotic varieties such as *mamotes, pejibayes, chiverres* and *carambolas,* I highly recommend trying them whenever offered.

You can learn more about tropical forests at www.nature.org. For those of a scientific disposition, **NatureServe** (www.natureserve.org/infonatura) has a searchable database of every species of bird, mammal, and amphibian found in Honduras and neighboring countries.

Marine Life

The magnificent menagerie doesn't end at the water's edge. **Manatees** paddle around the mangrove estuaries of the Caribbean.

Nine types of **dolphin** make their homes in Honduran waters, and several species of whales, including **sei, sperm, killer** and **pilot whales**, visit from time to time.

There are seven sea turtle species in the world, and four of them nest on Honduras's beaches. Female sea turtles return year after year to the beaches where they were born, and lay their eggs in the sand. When the babies hatch, they scamper to the sea en masse.

Once upon a time, **hawksbill, loggerhead, green and leatherback sea turtles** were common visitors to both the Caribbean and

Pacific coasts. Unfortunately, they have been hunted almost to extinction, both for their meat and for their eggs, which some fools believe to have aphrodisiac properties. On the beaches of **Plaplaya** in La Moskitia, a wildlife organization runs a protection program, guarding the nests from poachers so the turtles can do their thing undisturbed.

Some of the most impressive ocean wildlife is to be seen beneath the surface. The **Bay Islands** are one of the top diving destinations in the world, with an extensive fringing reef system that features walls that drop off to thousands of feet in depth.

Divers will see a rainbow of **coral** and **tropical fish**, including gobies, blennies, sergeant-majors and angelfish, to say nothing of lobsters, octopi and colorful little shrimp. Coral around the world is dying from increased water temperatures, but Honduras still has a lot of live coral.

The largest fish in the sea, the **whale shark**, frequents the area around Guanaja at certain times of the year, and divers can swim with these gentle giants.

Anglers haul in a vast variety of species. Familiar game species such as **sailfish**, **marlin**, **tuna**, **wahoo**, **jack**, **tarpon**, **snook**, **snapper**, **grouper** and **dorado** (the local name for the colorful and delicious fish also known as dolphin or mahi-mahi) are plentiful and large.

What is Ecotourism, Anyway?

Ecotourism is a term that you'll hear kicked around quite a bit on your travels in Honduras. Of course, most visitors to the country are here to enjoy the natural wonders, but does that make us all ecotourists? Does spending a couple of hours strolling through the forest with a herd of other Gringos make you an ecotourist? Or must you spend a week helping the students with their research at some remote biological station to earn the title?

In fact, ecotourism is a state of mind, **an ideal of sustainable, minimally invasive tourism** that both visitors and those in the tourism industry should strive for (alas, both groups often fall far short of the ideal). Ecotourists leave no litter, don't feed or interfere with the animals, and consume nothing but products that are harvested in a sustainable manner. A true ecolodge recycles and conserves, releases no waste into the environment, strives to use renewable energy, and generally tries to have as little impact on the natural habitat as possible.

Ecotourism is also about preserving a very important species called local workers. One of the central concepts of ecotourism is the idea that local people can make a better living by helping tourists enjoy the rain forest than they could by chopping it down. Good ecotourists patronize local businesses, and buy local products whenever possible.

The **International Ecotourism Society** defines ecotourism as "responsible travel to natural areas that conserves the environment and improves the well-being of local people." Their web site at www.ecotourism.org includes lists of environmentally friendly lodges and tour operators.

4. THE BAY ISLANDS

The **Bay Islands** are the most visited part of Honduras, and one of the Caribbean's top destinations for divers and snorkelers. Magnificent reefs lie just offshore. Anglers seeking gigantic bonefish, tarpon, tuna or marlin know the secrets of the islands' rarely visited flats and offshore trolling areas.

Roatan is growing tourist-related businesses with the speed of tropical plants in the sun, making it an interesting destination for those who seek the island experience (hammocks, umbrella drinks, seafood restaurants and funky seaside bars). People like myself, who evaluate spectacular beaches around the world, consider the beaches in Roatan to be as stunning as those found anywhere, rivaling those of Tahiti and the Seychelles.

Utila is known as a target for budget travelers and a haven for alternative lifestyles. It's also known for swimming with whale sharks, great diving and fishing. **Guanaja** has no roads, a few chickens and pigs, a few wonderful dive resorts and great fishing. There's not much else, but isn't that enough? The tiny **Cayos Cochinos** have a biological research station and a single resort.

All three islands have **spectacular diving, fishing and beaches**. Roatan is far more developed with tourist infrastructure, and has more "things to do" than the other much smaller islands. This might make for a good reason to spend most of your holiday time on Roatan – or a good reason to skip the bigger island and head for one of the smaller alternatives, away from the crowd.

Utila and Guanaja offer resorts of similar quality, more peaceful surroundings and, if anything, even better diving and fishing than Roatan. Many popular dive activities, swimming with whale sharks for instance, happen near the smaller two islands, with Roatan-based divers travelling by boat for an hour each way.

Of course the larger tourist crowds on Roatan also mean more nightlife, shopping and touristy "attractions." If you want to party, party, party in the bars, or if you have non-diving family members or kids who are going to want some other tourist activities, then Roatan is the place for you. If you want peace and quiet in the evenings after a day of diving or fishing, and are satisfied to hang around your resort bar in the evening, then go to one of the smaller islands.

It's easy to get from island to island, with boats leaving at various times every day. Roatan itself is large enough that you need to think about where on the island you want to stay in order to be close to the activities you are interested in. It's only about 30 miles long, but it can take an hour to get from one part of the island to another, so you should plan to stay close to the dive or fishing operations you plan on using.

ONE GREAT DAY IN ROATAN

If we plan carefully, we can have a quick visit with the inhabitants of the coral reef and the tropical forest, eat a lot of great seafood and lie around on one of the world's finest beaches – all in one day!

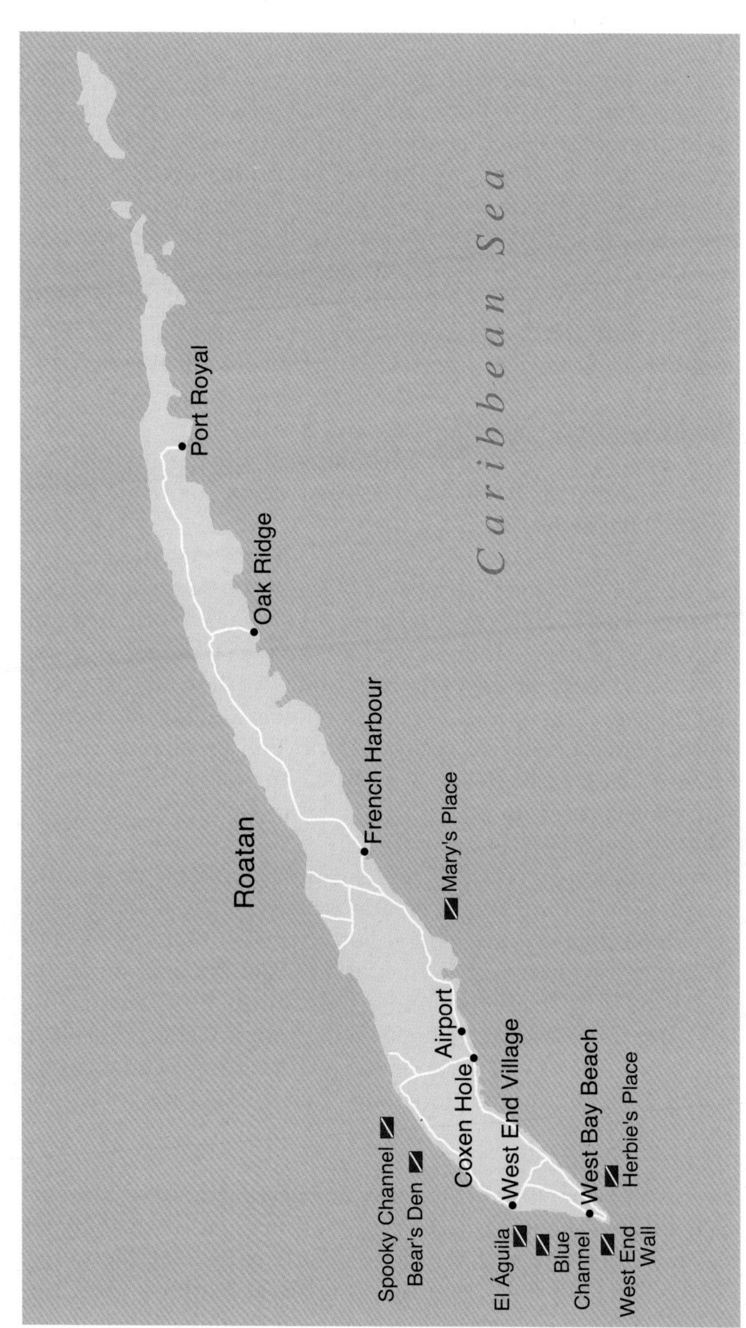
Caribbean Sea
Roatan
Port Royal
Oak Ridge
French Harbour
Mary's Place
Airport
Coxen Hole
West End Village
West Bay Beach
Herbie's Place
Spooky Channel
Bear's Den
El Águila
Blue Channel
West End Wall

Morning

The best way to be sure we get to do everything we want in one day is to hire a car and driver, who will pick us up and drop us off at any of the island resorts or the cruise ship dock. We can arrange for a van through **Librería Casi Todo**, Coxen Hole (Tel. 445-1944) for about $40 per person. Or, try **Theris** (Email therisdixon@yahoo.com) for a private tour. Or we could simply take taxis from place to place, which is fairly economical if we can split the cost among a group of three or four people. Our driver will certainly give us the inside scoop on island culture, telling us about their pirate past and their Hurricane Mitch experiences.

The living coral reefs that surround Roatan are what makes it such a magnificent tourist destination. Enjoying the reefs by snorkeling, scuba diving or, at the least, seeing them from a glass-bottom boat is the first thing to do.

For a self-guided snorkeling tour of the reefs, **Bay Island Beach Resort** (Tel. 445-3020) maintains an underwater snorkeling trail with small numbered signs pointing out the sights and explaining some of the ecology of the reef system. All the snorkeling stuff you'll need, a place to change and showers are available right there. Cold drinks and good seafood are also handy at Bay Island's **Deep Ted's Beach Bar and Grill**. Scarf a fish sandwich and some conch fritters.

If you are scuba certified, you can do a two-tank dive in the morning, with Bay Island or almost any of the island's other numerous dive centers. You should be able to rent all of your equipment, get in two boat dives and be back just after lunch, for under $80 per person. Pick a dive operator such as **Bananarama Dive Beach Resort** (Tel. 445-5005) or **Anthony's Key Resort** in Sandy Bay (Tel. 445-3003), and you can rent the latest underwater digital cameras for vacation snaps that will impress everyone back in Ardmore.

If you don't want to get your feet wet, but want to see what all the excitement is about, a trip over the reefs in a glass bottom boat is the way to go. **Underwater Paradise** is based at Half Moon Bay Cabins (Tel. 445-4047), and the **Coral Reef Explorer** (Tel. 336-

5597) is located at West Point. Call them to confirm departure times. Both go out for about an hour and are definitely worth the trip. You get a good look at the reef and will probably get to see dolphins whizzing by at some point. The water is quite clear and the shallow reefs the boats float over are where the fanciest coral and prettiest colors are.

We've got time to have lunch at only one place on Roatan, so that needs to be **Hole in the Wall**, where we'll chase down our favorite tropical beverages with a fish or lobster sandwich. Be sure to try the conch fritters.

Afternoon

Now we'll enjoy some of the aboveground natural wonders of the island. **Carambola Botanical Garden**, just across from Anthony's Key in Sandy Bay, offers a one-hour walk through tropical gardens and a splendid view over the bay from the top of the ridge. *Info:* Tel. 445-3117. $5.

Tropical Treasures Bird Park, also in Sandy Bay, has a variety of macaws and other colorful birds from Honduras and all over the tropics. *Info:* Tel. 445-1314.

If you have kids in tow who need to be tired out, try **Gumbalimba Park** (www.gumbalimbapark.com; Tel. 914-9196) for a hike through their gardens and a screaming ride on the ziplines. The entry fee is a stiff $40, but the park goodies include 11 zipline platforms, a climbing wall and nice trails through tropical forests.

Evening

After all that action and adventure, we'll take a stroll on the beach near West End and consume more tropical beverages at a small bar such as **Foster's**, then head back to the ship or our resort for some hammock time. We deserve it after such a long and strenuous day.

A FANTASTIC ROATAN WEEKEND

There's plenty to do on Roatan, and a whole weekend gives you enough time to get a good sample of all the island has to offer: **snorkeling, scuba diving, fishing, swimming,** eating seafood in **funky beach restaurants** and sipping umbrella drinks by the pool.

Friday Evening

Unless you get in early enough to go diving, spend Friday afternoon checking out the beach at West End and sampling the delights of any tropical bars in the area that catch your eye. Try the piña coladas at the **Monkey Bar**. Enjoy your resort's pool and hammocks or have an introductory snorkel – there are wonderful shallow reefs just feet off the beach.

Indulge yourself in a wonderful seafood dinner at **Chez Pascal** in the Island Pearl Hotel. Since you're on vacation, it's okay to splurge on the lobster. And the fancy drink afterwards. Leave a nice tip. Drift off after dinner for tropical drinks at yet another funky beach bar like **Al's Disco** in French Harbour. Their conch fritters are famous. Go back to your resort relatively early, to be up early for a full morning of diving.

Saturday Morning

In the morning one of the many dive operators will pick you up at your hotel for a ride to the dive boat. If you're staying at a dedicated dive resort, you probably won't have to do any more than walk to the end of the dock to get to your dive boat. Carb up at the breakfast buffet – you'll be burning plenty of calories soon enough.

If you've made arrangements in advance with your dive operator, you'll be able to make the most of your dive time. Choose most of your dives in advance, working with your divemaster to make sure you don't spend too much time zipping around in the boat between sites that are spread out around the island. The best thing is to give your divemaster a list of the sites you particularly want to see and the type of diving that interests you and your group the most.

An easy start to the day's diving is **Valley of the Kings**. This site is near both CoCo View and Fantasy Island resorts. The dive profile begins quite shallow with plenty of coral and small fish. You can push on down over the top of the wall as deep as you feel comfortable. This is a great combination of a shallow dive with a massive wall nearby. Look underneath the huge coral formations to spot octopi, lobsters and perhaps a large grouper.

A good nearby choice for a second dive is the **Prince Albert.** This wreck was sunk in about 85 feet of water and is mostly in one piece. Follow the buoy line down to the bottom and head south. The wreck will loom up in front of you. If you are quiet about it and get to the wreck before too many people have scared them off, you might see some really huge grouper or pelagics that like to hang near the wreck snagging small fish. These fish are attracted to structure and the small fish it holds, but they are going to spook quickly when the gringo divers show up, so it's nice to get down to the wreck area quickly and as unobtrusively as possible.

After the morning dives, resist any soggy sandwiches offered on the boat and hold out for a good seafood lunch at **Casa Romeo's** (Tel. 455-5518). Try the conch chowder and go ahead and splurge on squid appetizers and a lobster entrée. The restaurants at both **CoCo View** and **Fantasy Island** will always have a seafood selection on the lunch buffet. I suggest gorging on seafood as much as possible while you are on your all-too-brief vacation in the Caribbean - once you get back to Carbondale fresh yellowtail won't be on the menu at your local Captain D's. Sample fritters every day.

Saturday Afternoon

In the afternoon, it's time to enjoy some of the finest beaches in the Caribbean. The finest beaches in the Bay Islands are at West Bay, and they are right up there with anyone's opinion of the most beautiful beaches in the world. Alas, their beauty is no secret, and they are mobbed most of the time.

West End Beach is the place to see and be seen. The beaches in front of Tabanya Beach Resort and the Henry Morgan resorts are where most of the cruise ship visitors end up. **Keyhole Beach** near Mar Vista Bay is one of my favorites. It's small but secluded and usually empty.

If you don't make it to West Bay, the beach in front of your resort will do just fine. Spend the afternoon swimming, strolling on the sand and slurping umbrella drinks. And remember that there are excellent little reefs in easy swimming distance from many of Roatan's beaches. I highly recommend getting in some snorkeling.

Be aware that although many of the resorts in the Bay Islands are right smack dab on a beautiful beach, many of them are not. Be sure to check web sites, correspond with other travelers and call ahead to be sure your destination is blessed with beautiful white sand.

Saturday Evening

Dinner in the village at a funky palm-roofed, open-air restaurant such as **Eagle Ray's Bar & Grill**, West End, is what's on for tonight. Seafood is what's on the menu. They usually have a couple of lobster plates, and the fresh fish sandwiches are legendary. They are known for their tropical fruit drinks. There is a vast, relaxing view out to sea. Get a table on the patio so you can soak up the tropical ambiance.

Check to see if they have any live music planned for the evening. If they do, order another round of drinks after eating and relax.

If not, ask who's playing at **Foster's**. Foster's is a good place to sip brew, rum or tequila and soak up some good sounds in the casual island atmosphere. Occasionally, musicians in the islands on their own tropical holidays pass through and may sit in. Take a taxi back to your resort. Resist the temptation to walk on the beach in the moonlight unless you have a large dog with you.

Diving & Flying

You don't want to get the bends at 30,000 feet on the flight back to Newark. This means it is a bad idea to scuba dive on the same day as flying. The pressurized cabins of modern airliners are usually pressurized at significantly less than sea level. If your body is still slowly expelling nitrogen absorbed while breathing compressed air on a recent dive, flying with a low atmospheric pressure could trigger problems that would not occur at sea level pressures. This doesn't apply to snorkelers, because they don't breathe compressed air. **So: Scuba divers shouldn't dive within 24 hours before a flight!**

Sunday

If you are flying, skip scuba diving today. You'll probably be checking out of your lodge around noon, so morning activities are limited. For a change, try some breakfast goodies at **Rudy's** in West End. Go for the banana pancakes and pick one of their fresh fruit juices. They do not serve conch fritters at breakfast. Take a long walk on **West Bay Beach**. On the way back to your resort you should stop at **Tropical Treasures Bird Park** in Sandy Bay (Tel. 445-1314) to see scarlet macaws, great green macaws, blue and gold macaws, and even Hans macaws. You can get some great photos here.

A WEEKEND OF DIVING ON ROATAN

A weekend is just enough time to see a good sampling of the **dive sites around Roatan**. The diving is so good around Roatan that there's really no need to travel to Utila or Cayos Cochinos, as good as they are, for memorable reef visits.

Friday Afternoon & Evening

Assuming an arrival in early afternoon, the best thing to do is head immediately to your lodging of choice to drop off your luggage and head for the dock.

If you can, **communicate with the divemaster at your resort** by email or phone before your arrival. With the divemaster's advice, select the dive sites you are most interested in. Caves, walls, a wide variety of wrecks, drift dives, dolphin dives, shark dives – the list of dive types and marked dive sites goes on and on.

Diving Buddy Selection!

It's a good idea to be sure the people you are diving with over a few days have **similar interests and skill levels** as yourself, so you won't spend your valuable vacation time diving in areas that hold little interest for you. If you like drift dives best, floating around quietly looking at fish and coral, you do not want to spend your time poking in and out of caves. So select your dive buddies with care!

The fewer other divers in the boat with you, the better. **Try to arrange in advance for a "four pack" or "six pack" boat.** You also need to consider the skill levels of the people you are diving with when selecting sites. Beginners are either bored or scared at some of the deeper sites, while advanced divers may get bored spending hour after hour in shallow water. Roatan is narrow but about 30 miles long, with reefs surrounding just about the whole island. You could spend an entire day just motoring around without even getting

much diving done. Try to pick a group of sites for your weekend that are more or less in an area not too awfully far from your resort. The west end of the island has a few more famous dive sites, but those sites are also the most frequented by divers, so some of the bigger and more elusive fish may prefer to hang around elsewhere.

If you haven't been diving for a few months, a good site to warm up on is West End's spectacular **Blue Channel**. This dive has some shallow areas with a gradually widening opening leading through the coral formations and sea fans rising on both sides. The channel ends at a large sandy area with several small caves and swim-throughs. The wall drops to a sand base at only about 50 feet. There is rarely any current or wave action so a relaxing dive is to be expected. A sharp eye will find a few lobsters sticking their feelers out at the base of some of the coral formations. Look for moray eels guarding the tasty crustaceans.

Very close to Blue Channel is the wreck of the *Eagle*. **El Águila**, as it is known locally, was a 300-foot freighter sunk intentionally for a dive site and conveniently broken up into a couple of large chunks by Hurricane Mitch. The wreck is at the base of a long coral wall and is infested with large green morays. If you get to the wreck early in the day you might see some of the resident grouper. If you arrive with a crowd, these guys will see you, but you will not see them.

Let's go ahead and do a **night dive** on day one. If you are flying on Sunday, a night dive on Saturday night would be a bad choice. It's best to get most of your diving done early on in the weekend trip, allowing all of Saturday night and Sunday morning for breathing off any excess nitrogen that might accumulate. So Friday night is the night.

One of the best things about night diving is the amount and variety of fish, crustaceans and small critters that come out and prowl around after dark. Shallow dives are usually best for night dives, as most of these critters hang out on the shallow reefs. **Sea Quest** is a fairly shallow dive with plenty of coral and lots of small fish. At night you can see tiny shrimp prancing around in front of cracks in the coral. There is a wall that descends to a sand base. Small rays cavort around on the sand. Sometimes you can only spot them by the shine of their eyes in the flashlight. If you are sharp-eyed you may spot the weirdly elegant movements of an octopus or the lurching jerks of small squid.

Back at the resort, have a soak in the hot tub or pool, the perfect way to wash off the salt and soothe aching muscles. Have a decompression drink or two, but head for bed early for a full day of diving tomorrow.

Saturday

We're going to squeeze in three dives today: two in the morning and a third very shallow dive in the early afternoon. Flying on pressurized aircraft means your blood could be bubbling like champagne at cruising altitude if you do too much diving, especially deep diving, close to departure time.

Everyone loves **Mary's Place**, near French Harbour. A large crack in the reef wall leads you to an opening in the face of the wall at about 70 feet. The wall goes on down to the sand at something over 130 feet. The passage is not particularly narrow but it is important to be sure you have plenty of air left before going through it in either direction. Stay at least 25 feet from any other divers. Don't crowd each other! You don't want to be banging into the walls or have your face mask knocked off this deep in what is basically an underwater tunnel.

West End Wall is one of the best drift dives in the Bay Islands. You will almost certainly see a bunch of turtles as you zoom along with the strong current. You will see lots of sea fans leaning in the underwater wind. Keep your eyes open for **Old Silver Sides** on this dive. This is one of my favorite dives in Roatan since you don't have to work too hard and you can never be sure what types of exotics you will see. You get to cover quite a bit of territory without stirring up too much commotion, so you can sort of sneak up on some shy sea life you would ordinarily scare off.

I'm not a big fan of one-handing a baloney sandwich in the boat while wearing my wet suit. And why should I, when we can have one of the best seafood meals available on the planet? **Half Moon Bay Cabins** has fish, shrimp and lobster that have just been gently lifted from the sea yards from where you are sitting. The fish sandwiches are so juicy it drips off your elbow as you take your fist bite (see *Best Eats*).

After lunch, find your way to the end of the dock for yet another dive in the crystal-clear Caribbean waters around Roatan. With all afternoon and only one dive to do, it is possible to reach one of the more distant dive sites on the list.

One of the most popular sites, and thus one of the busiest, is **Herbie's Place**. It's such a nice dive that it's worth ignoring the other sheep in the water with you. It is a great drift dive at the extreme southwest end of the island. You can lazily drift over shallow beds of coral and sea fans or swim out a little to the edge of the reef where it drops off into the blue. The dive boat drifts along with the divers. A long safety line with a buoy trails out behind the dive boat. This is for experienced divers only.

Drift Dives

A relaxing way to see a lot of reef is by simply **floating along with the current** while your dive boat floats along with you. When there is a stiff current running and good visibility, you can cover quite a bit of reef and can sneak up on shy pelagics, turtles and rays.

With luck, you'll be back from your afternoon dive well before sundown. Hammock, pool and beer are next on the list. The **Chez Pascal** in the Island Pearl Hotel is the best place to eat on Roatan. Yes, the lobster is a little on the spendy side but you are on holiday, so splurge. Have a fancy dessert and a fancy drink afterwards.

Drift off after dinner for your favorite tropical drinks at yet another funky beach bar like **Al's Disco**, French Harbour. Their conch fritters are famous. Don't stay up too late or drink too much since tomorrow includes a morning of vacation fun followed by boo hoo time: back to Carbondale.

Sunday

No one says you can't **snorkel** just before flying, so Sunday morning is a perfect time for frolicking with dolphins. Skip the demeaning dolphin shows involving captive dolphins but definitely sign up to swim with them in the wild. When you call for reservations, be sure you determine that the dolphins you will be interacting with are in no way penned up. A couple of dolphin attractions offer beach or reef "encounters." Although their pens are quite large, indeed enclosing parts of a beach and some reef chunks, the dolphins are captive and cannot visit the open ocean. They visit with tourists for fish treats instead.

You want to be in a boat looking for dolphins swimming around on their own offshore. When spotted, the boat slows down and, frequently, the dolphins will come closer to see what's up. Snorkelers then plop into the crystal clear water and watch as the dolphins cavort in the immediate vicinity. Unlike captive dolphins, **wild dolphins almost never come close enough to touch**.

ALTERNATE PLAN

Forget for a moment, if possible, all about diving and spend the morning **fishing along the reef edge** for dorado, grouper, yellow tail or possibly a wahoo. **Captain O**, Tel. 403-8887, is a leading charter captain in the islands and can provide all the tackle, bait, lunch and beer you will need for offshore trolling. If you are a fly-fishing fanatic you should bring your own rods, reels, tippets, etc.

There's no clinging to their fins for a friendly, cross-species ride, but it's awesome to see them zipping around you in the open sea, even if they are only at the limits of underwater visibility. **Anthony's Key Resort** and **Paradise Beach Club** both can arrange for this type of wild dolphin encounter.

Conch Fritters

Conch fritters are balls of conch meat, corn meal or flour and perhaps a little egg formed into balls and dropped into hot oil to cook. People love to eat them and drink beer. Almost all the bars and restaurants in the Bay Islands claim them as a specialty. Try them everywhere you go.

Lunch involving seafood, beer or tropical spirits is the last thing to do before heading for the airport. For your last island meal, it's important to do it right. Few places do the last meal on the island thing better than **Casa Romeo's** (Tel. 455-5518). Try their whole roasted fish and conch fritters. Suck down a couple of the local **Imperial** beers or your favorite umbrella drinks fueled by **Flor de Caña**, the local rum.

Head back to your resort or hotel to check out. Grab a taxi to the airport. Bye bye.

A WEEKEND OF DIVING ON UTILA

Utila is far less touristed than Roatan. Here you'll see no cruise ship tourists, but rather a mix of backpackers and alternative-lifestyle gurus attracted by the famously cheap diving, the late-night trance parties and the drum circles on the beach. Another frequent visitor around Utila is the largest fish in the sea, the **whale shark**.

Friday Afternoon & Evening

Most visitors stay in dedicated dive resorts or small hotels/ cabins. There are no fancy places on the island but there are plenty of pleasant places to stay, eat and recreate. Both **Coral View Beach Resort** in Sandy Bay, and **Deep Blue Resort** are dedicated dive resorts with comfortable lodging, restaurant, bar and complete dive operations (see *Best Sleeps*).

We've arranged lodging in advance, so we'll be met at the airport or dock and taken directly to our resort. The best thing to do is not delay this process. Guzzle the complimentary welcome drink, dump your stuff in your room and get to the end of the dock to start diving as quickly as possible.

Even though you're gung-ho and ready to dive, dive, dive, we should probably start off with an easy dive or two. **Stingray Point** is a sandy slope with a nice reef angling down to about 100 feet. You can take your time and go as deep or shallow as you like and not run out of reef to explore on one tank. You're guaranteed to see lots of small stingrays and possibly a few spotted eagle or leopard rays.

The wreck of the 211-foot *Halliburton* is located on a patch of sand varying from 60 to 100 feet. There is some nearby coral, and the wreck has been down since 1991 so there is a good amount of fishy activity in spite of the fairly barren surroundings. If you're a wreck-head you'll like this one. You can swim down into the hold and look around a bit.

Saturday Morning

We'll be up bright and early to enjoy a spectacular Bay Islands sunrise, a cup of rich Honduran coffee and a breakfast of ripe and juicy tropical fruits. Then it's back in the boat for another day of world-class diving.

It's best to get your deeper diving done early in the weekend trip, allowing all of Saturday night and Sunday morning for breathing off excess nitrogen before you fly. We got warmed up yesterday, so let's do a fairly deep dive on a top site called **The Pinnacle**.

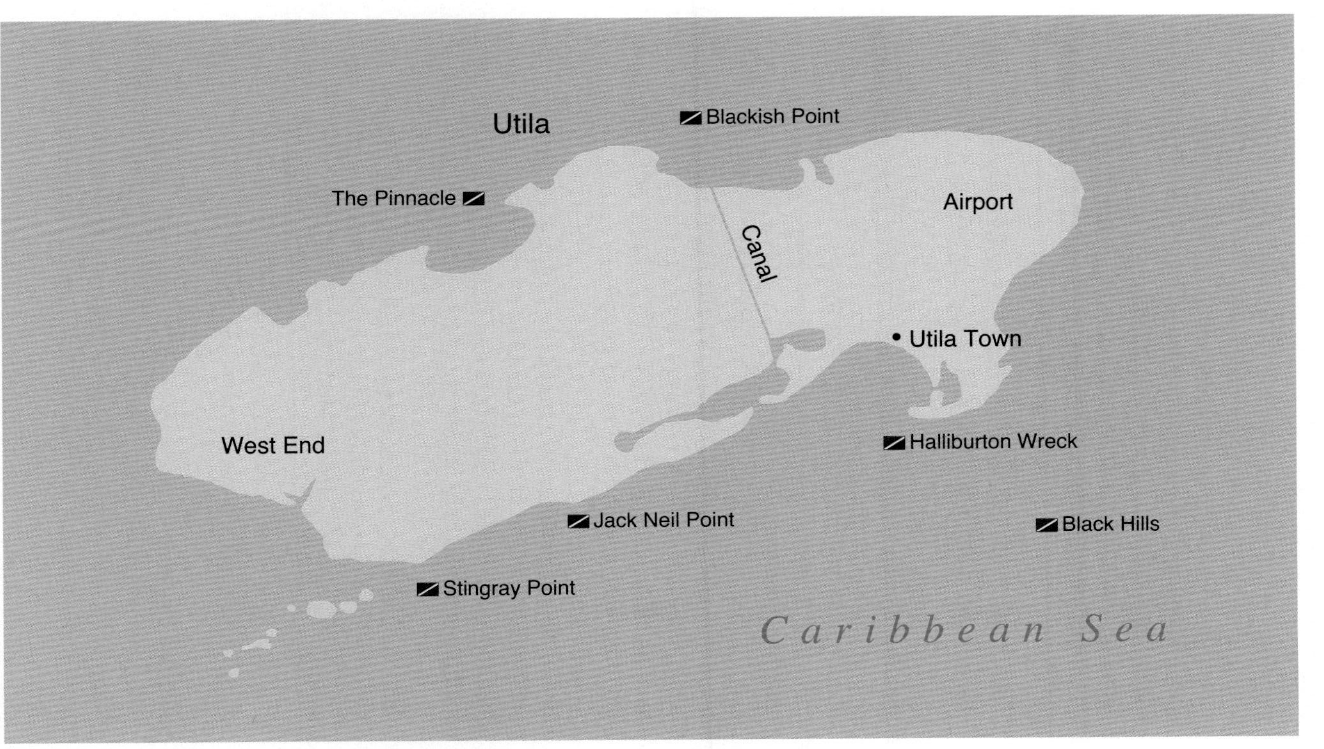
Utila
Blackish Point
The Pinnacle
Airport
Canal
Utila Town
West End
Halliburton Wreck
Jack Neil Point
Black Hills
Stingray Point
Caribbean Sea

For this dive you need to depend on your divemaster to lead you through the good parts. The site is primarily a deep wall that you access through a deep-entry swim-through. This leads across a deep channel to a coral pinnacle rising up to within a few feet ofthe surface from well below 150 feet. It's great to slowly spiral your way around the pinnacle as you rise to the surface. You should see lots of lobsters, crabs and tiny, colorful shrimp. A sharp eye may see pelagics at the extreme edge of visibility. The usual butterfly fish and French angels abound.

Saturday Afternoon

After lunch, we're going to try to find a whale shark. At most times of the year the giant fish migrate through the waters around Utila and will sometimes consent to be snorkeled with. **Whale sharks** eat plankton and nekton, which includes occasional small fish – they don't take bites out of people.

Whale shark encounters are much like dolphin encounters: your boat cruises around in likely-looking areas while your skipper looks for the tell-tale boil in the water that indicates the presence of the enormous fish. When they are located, snorkelers and scuba divers plop over the side and, hopefully, swim quietly while the giant fish lurk around. Whale sharks are usually slow swimmers but may not show much interest in visitors. Be sure to take an underwater camera along on this outing.

All of the dive operators on the island are in on the whale shark action so you should have no trouble setting up an excursion.

Saturday Evening

We'll have a fantastic seafood dinner at our lodge or at any of a variety of local *champas*, perhaps the **Island Café** near Coco Loco, **Susan's Restaurant** on Suc-Suc Cay, or the romantic **Mango Café**.

Somehow, we still have some energy left after the hard day's diving, so we'll stop by the **Tranquila Bar** and scout out the scene for a trance party or a drum circle on the nearby beach. Even if you don't have many pierced body parts, it's a fun scene and besides, it's about all the nightlife there is on Utila.

Sunday

If you're flying today, better skip the diving, but there's no reason you can't have a final **snorkel** near your resort. On the other hand, if you're not flying, you could get in another two-tank dive in the morning – there are plenty of other awesome sites!

Unlike Roatan, Utila does not have much in the way of "activities" or things to do with bored kids. Fortunately, the beaches are grand, so no member of the family is likely to complain if you spend your last morning in the Bay Islands swimming and sunning on the beach.

ALTERNATE PLAN

Utila is also a **dream destination for anglers**, with almost perfect fishing conditions for several distinct types of fishing. You can stalk bonefish, permit and tarpon on the flats in the morning, hunt for grouper and snapper on the reefs in the early afternoon, then troll offshore for billfish and dorado before heading back to the dock for a well-deserved fish dinner. This is one of the few places in the world where you might hope for a Grand Slam!

A WONDERFUL WEEK IN THE BAY ISLANDS

You could easily spend a week (or more) diving without visiting the same place twice – Roatan alone has around 100 buoyed dive sites, including a dozen wrecks. For most of us, a mere several days **diving** will be sufficient, leaving time for a day or two of **fishing**, a couple of afternoons seeing the **sights on shore**, and plenty of time hanging around on the beach or at the pool with a cold one in your hand.

RECOMMENDED PLAN: You could easily divide up your week and visit two or even all three islands. But unless you're the type who likes to check off lists of destinations, there's little reason to do so. All three islands have excellent diving, fishing and beach lounging, so choose one and take a day trip to one of the other islands for a change of pace. **Roatan** is by far the largest island, and has the biggest tourist scene, with a wide variety of "things to do." **Utila** has the youth scene and is beloved of the backpacker set. **Guanaja** doesn't have much of anything but diving, fishing and beaching.

ROATAN

The main dock for Roatan is in **Coxen Hole** and the airport is only about two miles outside town. What would normally be a sleepy, somewhat grubby village has been tarted up a bit to lure the thousands of tourists who pass through every week on cruise ships. There a few bars and restaurants in Coxen Hole that are okay, but there really isn't much of interest. It is wise to avoid the village after dark unless you are with a well-trusted local.

A reasonable road runs north out of Coxen hole to Sandy Bay and West End, nice villages on the north side of the island with bars, restaurants and wonderful beaches. **West End** has plenty of everything you'll need to dive, fish, drink rum drinks and eat conch fritters. It's a small, laid-back village, but things that appeal to tourists on tropical holiday abound. Life can be quite slow in West End – it's a good place to let yourself go to seed. Sandy Bay is a slightly larger village, but isn't particularly tourist-oriented.

If you drive east from Coxen Hole past the airport, you'll pass a few resorts and attractions vying for your touristic attention. Blink and you'll miss the tiny village of Brick Bay, but continue on to the slightly larger, slightly smelly fishing town French Harbour. Keep going. The road gets worse as it heads east to Oak Ridge and some lovely beaches like **Camp Bay**. Poke around the waterfront a little in Oak Ridge and you may see guys more or less hard at work building fishing boats. A remnant of the once thriving boat building business remains. There's not much happening in Oak Ridge besides a few dive resorts and a small fishing fleeet operating out of the small harbor.

A resort a little away from the action, but close enough for quick visits as needed, is a good selection criterion for Roatan. **CoCo View Resort** and **Palmetto Bay Plantation** are both good choices (see *Best Sleeps*). This is a laid-back tropical island as well as a top diving and fishing destination. Even with three or even four dives on most days, there will be plenty of hammock and pool time. It is also wise to plan for at least one day spent fishing. Other island attractions include tropical parks, a bird sanctuary, iguana preserve, zipline parks and funky tropical beach bars serving umbrella drinks. The beaches of Roatan are of legendary beauty.

Don't Miss ...

Drift Dive at West End Point - Relax as you sweep across the face of the wall.
Night Dive at Spooky Channel - Hold on tight to your buddy and drift through a dark tunnel.
West Bay Beach - Roatan's finest beach is a true tropical paradise.
Flats Fishing - Casting for bonefish and permit on the flats is one of the world's top fishing experiences.
Offshore Trolling - Have an epic battle with a billfish, or snag some wahoo or dorado for dinner.
Whale Shark Encounters - Utila is one of the few places in the world where you can get a close-up look at the largest fish in the sea.

Most of the resorts on Roatan focus on diving, and offer **seven-night all-inclusive packages** with around 20 dives, accommodations, airport transfers, most meals and a few other little extras. You can expect to pay in the neighborhood of $1,000 for this type of deal. Fishing packages usually run substantially more but are still quite reasonable.

There's a good directory of Roatan businesses and travel information at www.roatanet.com.

Roatan Dive Sites

Scuba diving on Roatan is some of the best in the world. There are over a hundred named dive sites with walls, tongue-and-groove reefs, shark dives, wrecks, caves, etc. The reefs go all the way around the island and no part is far from top-quality diving. Utila (famous for dives with whale sharks), Guanaja and Cayos Cochinos are close by, and most Roatan dive operators offer day trips to these unique dive areas.

The snorkeling is easy and wonderful. Some of the most beautiful reef structure is quite shallow. If you don't scuba, you can snorkel to wonderful reefs only a few feet from almost any of the beaches on Roatan.

Bear's Den has coral formations with **gigantic caves**. Sponges, grouper, the ubiquitous parrot fish, surgeon fish and squirrel fish abound.

Spooky Channel consists of a wide, long dark tunnel that you swim through to get to the face of the reef. It starts at about 30 feet and slopes gently down to exit on the reef face at about 95 feet. Keep close to your buddy on this one, and watch for boats zooming around when you surface. This is **a great night dive** for advanced divers. At night, octopus, squid, lion fish and the occasional shark make their appearance. There's also less boat traffic.

Barry's Reef is a nice wall dive that starts out fairly shallow. The wall goes down to the sand at about 80 feet, so it's not too deep to prowl around the bottom of the wall and look for the critters that like to hide in the dark crevasses. With a sharp eye you can see several types of crabs.

Roatan's Best Dives

Make sure you don't leave Roatan without experiencing these dives: **Bear's Den**, **Spooky Channel**, **Barry's Reef**, **West End Wall**, **Morat Wall**, and **CoCo View**.

Large schools of barracuda congregate just above the top of the reef. Curious, they will follow you around as you explore.

Few drift dives are better then the one called **West End Wall**. The direction of the drift is dependent on the tide, but you can expect to drift at one or two knots along the face of a deep and spectacular wall. I like to try to stick as close to the wall as possible so I can check out the weird coral, sponges and tiny shrimp as I float by. You'll see **huge barrel sponges and schools of triggerfish**. As you move away from the wall, a panorama opens up at the edge of the deep blue drop-off. If you look carefully, you may see large fish such as tuna or amberjacks swimming by just at the limit of visibility.

The **Prince Albert**, directly in front of CoCo View Resort, is a 145-foot freighter intentionally sunk in about 85' of water. The ship is mostly in one piece, and you'll see the shadow of it just a minute or two after you start swimming from the mooring line. There are some **enormous grouper** that make a home here, but you're unlikely to see them unless you dive early in the day and approach quietly and slowly. Sneak around the bottom of the wreck and you may see a couple of them before they head off into the blue. They used to hang around cadging snacks from divers, but the action got a little too frantic, with jacks and other fish trying to get in on the action. The grouper feeding has been stopped and the grouper are shy again.

Another nice wreck is the *Eagle*, a 300-foot freighter sunk intentionally for a dive site and conveniently broken up into a couple of large chunks by Hurricane Mitch. The wreck is at the base of

Deeper Than Thou

Many divers, often relative newbies, seem to think dives must be deep, in caves or on wrecks to be good enough for them. They pride themselves on the danger quotient of the dives they talk about. Here's a hint from experienced divers: **deep dives are shorter**. You see fewer fish and other marine life on deep dives. **Colors fade with depth** so deep dives are colorless. My favorite dives are in 30 feet or less. I get to stay down much longer and see many more fish and lots of colorful coral. Let the braggarts brag. The best dives are usually fairly shallow.

a long coral wall and is infested with large green morays. The morays make for great photographs but it is unwise to try to feed them. There is a lot of jagged metal and junk on and around the wreck, so be careful.

One of the best dive sites on the island, **Morat Wall** is a three-mile long reef at the extreme northeast end of the island. Few dive operators go here, so it gets little traffic, meaning that you'll see **more fish and exotic creatures**. You will almost certainly see **turtles**. The wall is a good drift dive, depending on which part of the reef you start on and the way the current is running. Try to stay close to the wall so you can see the gigantic sponges and gorgonians, and the large gardens of elkhorn and staghorn coral. You might see tarpon roaming around at this site.

Sassy's Bight is rarely visited: few divemasters on the island have been there and those who have keep the secret for special clients. Somewhere near the northeastern tip of the island, Sassy's Bight is a sand-floored conduit channeling strong currents between **two enormous coral mountains**. Schools of bait fish attract large predators such as tarpon, enormous snook, jack, tuna, sailfish, and occasionally marlin. Drift through as if you are just another bait fish, and hope there's nothing big enough to eat you waiting on the other side. Ask your divemaster if you can get up a special trip to this secret dive site.

Roatan Dive Operators

It's convenient and usually economical to stay at a dedicated dive resort and spend all your time with them in an all-inclusive package. You get to leave all your gear at the dock at the end of the day and stagger back to your room for a beer and a shower without having to think much. Most resorts will wash your gear and have it ready for your diving the next morning. All you have to do is grope your way to the end of the dock and step into the boat. There are a variety of resorts that cater almost exclusively to divers.

Competitive Prices!

Beware: the competition between dive operators in the Bay Islands is intense, driving down prices to almost unsustainable levels. Most dive packages start around $800 per week for lodging, food, and almost too much diving time. **If you see prices lower than that, there may be shortcuts taken somewhere**: crummy rooms or food, beat-up equipment, inadequate staffing levels, or possibly shortcuts on safety issues. Avoid seemingly impossible bargains. Go ahead and let yourself pay a little bit more for a top-quality dive and vacation experience; our *Best Sleeps and Eats* chapter will steer you right!

On the other hand, it is quite possible to stay at any resort or hotel on the island and do your diving with one of the independent dive operators. The dive shops will pick you up and drop you off at your hotel and give you pretty much the same kind of diving and service you get from an all-inclusive. All of the hotels and resorts work with the dive operators and can put together a dive package for you. The lodging and food side of the dive resorts is covered in the *Best Sleeps and Eats* chapter.

The Bay Islands are famous for being **the cheapest place in the world to dive**. There are dozens of dive operators competing with each other, so the prices tend to stay low. It is possible to become certified for $100 including instruction, equipment and dive trips. What a deal!

For full details on diving and fishing resorts and independent operators, see the *Best Activities* chapter. Here are my favorites:

- **Anthony's Key Resort** (www.anthonyskey.com; Tel. 445-3003) has (at last count) 14 dive boats taking up to 20 punters each, and a large snorkel boat herding 30 snorkelers.

- **Bananarama Dive Beach Resort** (www.bananaramadive.com; Tel. 445-5005 or 727/564-9058 US) has an excellent reputation, and they have all the usual water sports equipment handy.

- **Bay Island Beach Resort** (www.bibr.com; Tel. 445-3020 or 800/227-3483) offers great deals on week-long diving packages.

- **CoCo View Resort** (www.cocoviewresort.com; Tel. 455-7502 or 800/510-8164 US) offers a variety of rooms and flexible dive plans. It's a good resort, and the dive operation is one of the best in the area. There's excellent diving directly in front of the resort.

- **Fantasy Island** (www.fantasyislandresort.com; Tel. 455-7499 or 800/676-2826 US) is a dedicated dive resort with PADI training at all levels.

Roatan Fishing

Although most businesses in the area focus on attracting divers, the Bay Islands are also an angler's paradise. Bonefish and permit on the flats, tarpon in the channels, billfish and dorado offshore, and snapper and grouper over the reefs are all wonderfully plentiful. With luck, an elusive Grand Slam could be achieved here.

There are several charter captains and a few small operators who can take you out for half or full days providing beer, bait and tackle. This type of resort fishing is cheaper in the Bay Islands than in other Caribbean or Central American destinations.

You don't need a fishing license for sport fishing in Honduras, so if you're really hard-core you can bring your own tackle and fish from the beach for tarpon and snook. Try any of these folks first:

- **Crystal Beach Cabins** (Tel. 403-8847) arranges trips with Cap'n Sam, who knows the local waters and how to catch the fish – he was 2003 Bay Islands Billfish Tournament champ.

- Captain Loren Monterroso works out of **Early Bird Fishing Charters** in Sandy Bay (Tel. 955-0001 or 445-3019). He has a fully-equipped 24-foot Grady White explorer with full electronics and all the tackle you might need for offshore pursuits. Fly and live bait flats fishing is also offered.

- **Captain O** (Tel. 403-8887), knows where the big 'uns are, and focuses on taking clients to the areas where the fishing is best. He has 27' and 25' sport fishers, and offers very reasonable prices. If you've dreamed of catching a marlin, sailfish or wahoo, the Captain knows all the trolling tricks.

- **Mango Creek Lodge**, near Oak Ridge (www.mangocreeklodge.com; Tel. 435-2576), is for serious anglers. They specialize in fly-fishing on the extensive flats close to the lodge. The resort is very privately situated. Lodging and food are nice but not luxurious.

- **Marco & Carlos Fishing Charters** (Tel. 445-4171), with two boats and top-notch tackle, will take you trolling for dorado, marlin and wahoo or bottom fishing for jacks, grouper, snapper and barracuda.

- **Subway Watersports** (www.subwaywatersports.com; Tel. 387-0579 or 359-4190) is the fishing operator for Palmetto Bay Plantation, Barefoot Cay, and Turquoise Bay Resorts. They offer flats and offshore fishing trips with all equipment included. The best thing about them is their light trolling along the reef trips, which are a real bargain. Cruise ship visitors can go on a half-day trip for only $200.

Roatan Dolphins

Wild dolphin encounters can be the highlight of anyone's trip. Snorkeling around in the open ocean with frisky wild dolphins zooming around to check you out is an unforgettable, cross-species communication experience.

The most famous place in the Bay Islands to interact with dolphins is at **Anthony's Key Resort**, where they have several of

Do Right by Dolphins

Swimming in the open ocean with **truly wild dolphins** seems more acceptable to me than swimming with them in pens, and several places in the Bay Islands offer such opportunities. Wild dolphins may cavort around a bit when snorkelers appear in the water with them, but they don't come close enough for you to rub them on the tummy.

Some resorts use misleading wording in their promotional efforts to make you think the dolphins you will be swimming with are truly "wild," neglecting to mention that the dolphins are actually penned in and have little choice but to cooperate with their captors by entertaining the tourists for fish treats. So reject the dolphin prisons. Before agreeing to participate in any dolphin "encounter," **ask whether they are in pens**. Dolphin snorkels or beach dives may sound as if the dolphins are participating willingly, but in most of these cases the dolphins are in cages - large ones perhaps, but cages just the same. If they are in pens, just say no.

them penned up for your enjoyment. Perhaps there is some therapeutic value in this ridiculous attempt to legitimize enslaving intelligent wild animals for profit. Call to check for show times.

A much better alternative is to take one of the **snorkeling trips** that go just offshore **looking for schools of wild dolphins** willing to swim around nearby while tourists snorkel. The dolphins are not usually harmed or coerced in the process. My experience is that wild dolphins will zoom around delightfully close enough to enjoy while snorkeling. Anthony's Key Resort arranges these types of trips as well as the other, more exploitive types of dolphin worship.

Paradise Beach Club (www.paradisebeach.com; Tel. 403-8062) in West Bay offers pretty much the same dolphin options for slightly less money.

Glass Bottom Boat Trips

Two different boats sport glass bottoms and can show anyone who is unwilling to get wet a very close-up view of the spectacular reefs just offshore. Both boats are air-conditioned and comfortable. **Underwater Paradise** (www.halfmoonbaycabins.com; Tel. 445-4047) is based at Half Moon Bay Cabins, and the **Coral Reef Explorer** (www.roatancoralreefexplorer.com; Tel. 336-5597) is located at West Point. An hour-long trip will cost you around $20.

Other Water Sports

Subway Watersports (www.subwaywatersports.com; Tel. 387-0579) has everything you need for sailing, kayaking, scuba, snorkeling, water skiing, etc. They have several locations, including Palmetto Bay Plantation, Barefoot Cay, and Turquoise Bay Resort.

They also do a **lovely sunset sailing trip** for $35 pp with drinks, snacks, and snappy commentary.

Cruise Ship Avoidance!

You can find **cruise ship schedules** for the port of Roatan at www.cruisecal.com/dnn/Default.aspx?tabid=179. You may want to avoid the beaches near the port when the ships are in town.

Zipping Around on Scooters

What could possibly be more fun when visiting the tropics than to rent a scooter or ATV and zoom noisily around the island? **Captain Van's Rentals** (www.captainvans.com; Tel. 403-8751 or 445-4076) offers motorcycle, moped and bicycle rentals. They have two locations on Roatan: West End and West Bay Beach.

Roatan Beaches

Most of the best beaches in Roatan are on the north side of the island. The south tends to be rock, with not much in the way of sandy beaches. **West Bay** has the finest beaches in the Bay Islands, and they are beauties. These beaches are simply spectacular and will be right up there with anyone's opinion of the most beautiful beaches in the world. Be aware that although many of the resorts in the Bay Islands are right smack dab on a beautiful beach, many of them are not. Be sure to check web sites, correspond with other travelers and call ahead to be sure your destination is blessed with beautiful white sand.

West Bay has the classic tropical beach with waving palm trees. **West End Beach** is the one you want if you want to be close to the scene: see and be seen. The beaches in front of **Tabanya Beach Resort** and the **Henry Morgan Resort** are where most of the cruise ship visitors end up. **Keyhole Beach** near Mar Vista Bay is one of my favorites. It's small but secluded and usually empty.

Roatan Attractions

Roatan has no shortage of pastimes on shore: botanical gardens, bird and butterfly parks, iguana shows, dolphin worship, kayaking through the mangroves and zipping around on scooters or ATVs. Newer attractions include paintball, flying around in ultra lights, and of course, a couple of ziplines.

Roatan is almost 30 miles long and several miles wide, so it is big enough to rent a car or jeep and zip around on your own checking out beaches, funky bars, snorkeling spots and shops. Not even counting diving or fishing, you could exhaust yourself pursuing holiday activities for several days and not see and do all of the tourist things.

Carambola Botanical Garden

Just across from Anthony's Key in Sandy Bay, Carambola Garden offers a one-hour walk through tropical gardens. The plants are not particularly well marked but the walk does allow you to identify most of the more interesting plants you see in the area. The views over the bay from the top of the ridge are great. It is certainly worth the $5 entrance fee. *Info:* Sandy Bay. Tel. 445-3117.

Sherman Arch's Iguana Farm

Iguanas are considered a great thing to eat in much of Central America, and they need a safe harbor. About 18 years ago Sherman Arch decided to put his iguana hobby on a firmer footing and opened his iguana preserve to the public. His entire family now participates in feeding and caring for some **3,000 iguanas**.

Wild iguanas come here to avoid being eaten by the iguana meat-hungry islanders who consider them not just a delicacy but a staple. Many of them are tame enough for tourists to handle. This is a great stop for close-up photos of these Godzilla-like creatures. *Info:* French Harbour. Open 8am-4pm. $5.

Tropical Treasures Bird Park

This park in Sandy Bay offers exciting guided tours through **outsized aviaries** with birds from Honduras and other parts of the tropics. The lovely park is at the edge of the beach and houses literally hundreds of bird species. The beauty of the park itself and the setting make the trip worthwhile.

Roatan Bruce!

On station 106.5 FM - Monday to Friday, 10 am to 1 pm, **Bruce Starr** does the Roatan Bruce Show, which is a local English-language talk show. This is a good way to keep up with local issues if you don't speak Spanish.

You'll find all the macaws here, including scarlet macaws, great green macaws, blue and gold macaws, and Hans macaws. There is also a plethora of parrots, with white-crowned parrots, orange-chinned parakeets, white-fronted parrots, mealy parrots, red-lored parrots, and yellow-crowned parrots, a species particular to the Bay Islands. Of course toucans are here as well. Be sure to bring your camera. It's hard to get close-ups of tropical birds flying around in the rain forest, but it's easy to get nice and close in the bird park. *Info:* Sandy Bay. Tel. 445-1314.

Canopy Tours (Ziplines)

There are several canopy tours on Roatan. One is near West Bay and one is at Palmetto Bay. The one at Palmetto Bay is the most challenging, as it has a rock wall and several types of rope bridges incorporated into the tour amidst the different zipline stops.

- **Gumbalimba Park** (www.gumbalimbapark.com; Tel. 914-9196) has 11 zipline platforms and various other activities at the park, but it costs a steep $40 per person!

- **Roatan Jungle Canopy** (Tel. 991-0161) near French Harbour, has 13 zipline platforms, 6 bridges, wall climbing and even more thrills.

UTILA

Utila is far less touristed than Roatan. No cruise ships dock at Utila. The island attracts an international mix of **backpackers** looking for cheap diving to alternative-lifestyle gurus attracting a crowd around them for **late-night trance parties** and drum circles around a bonfire on the beach. Utila also has great diving and fishing.

While I have not personally sampled the trance side of things, I

can say the fame for the rest is well deserved. But realize, after diving, fishing, eating, drinking and listening to a little live music, there is really not much of anything to do on Utila. But that's okay. The diving and fishing are enough by themselves to make a trip worthwhile.

Utila Diving

The reefs around Utila rival those anywhere in the world. Larger Roatan has more reef acreage, but Utila is visited less and doesn't have cattle boats churning things up and scaring away the big fish. In my opinion, the diving in general around Utila and Guanaja is better than Roatan for the simple reason that there are fewer divers in the water.

There are more than 50 buoyed sites, representing a variety of wall dives, caves, wrecks, stingrays, sharks, deep, shallow – something for all diving levels and interests. The web site at www.utiladivebuoys.com lists all the buoyed sites with excellent interactive maps. Awesome steep walls line the north side of the island. You could spend a week just diving different walls.

Top dive sites around Utila include **Stingray Point**, **Jack Neil Point**, **Pretty Bush**, **Black Coral Wall**, **Airport Caves**, **Black Hills**, **Blackish Point**, **Willie's Hole** and **Ragged Cay**.

An easy dive where you will definitely see lots of small stingrays and possibly a few spotted eagle or leopard rays, **Stingray Point** is a sandy slope with a nice reef angling down to about 100 feet. You can take your time, go as deep or shallow as you like and not run out of reef to explore on one tank.

The wreck of the 211-foot *Halliburton* is located on a patch of sand varying from 60 to 100 feet. There is some nearby coral and the wreck has been down since 1991, so there's a good amount of fishy activity in spite of the fairly barren surroundings. If you're a wreck-head you'll like this one. You can swim down into the hold and look around a bit.

Ron's Wreck is a small boat sunk fairly recently and not really worth the effort unless you just really like to dive on wrecks. There are much better sites around and you only have a week, so ...

Sturch Bank is a little offshore and a good spot to see manta rays. Sometimes they'll swoop around divers, doing rolls and hanging around like curious dogs. Whale sharks and dolphins are also common companions. This is one of the best dives in the Bay Islands.

You've done the dolphin thing on Roatan and got your T-shirt. How about **whale sharks**? Cute and cuddly whale sharks migrate through the waters around Utila throughout much of the year, and will sometimes consent to be snorkeled with. You may have to work a bit to keep up but the whale sharks seem curious too and circle around for another look at the crazy gringos. Almost any of the dive operators on the island will arrange such an expedition for you.

Utila is famous for offering the cheapest diving and dive courses in the entire Caribbean, perhaps anywhere. European and American budget travelers make up the majority of Utila's visitors. There are no fancy places on the island, but there are plenty of comfortable places to stay, eat and recreate. Both **Coral View Beach Resort,** in Sandy Bay (Tel. 425-3783) and **Deep Blue Resort** (Tel. 425-2015) are dedicated dive resorts with nice lodging, restaurant, bar and complete dive operations.

Dive shops and outfitters abound on the small island. **Alton's Dive Shop** (www.altonsdiveshop.com; Tel. 425-3704) is a PADI, DAN, NAUI Pro Platinum Training center with courses covering everything through NAUI Assistant Instructor, NAUI Master Scuba – the list of specialty courses goes on and on. They have all the right rental stuff, Nitrox fills, and photo facilities.

Captain Morgan's Dive Shop offers a full line of PADI certified courses from Open Water to Divemaster. They accommodate their divers at the lovely Hotel Keyla.

The *Utila Aggressor* live-aboard boat (www.aggressor.com; Tel. 800/348-2628 US) leaves from La Ceiba for seven-day trips to rarely explored spots around Utila.

See *Best Activities* for full details on diving and fishing operations.

Utila Fishing

Fishing around Utila is nothing less than fantastic. The deep trough directly offshore funnels migrating pelagics past Utila, just a little out from the plunging reefs. Currents form gigantic eddies off the southwest end of the island past Diamond Cay and Stingray Point. The eddies pull together baitfish and plankton in huge schools which attract passing billfish, tuna, whale sharks, dolphins and other pelagic fish.

The reefs in the same area hold another trove of baitfish and their predators: grouper, snapper, sharks, barracuda and a myriad of vivid reef fish. There are also huge areas of flats, teeming with bonefish and permit. You can easily stalk bones and permit on the flats in the morning, hunt for grouper and snapper around the reefs in the early afternoon and spend a couple of hours trolling for billfish and dorado before heading back to the dock for a well-deserved fish dinner. **Coral View** in Sandy Bay, **Deep Blue** and **Laguna Beach Resort** are all resorts that cater to anglers and are close to the action (see *Best Sleeps*).

GUANAJA

There's not much in the way of things to "do" on Guanaja other than diving, fishing, drinking umbrella drinks and lying around in hammocks. That seems to be more than enough for most visitors to this laid-back island paradise. There's a small waterfall with some pools you can hike to near **End of the World Resort**, and some modest Mayan ruins to poke around in. That's about it.

Guanaja Diving

The best dive sites in the Guanaja area include the wrecks around Pond Cay, the wreck of the **Jado Trader**, **Jim's Silver Lode**,

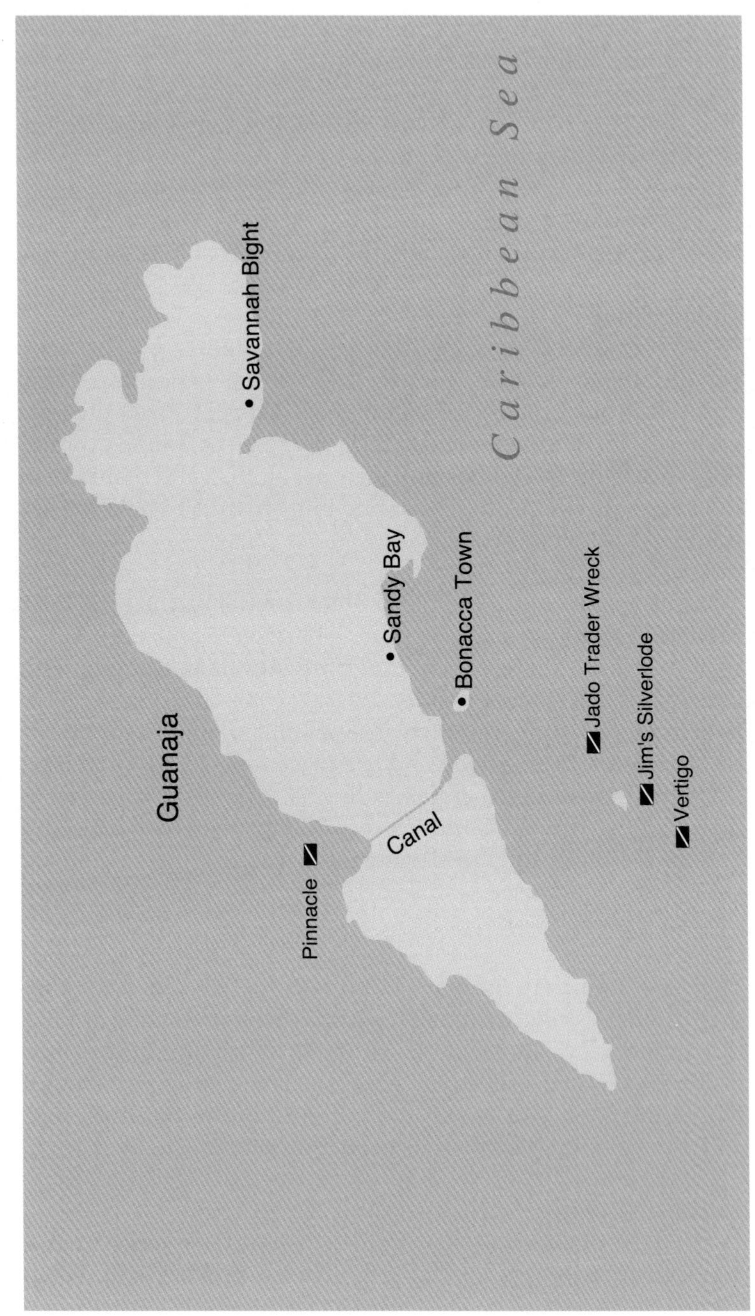
Caribbean Sea
Savannah Bight
Sandy Bay
Bonacca Town
Guanaja
Jado Trader Wreck
Jim's Silverlode
Vertigo
Canal
Pinnacle

Vertigo, Final Wall, Pinnacle, Volcano Caves, and **Siberia Eel Garden.**

There are a couple of dedicated, all-inclusive dive resorts. **End of the World Resort** charges $900 for seven-night diving packages. Divers are catered to carefully with a full line of rental equipment and the usual panoply of courses. You can't get to **Nautilus Resort,** near Bonacca Town (Tel. 453-4389), by car. You'll need to hop a ride on one of the resort's boats to get to the 60 acres on a hill overlooking the long, white sand beach that are the setting for Nautilus's seven rooms, some with AC. Of course, diving is the thing here and all the usual rental equipment and certification courses are available.

Guanaja Fishing

Some of the best bonefish and permit fishing in the world is found on the miles of sand and turtlegrass flats around Guanaja. Wading or poling small flats skiffs gets you within fly-casting distance of schools of three- to seven-pound bonefish. Permit up to 25 pounds and tarpon up to 90 pounds lurk nearby, making an elusive Grand Slam a distinct possibility. Reportedly, the **world record bonefish** was caught recently in front of the **Nautilus Resort** on Guanaja. Good luck.

Almost any of the resorts or hotels on the island can set you up with a fishing trip to either the flats or trolling offshore. **End of the World Resort** (www.guanaja.com; Tel 991-1257) offers seven-night fishing packages with all the goodies for $1,500. Captain Brian arranges flats, reef and offshore trips. **Coral Bay Dive Resort** (www.coralbay.ca; Tel. 877/682-9054 US) has similar deals. Most resorts provide all the spinning and deep-sea tackle you'll need. If you prefer fly-fishing, you will need to be self-sufficient with most tackle.

Cayos Cochinos Marine Reserve

The Cayos Cochinos (Hog Keys) are a group of tiny islands about midway between Roatan and the mainland. Remote and little-visited, the reefs are pristine, and diving and fishing are spectacular. The islands are a UNESCO World Heritage site and a protected marine reserve. The Honduran Coral Reef Foundation administers the park, and has a research station there (not open to the public). *Info:* www.cayoscochinos.org.

The islands are uninhabited except for a dive lodge called **Plantation Beach Resort** (see *Best Sleeps*). Dive boats from Roatan visit here on day trips. **Destinos de Exito** (www.destinosdeexito.com) runs full-day tours of the keys from La Ceiba, with snorkeling, a hike and a stop at Plantation Beach for lunch.

5. THE NORTH COAST

Here you'll find **beautiful Caribbean beaches** and some of the country's most interesting and easily accessible **nature reserves**. This is the home of the fascinating and friendly **Garífuna people**, so be sure to pay a visit to one of their traditional villages, and feast on grilled fish on the beach.

The main transport hub here is **La Ceiba**. With its airport and ferry terminal, it's the gateway to the Bay Islands and to the Moskitia region to the east. Ecotourists flock to nearby **Pico Bonito National Park**, and adventure sports fans dig the whitewater rafting on the **Cangrejal River**.

The area around **Tela**, to the west, is more of a beach scene, with several nice waterfront resorts. There are also plenty of ecotourism opportunities, including **Jeanette Kawas National Park**, **Punta Izopo Wildlife Refuge** and **Lancetilla Botanical Gardens**.

At the western end of the coast, the pleasant little beach town of **Omoa** is now a favorite with the backpacker set. To the east, **Trujillo** also has fine swimming beaches and is near the seldom-visited **Capiro y Calentura National Park**. Each of these towns features a classic old Spanish fortress.

ONE GREAT DAY IN PICO BONITO

One of Honduras's finest parks is just a short plane ride away from the teeming tourist resorts of the Bay Islands. Thanks to the convenient airport at La Ceiba, a day trip to **hike in the rain forest or run the rapids** is quite feasible.

Morning

Get up bright and early, have a couple of cups of rich Honduran coffee, and catch an early flight to the airport at La Ceiba. There are morning flights from Roatan, Tegucigalpa and San Pedro Sula. As you fly in, you can't miss **Pico Bonito**, a steep green mountain not far from the airport. That's where you'll be hiking later today!

There are several good tour operators based in the area. **Omega Tours** (www.omegatours.hn; Tel. 440-0334 or 965-5815) and **Jungle River Lodge** (www.jungleriverlodge.com; Tel. 440-1268 or 398-7641) both offer rain forest tours as well as whitewater rafting trips. You can expect to pay $35-50 for a 4-5 hour hiking trip.

Here's a bit of general advice: any time you plan to travel from one area of Honduras and back again in a day, don't try to make the travel arrangements yourself - let a local tour company handle it, and you'll save yourself a lot of hassle. Honduras is not Switzerland - flight times can change, buses can be late, and all kinds of other crazy things can happen. You *do not* want to be stranded at some grass airstrip in the middle of the jungle with the tropical night coming down. Most tour operators are happy to arrange a seamless door-to-door trip for you, and they may even save you a buck or two.

Afternoon

Okay, we had an uneventful flight into La Ceiba, the tour company met us with a van at the airport and whisked us up into the hills. After a light picnic lunch, we're ready to explore **Pico Bonito National Park**.

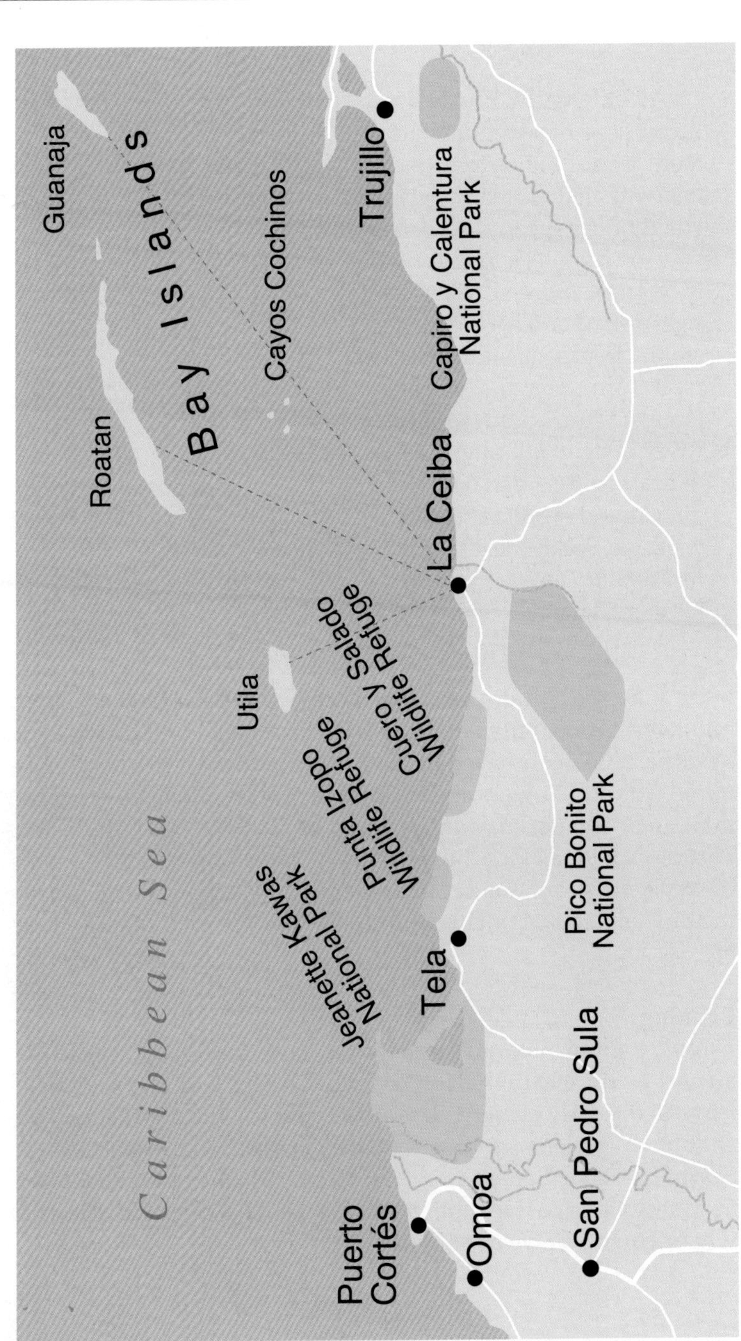
Guanaja
Roatan
Bay Islands
Cayos Cochinos
Trujillo
Capiro y Calentura National Park
La Ceiba
Utila
Cuero y Salado Wildlife Refuge
Punta Izopo Wildlife Refuge
Jeanette Kawas National Park
Caribbean Sea
Tela
Pico Bonito National Park
San Pedro Sula
Omoa
Puerto Cortés

ALTERNATE PLAN

If your idea of adventure has more to do with adrenaline than with animals, then maybe you'd rather spend the afternoon on a whitewater rafting trip. The **Cangrejal River** is right on the border of the park, and it offers some of the best river rafting in the world. **Omega Tours** and **Jungle River Lodge** both offer half-day rafting trips, and both beginners and expert rafters are welcome. See the next section *(A Fantastic La Ceiba Weekend)* for more details.

Pico Bonito is the third-largest protected area in Honduras, and has the greatest difference in altitude. It includes nine impressive mountain peaks, which are drained by 19 major rivers, with hundreds of magnificent waterfalls. It has at least eight distinct ecosystems, including tropical broadleaf and pine forests, and cloud forest at the higher elevations.

Parts of the park are still primary forest (never logged). The remote and unexplored regions are home to all kinds of animals, some of them very rare elsewhere. The patient hiker may see *pizotes*, agoutis, sloths, white-faced and spider monkeys, tapirs, anteaters and wild boars. Over 300 species of birds have been observed in the park. Colorful butterflies, hummingbirds and flowers such as orchids and bromeliads are common. *Info:* The park is administered by **FUPNAPIB** (Fundación Parque Nacional Pico Bonito), www.picobonito.org; Tel. 442-0618. The Visitors' Center (**Campamento Curla**) is located near the tiny village of Armenia Bonito. The park entrance fee is about $6.

Evening

If you've flown into the region for the day, you'll head back to the airport, as the last flights for Roatan, San Pedro or Tegus usually leave in the early evening. If you're spending the night here, you should have plenty of time to visit one of the Garífuna villages east of La Ceiba. **Sambo Creek** and **Corozal** are popular spots for an afternoon trip. They both have beautiful beaches with *champas* where you can have a seafood dinner.

A FANTASTIC LA CEIBA WEEKEND

With a weekend to spend, we won't have to choose between a hike in the forest and a whitewater rafting adventure. We're going to do both!

Friday

We're staying at one of the **jungle lodges** in the area. There are good options in all price categories, so why not sleep where the action is? There are some good hotels right in La Ceiba as well, but we're here to see the rain forest and ride the river, not to study the (doubtless fascinating) political economy of a Central American port city. We'll choose either the first-class **Lodge at Pico Bonito** or the bargain-priced **Omega Lodge** (see *Best Sleeps*).

We've made all our arrangements beforehand, so the staff from our lodge will meet us at the airport, ferry terminal or bus station, and whisk us straight to our cozy rain forest hideaway. Even if you're an experienced independent traveler, I highly recommend doing things this way in Honduras. Many budget lodgings include local transfers in their prices, so it's a waste of money and time to take a taxi. But even if you have to pay an extra fee for your lodge to pick you up, it's well worth it to avoid the chaotic hurly-burly of taxi drivers, touts and hustlers at the airport or (worse) the seedy neighborhoods that are found around bus stations.

Saturday

We've made arrangements through our lodge for an English-speaking guide to accompany us to the rain forest. **Pico Bonito** is not a difficult park to visit on your own, but we'll see more wildlife and learn more interesting stuff about the region with a local guide. Besides, we want to support the local economy, in hopes that the rain forest will be here for our grandchildren to enjoy some day.

There are several good tour operators based in the La Ceiba area. **Omega Tours** (www.omegatours.hn; Tel. 440-0334 or 965-5815) and **Jungle River Lodge** (www.jungleriverlodge.com; Tel. 440-1268 or 398-7641) both offer rain forest tours as well as whitewater rafting trips. You'll pay about $35-50 for a 4-5 hour hiking trip in the forest, including transport from La Ceiba, park entrance fees and a light lunch.

Morning is always the best time to spot wildlife, so we'll head into the forest bright and early. Although it's easily accessible from the travel hub of La Ceiba, Pico Bonito is actually a vast and mostly unexplored wilderness area. It's the third-largest protected area in Honduras (265,000 acres), and has the greatest difference in altitude. To reach the summit of the namesake mountain (2,435 meters) requires a week-long trek through trackless jungle. The park's highest peak, the 2,480-meter **Montaña Corozal**, has never been climbed, according to the locals.

Pico Bonito National Park includes nine impressive mountain peaks, which are drained by 19 major rivers, with hundreds of magnificent waterfalls. It's one of the most diverse parks in the country, with at least eight distinct ecosystems, including tropical broadleaf and pine forests, and true cloud forest at the higher elevations.

Parts of the park are still primary-growth forest (never logged). The remote and unexplored regions are home to all kinds of animals, some of them very rare elsewhere. The patient hiker may see *pizotes*, agoutis, sloths, white-faced and spider monkeys, and wild boars. If you're really fortunate, you may get a glimpse of a tapir, a giant anteater, a jaguar, puma or ocelot. Over 300 species of birds have been observed in the park. Naturally, orchids, bromeliads and other resplendent flowers are common, especially in the high cloud forest. Colorful butterflies and hummingbirds flit about.

The best-known area in the park, and the destination of many a day-tripper, is the **Río Zacate**, which has a series of waterfalls, some with nice pools for swimming. The highest, known as **La Ruidosa** (the noisy one), is 130 feet high. It's about an hour walk up the river, along a well-maintained trail through the lush rain forest. The trail offers spectacular views of the jungle and the Caribbean Sea below, as well as a good possibility of seeing some monkeys or other jungle denizens. *Info:* The park is administered by **FUPNAPIB** (Fundación Parque Nacional Pico Bonito), www.picobonito.org; Tel. 442-0618. The visitors' center (**Campamento Curla**) is located near the tiny village of Armenia Bonito. To get here, take the highway towards Tela about 12 miles west of La Ceiba, to Colonia Primero de Mayo. From here, a dirt road leads to Armenia Bonito. The park entrance is a half-hour walk further on. Buses for Armenia Bonito leave from the Central Plaza in La Ceiba every hour. The park entrance fee is about $6. The visitors' center has very basic overnight lodging for around $10 per person.

AMARAS (Tel. 443-0329) rehabilitates and releases animals and birds into the wild. It's worth a short visit to their facility, 12 km west of La Ceiba, along the highway to San Pedro Sula.

Sunday

The **Cangrejal River**, on the eastern border of Pico Bonito, offers some of the best whitewater river rafting in the world. In addition to thrills and spills, a rafting trip gives you another perspective on the rain forest, it's a chance to stay cool in the tropical heat, and it's just jolly good fun all around.

The river has class III and IV rapids, and is runnable year-round (the high water season is September through January). It's a double adventure to navigate the rapids while racing through the extravagant vegetation of the rain forest.

If you've never rafted before, don't worry – it's not as dangerous as it

Soaking Wet?

Rafting is guaranteed to get you soaking wet. That's okay. Outfitters will carry your dry stuff in sealed, waterproof bags. Wear shorts and a T-shirt, with sandals or tennis shoes. If you bring a camera, make sure it's waterproof!

sounds (or perhaps we should say that it's only as dangerous as you choose to make it). You'll be riding in an inflatable rubber raft with an English-speaking guide, and wearing a helmet and life jacket. Your guide will give you a short training course before you plunge into the whitewater. After you've shot the rapids, you can relax with a peaceful swim in the river. A half-day rafting trip takes around four hours, and will cost you $50-70 per person, including transportation and a light picnic lunch. Experienced rafters or kayakers can take a full-day trip, starting further up the river, with more intense rapids and technical whitewater.

The Cangrejal also has plenty of nice swimming places, and waterfalls, inluding the 240-foot high El Bejuco, so even if you're not rafting, it's nice to go for a hike along the river and a refreshing swim.

The two main rafting tour operators are **Omega Tours** and **Jungle River Lodge**. Both have basic but comfortable lodges right on the river. Our trip begins with a short warm-up, floating through some very mild rapids, and an instruction session with our bilingual guides. Now that we have a clue what to do, we're ready to run the class III and IV rapids, with steep drops, long wave-trains, waterfalls, and passages through narrow gorges with rocks towering hundreds of feet overhead.

About halfway down, we'll leave the rafts and hike up a small creek to a 10-meter-high waterfall thundering into a deep pool, the perfect place for a swim. The water is crystal clear and warm, and the lush green jungle is all around us.

At the end of the day, soaking wet, tired and maybe just a little bit sore, but happy, we head back to our jungle lodge for an ice-cold beer and a hearty dinner. We go to sleep to the sounds of the jungle, wishing we didn't have to leave in the morning. See *Best Activities* for details.

A FANTASTIC TELA WEEKEND

If the rain forest and rafting are your things, stick around La Ceiba – there's plenty in that area to keep you busy for a weekend, or much longer. However, if you want to see the **coastal ecosystems**, and get in some **beach time**, the **Tela area** is your best bet for a weekend trip.

Friday

Tela is about equidistant from La Ceiba and San Pedro Sula, and it's easy to get there by bus from either airport. If you want a beach resort with lots of action, stay at **Villas Telamar**. If you prefer an economical B&B that's loaded with character, try the **Maya Vista**.

We'll line up a tour of **Punta Sal** for tomorrow morning, then have a beer on the beach and an early dinner. The famous Tela nightlife will have to wait for tomorrow night, because we're getting up at the crack of dawn for the best birding.

Saturday Morning

Jeanette Kawas National Park, located on the western end of the Bay of Tela, is one of the country's most important protected areas. It's easy to visit and provides a good contrast to mountainous Pico Bonito. In one day, you can visit several different ecosystems, observe tropical birds, monkeys and other wildlife, take a swim on a beautiful beach, do a bit of snorkeling, and experience a bit of the fascinating Garífuna culture.

Formerly called Punta Sal, this park was renamed for **Jeanette Kawas**, a local environmental crusader who was murdered in 1995, presumably by vested interests opposed to the creation of protected areas.

The 178,000-acre park includes 14 different ecosystems. Most of the park is a vast area of wetlands. **Mangroves** form a labyrinth of estuaries, lagoons, canals and flooded forests. Coral reefs lie just off the pristine beaches.

Mangrove swamps and coral reefs are two of the most critical habitats in the marine world. Thousands of species of fish and invertebrates spend part of their life cycles hanging around mangrove swamps, coral reefs, or both. Kawas includes one of the largest remaining expanses of mangroves on the entire Atlantic coast of America, and the largest area of coral reef in Honduras outside of the Bay Islands.

The diversity of life here is quite amazing. Within the boundaries of the park are over 500 species of plants, 49 mammals, 68 reptiles, 345 birds, 142 insects, 70 freshwater fish and 51 corals. Over 100 threatened and endangered species make their home here, including six species of sea turtle.

The waterways are thick with **dolphins** and **manatees**, and the beaches are crawling with crabs. In the forest live white-faced and howler **monkeys**, agoutis, *pizotes*, hummingbirds, oropendulas and toucans. The lagoons are teeming with **water birds** such as pelicans, herons, egrets, kingfishers, wood storks and roseate spoonbills. A vast profusion of vegetation – almond and coconut trees, orchids and bromeliads – covers every square inch.

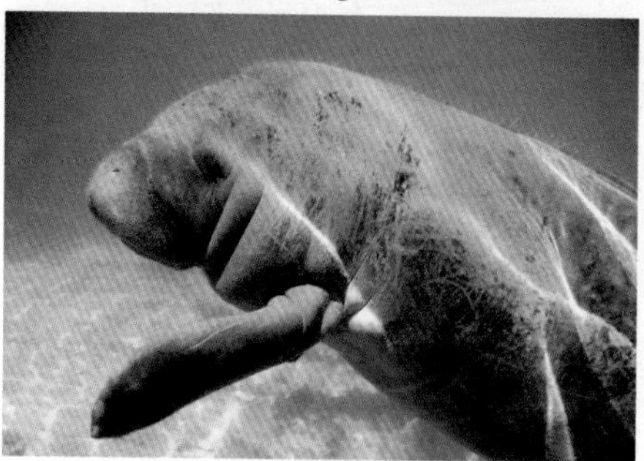

Several local tour operators offer trips to Punta Sal (as most locals still call it). Perhaps the best known is **Garífuna Tours** (www.garifunatours.com). Their office is near the central park in Tela, and they run daily boat tours that showcase the diversity of the area. **Coco Tours** (www.hondurascoco.com) is another possibility.

The best time to see birds and other wildlife is early morning, so we'll get up at the crack of dawn and be ready to go about 8am. We'll take a boat across Tela Bay, quite possibly seeing enormous pods of porpoises on the way. About a half-hour boat ride brings us to the peninsula of Punta Sal.

Now we hike across the peninsula. The path gets a bit steep as it winds up the hill, passing out of the mangrove forest and into tropical broadleaf rain forest. If we're lucky, we'll see some white-faced and howler monkeys. If nothing else, we're certain to hear the howlers in the distance, sounding like big dogs barking.

On the other side of the peninsula is **Playa Cocolito**, a classic Caribbean beach with snow-white sand and turquoise water. The coral reef is just offshore, so don mask fins and snorkel and check out yet another ecosystem. The snorkeling at Cocolito is okay, but it's nothing to compare with the scene on the Bay Islands. If you'll be visiting them at some point in your trip, then you may opt to skip the snorkeling interlude.

This tour winds up with a bit of lounging about on the beach, and a typical Garífuna lunch. We'll be back in Tela by midafternoon. This is Garífuna Tours' typical Punta Sal day trip, and it costs about $29 per person. Other operators do pretty much the same itinerary, with similar prices. Most tourists find that it makes a nice way to see the area, with a pleasant mix of activities and not too much strenuous hiking.

More adventurous travelers may find this itinerary a bit tame. No problem –

all the local operators have other options, or will even let you custom-design your own tour, for a price (remember, any of these tour companies will also arrange hotels, local flights, etc – a good way to make sure things go smoothly).

Bird lovers will want to take a boat tour to the **Micos Lagoon**, the best place to spot birds – over 350 species have been sighted here. Afterwards, make a stop in **Miami**, one of the most picturesque of the Garífuna villages, its people living in thatched huts just as they have for two centuries. There are a couple of little open-air *champas* here, where you can have a nice lunch of fresh grilled fish with rice and beans and fried plantains.

For many years, the only human inhabitants of the park were the Garífuna, but after the building of the railway around 1910, thousands of *mestizo* farmers began moving into the area and clearing the forest for farms and ranches. Huge areas were deforested, with ill effects for soil and water quality. Today a couple thousand Garífuna live in small villages within the park, and thousands of other local people live in adjacent buffer zones.

The organization called **PROLANSATE** founded the park in 1992 (the name is an acronym, signifying PROtection of LANcetilla, Punta SAl, and TExiguat). Today, PROLANSATE operates and protects five North Coast parks, with only 23 employees to patrol the parks and try to balance conservation with the needs of local residents and the demands of visitors.

As are all of Honduras's wilderness areas, Punta Sal is facing many threats. Local industries pollute the water, and fish farms have accidentally introduced exotic tilapia into the lagoons (tilapia are an insipid fish that are unfortunately becoming a staple on menus around the world, because they are cheap and easy to farm).

Deforestation has caused increased sedimentation, which is killing the park's coral reefs. Lethal Yellow Disease is killing coconut trees. Over-fishing, poaching and illegal logging are depleting the park's resources. But the gravest threat of all is simply the huge numbers of people moving into the area and clearing land for crops and cattle. PROLANSATE are doing their best to protect the park, but they are sadly short of money and resources. And the local powers-that-be have demonstrated in the most direct way possible that they won't tolerate interference with their business interests (see sidebar on this page).

Ongoing development threatens not only the natural resources of the park, but the Garífuna's traditional way of life as well. Part of PROLANSATE's mission is to protect their culture, teaching them sustainable farming techniques, hiring them as tour guides and park guards, and helping them to recover from the devastation of Hurricane Mitch. *Info:* Most visitors arrive by boat from Tela, but it is possible to drive to Miami (with 4WD) and hire a boat there. Entry fee is 30 Lempiras ($2). There's a bit of a visitors' center in Miami, but no other facilities. www.prolansate.org; Tel. 448-2042.

Sunday

I warned you to stay out of the discos in the **Zona Viva**, but you went anyway, didn't you? After dancing to *punta* music and slugging *mojitos* until

Eco-War

In Honduras, protecting the environment can be hazardous to your health. Some of those who profit from agricultural development, logging and other environmentally-destructive activities are willing to kill to protect their interests, and the authorities are powerless to stop them. **Jeanette Kawas**, the president of **PROLANSATE**, had campaigned against a plan to drain part of Punta Sal National Park for development. One day in 1995, she was shot dead at her home. Despite the fact that an eyewitness identified the killer, and informants named the person who ordered the hit, the case was dropped without explanation, and no one was ever charged.

This murder was no isolated case; other Honduran activists have been assassinated over the years, and various international bodies have accused the Honduran government of turning a blind eye. So, please treat Honduras's parks and preserves with respect, and do your best to support local businesses. The price to preserve these treasures is high.

almost dawn, you won't be making an early start today. That's okay. We still have time to balance beach and forest with a visit to **Lancetilla Botanical Garden**.

The largest botanical garden in Central America, Lancetilla has over 1,200 species of tropical plants from all over the world. It consists of two sections: the **arboretum** has six km of walking trails, with fruit trees, flowers and other plants neatly labeled. The adjacent **Lancetilla Nature Reserve** is much larger. There's a trail leading through it that requires about three hours to walk. Guided tours are available.

Lancetilla was founded in 1925 by the United Fruit Company. They had no altruistic purpose – their goal was to study the various diseases that afflicted banana plants, and to experiment with tropical plants from around the world to see which might profitably be grown in Honduras. Today the park is run by the National School of Forest Sciences.

Lancetilla has not only native Central American plants, but **exotic fruits from all over the world**, including such curiosities as mangosteens, keppel fruits, durians, rambutans and carambolas from Malaysia, pili nuts from the Philippines, Barbados cherries, and jaboticabas from Brazil. The akee fruit is poisonous until it ripens and the fruit cracks open, when it can be cooked and looks (and tastes) a bit like scrambled eggs.

There are other fruits growing here that you won't want to taste, or even touch, such as the round orange-green fruit of the strychnine tree, not to mention the deadly javiello, and termenalia trees with their poisonous sap.

Towering bamboo, fragrant jasmine, rustling palms and all the other wonders of the tropics are here in leafy profusion. Flower lovers will delight in the **National Collection of Orchids**, with over 1,000 varieties of orchids and other exotic flowers.

More than 200 species of birds have been identified in the park, including some that are very rare elsewhere. You may see several varieties of trogons, motmots, harpies, oropéndolas and toucans, to say nothing of swarms of hummingirds and butterflies.

The **Lancetilla River** runs through the site, and offers several nice swimming areas. A dip in the cool river water is just the ticket after an hour or two of wandering the paths in the jungle heat. *Info:* Located about 5 km southwest of Tela. www.lancetilla.org; Tel. 448-1740. Open daily 7am-3:30pm. Admission $6. Lodging is available in some small cabins and a guest house ($15 double).

A WONDERFUL WEEK ON THE NORTH COAST

A week gives you time for both the rain forest and the beach. Tour **Pico Bonito** and go rafting on the **Cangrejal**, then visit **Punta Sal** or less-touristed **Punta Izopo** or **Cuero y Salado**. Don't forget to leave plenty of time for lounging about on the beach near Tela.

RECOMMENDED PLAN: If you have a week, divide your time between **La Ceiba** and **Tela,** enjoying both ecotourism and water sports in both places. Stay at a jungle lodge near La Ceiba, explore **Pico Bonito National Park** and take a **rafting trip** on the Cangrejal. Stay on the beach near Tela, and visit the **coastal parks** Jeanette Kawas (Punta Sal) and Punta Izopo, and one or more of the nearby Garífuna villages.

If you have more time, you may want to head west to the funky little beach town of **Omoa**, or east to **Trujillo**, where an old Spanish fort dominates the town and a couple of less-visited wilderness areas are within easy reach.

LA CEIBA

The third largest city in Honduras (about 250,000 people) is a fairly young one, both historically and demographically. It was founded in 1872, and is named for an enormous Ceiba tree by the beach, where locals used to gather to trade. During the bad old banana days, it developed into a major port.

Today La Ceiba is known as Honduras's **ecotourism capital**, as the easily accessible Pico Bonito National Park is nearby. It's also the gateway to the Bay Islands, and to the wild eastern region of La Moskitia.

La Ceiba is also famous as the country's **nightlife capital**. As the locals (*ceibeños*) will tell you, "Tegucigalpa thinks, San Pedro Sula works, and La Ceiba parties!" With all this going for it, the La Ceiba area might just be the perfect base for a lengthy visit to the country.

Just outside of town is **Pico Bonito National Park**, its namesake 2,435-meter peak clad in cloud forests and watered by rushing mountain streams. Pico Bonito is one of the most diverse parks in Honduras and, although it still has vast areas of uninhabited, unspoiled wilderness, it's quite easy to visit.

Along the edge of the park, the **Cangrejal River** tumbles through the lush rain forest. This is some of the finest rafting and kayaking water in the world, with a wide range of rapids to suit all levels of skill (see *Best Activities*).

La Ceiba itself is a noisy and dirty port city - not very attractive. But it has plenty of stores, banks, internet cafés and other necessaries. Most of the hotels, restaurants and tourist facilities are located

Don't Miss ...

Pico Bonito National Park - some of Central America's most pristine rain forest
Jeanette Kawas National Park - coastal region of beaches, lagoons and mangrove swamps teeming with colorful birds and monkeys
Lancetilla Botanical Gardens - largest botanical garden in Central America famous for exotic plants and birding
Garífuna Villages - spend some quality time with the locals at a funky beachfront village

in the area around the **Central Park**, an agreeable shady plaza a few blocks back from the beach.

I strongly recommend staying at one of the **jungle lodges** – there are good choices in the budget, moderate and first-class categories, so why not sleep right in the rain forest? You might never have to come into town at all, unless you want to sample some of the notorious nightlife.

At night, join the rainbow mix of *catrachos, gringos* and *turistas* from all over the world slurping rum and dance to *punta* music in the clubs of the **Zona Viva** from midnight until dawn (see *Nightlife & Entertainment*).

Divers board the *Utila Aggressor* live-aboard boat (www.aggressor.com; Tel. 800/348-2628 US) in La Ceiba for seven-day trips to rarely explored spots in the Bay Islands (see *Best Activities*).

Most buses depart from the **central bus terminal** (unlike in San Pedro or Tegucigalpa). Hedman Alas runs first-class buses to San Pedro Sula and Tegus, which depart from their own terminal. There is daily **ferry service** between La Ceiba and the Bay Islands of Utila and Roatan. The ferry terminal (Muelle Cabotaje) is 8 km east of town.

La Ceiba's **airport** is a hub for all three domestic airlines, (Sosa, Atlantic and Isleña, see *Practical Matters*) and you can fly to Tegucigalpa, San Pedro Sula, Roatan, Utila, Guanaja, Trujillo, and the Moskitia region.

There's a **tourist information center** on the Central Park, on the first floor of the Banco de Occidente building. Open Mon-Fri 8am-4pm; Sat 8am-noon. www.laceiba.com.

NEAR LA CEIBA

The Garífuna beach villages of **Sambo Creek** and **Corozal** are popular spots for an afternoon trip. They both have nice beaches and *champas* where you can have a seafood dinner.

Río Maria, about 8 km from of La Ceiba on the road to Trujillo, makes an easy day trip. 45 minutes' hike along the river, passing some beautiful ocean views, brings you to a chain of clear and idyllic pools in the river – the perfect spot for a swim amid the green of the rain forest. As at any isolated area in Honduras, it's safer to go with a local guide.

A local tour company can also take you to **Cacao Lagoon**, about 24 km from town, for a canoe trip around a mangrove-lined lagoon. You'll see vast flocks of wading birds, as well as white-faced and howler monkeys.

The Lodge at Pico Bonito is well worth a visit, even if you aren't staying there. For a small fee, you can hike their well-maintained trails and visit their butterfly farm and serpentarium.

The Garífuna People

The **Garífuna**, also known as Garinagu, have a very colorful history. Their ancestors were indigenous Caribs on the Caribbean island of St. Vincent, and blacks from West Africa who arrived on the island in the 1600s when slave ships bringing them to the West Indies wrecked on the coast. During the Napoleonic wars, the Garinagu allied themselves with French settlers on the island, and fought against the British. As punishment, the British deported them to the island of Roatan.

When Roatan proved to be too small and infertile to support them, the Garinagu began to migrate to the mainland. Today they live all along the Caribbean coast of Central America, from southern Belize to northern Nicaragua. They have preserved much of their traditional culture, including their own Garífuna language (most also speak Spanish or English).

Traditional Garif music has evolved into Punta Rock, a genre of music that combines traditional rhythms played on the *garawon* drum, rattles, and turtle shells with modern instruments such as guitars and synthesizers, often with socially conscious lyrics. The huge popularity of *punta* has been a major factor in the renaissance of the Garífuna culture.

Visitors also love the typical Garífuna cuisine, served at informal beach restaurants called *champas*: casava, coconut bread, conch soup and grilled fish.

To learn more about the Garífuna culture, check out the web portal www.garinet.com.

TELA

Tela is Honduras's premier beach destination outside of the Bay Islands, and there are many attractions in the area, including **Lancetilla Gardens**, **Jeanette Kawas National Park** and **Punta Izopo Wildlife Refuge**, as well as several beachfront Garífuna villages. Tela is easy to get to, about equidistant from the airports at San Pedro Sula and La Ceiba, and there's a pretty good selection of lodging places and facilities. With all this going for it, it's no surprise that Tela is steadily growing into a major tourist destination.

Conquistador Cristobal de Olid founded a town here in 1524, and called it Triunfo de la Cruz (Triumph of the Cross). Some say that the name Tela derives from a shortened version of this name. Today **Triunfo de la Cruz** refers to a village to the east of Tela, inhabited mainly by indigenous Garífuna people. The Bay of Tela was the scene of battles between English buccaneers and Spanish treasure galleons.

Later, Tela became a major center of the all-powerful banana business as the headquarters of the Tela Railroad Company (a division of United Fruit), which managed to convince (that is, pay off) the government to give it millions of acres of land for banana plantations in return for building a short stretch of railroad between the plantations and the port (most of which was later abandoned). In 1976, the banana barons moved out, their experimental farm became Lancetilla Botanical Garden, and some of their old housing became a beachfront hotel.

The area of Tela would make a good place to stay for a week or two, and use as a hub for day trips to the nearby wilderness areas, as well as overnight trips to Copán (three hours away) and the Bay Islands. The attractions of the area are outside of town – central Tela doesn't entice most visitors to linger for very long.

The center of town is a small grid of streets with a central square just two blocks from the water. Restaurants, bars and discos line the **beach boardwalk**, where local hustlers offer cheap hotel rooms and tours to the area's attractions (as well as other, less respectable diversions). The town is pretty grungy, and the beach right in town is not an inviting place for a swim – it's dirty, and there are sleazy characters hanging around just waiting to steal your stuff when you go in the water.

Once you get out of town, you'll find a **beautiful white sand beach** stretching for 40 km around a large bay. There are plenty of secluded swimming spots, but unfortunately it's not safe to swim or stroll on your own. A pleasant and safe place to enjoy the beach is by the **Villas Telamar** hotel, just west of the town center (see *Best Sleeps*), but of course it's crawling with other sun worshipers. If you want to enjoy some of the idyllic beaches out of town, talk to one of the officers of the local **Tourist Police**.

In the past, Tela had a serious problem with crime against tourists, which threatened to sabotage its development as the next hot Caribbean resort. The authorities established a new force called the Tourist Police, English-speaking officers who patrol the beaches and other tourist areas. If you want to take a walk on the beach, just ask one of the officers and they will actually accompany you. The program has been a great success, and crime has fallen off dramatically.

The **Garífuna Museum**, on the second floor of the **Mango Café**, has some moderately interesting exhibits on the history and customs of Honduras's Garífuna culture (open Mon-Sat 9am-10pm; free). The nearby Garífuna villages of **San Juan**, **Tornabé**, **Miami**, and **Triunfo de la Cruz** are popular stops for visitors.

After La Ceiba, Tela is the nightlife capital of the North Coast. The beach area has a plethora of discos that heave from midnight until dawn on the weekends. It's a colorful scene, to say the least, with hookers and dope freely available, and drunken disagreements often settled with knives or guns. Tela nightlife isn't like Cancun nightlife. Having a few drinks at the beach bars is safe enough, but venturing to the late-night discos is not for the faint-hearted, and definitely not safe for unaccompanied ladies. *Info:* Good roads connect Tela with La Ceiba and San Pedro Sula. The drive to either is about an hour. **Hedman Alas** runs a couple of buses a day to La Ceiba and San Pedro (via the airport). Their terminal is at the Villas Telamar hotel. **Garífuna Tours** runs a slightly more expensive shuttle service to La Ceiba, San Pedro and the airport.

The local **Chamber of Tourism's** web site at www.telahonduras.com has some information about area attractions and lodging.

PUNTA IZOPO NATIONAL PARK

This park on the eastern side of Tela Bay is smaller than Kawas, and sees far fewer visitors. Like its more famous neighbor, **Punta Izopo** consists of a sprawling expanse of wetlands formed by the estuaries of several rivers. A peninsula juts out into the sea, rising into the small mountain that gives the park its name. Rock and sand beaches are lined by coral reefs and backed by miles of mangrove lagoons and waterways.

The only way into the park is by boat. Most visitors will choose to put themselves in the hands of **Garífuna Tours**, which runs daily trips by kayak. You'll head out past the town of Triunfo de la Cruz, put in the kayaks and paddle into the mangroves. This is an excellent way to see the wildlife, as you can silently glide right up on birds and other local inhabitants that might be scared away by the noise of a motorboat.

Mangroves

Mangroves grow in saltwater coastal habitats, with their exposed roots right in the tidal water. The roots trap sediment as the tide flows in and out, so mangroves can actually build new islands.

The underwater forest of their roots makes a perfect habitat for filter-feeding organisms such as barnacles, oysters, sponges, and sea squirts, which anchor to the mangrove roots and filter out food from the water as the tide goes in and out. Adolescent **fish**, shrimp, lobsters and many other sea creatures find shelter and food among the mangrove roots. **Birds** and **monkeys** live in the trees.

Mangrove wetlands have many **ecological benefits**. They prevent coastal erosion, filter out pollutants, and absorb some of the wave energy of storm surges caused by hurricanes.

Most of the trees you'll see are the black, red and white **mangroves** that create their own unique ecosystem between land and water, but the area has over 500 plant species, including interesting trees such as mangos, marañon, coconut palms, guanacaste, cacao and sea grapes. The North Coast of Honduras has the largest remaining area of mangrove wetlands in the Americas.

Punta Izopo is particularly noted for its biodiversity, with many endangered and rare animals. The **32 mammal species** include monkeys (both white-faced and howler), nutrias, anteaters, sloths and jaguars. The waterways are home to manatees, dolphins, crocodiles, caimans and four species of sea turtles, two of which have been observed laying eggs on the beaches in the eastern regions of the park. There are over 70 species of freshwater fish. Fishermen will be excited by the tarpon and snook. Reptiles include iguanas, boa constrictors and Honduran pythons.

And birds? Over half of the species that exist in Honduras can be seen here. It's worth visiting for the wealth of water birds alone: roseate spoonbills, the rare jabirú stork, ibis, ducks, egrets and herons of all descriptions. You'll also see raptors such as eagles, many migratory species and, in the forests, hummingbirds, toucans and parrots. In March and April you may observe birds courting and building nests. Pelicans and other waterbirds put on their resplendent nuptial plumage during this season. *Info:* www.prolansate.org/htms/izopo.htm; Tel. 448-2041.

CUERO Y SALADO WILDLIFE REFUGE

This park is named for two of the rivers whose estuaries form a large area of wetlands about 30 km to the west of La Ceiba. Like Kawas, it's a labyrinthine network of mangrove-lined rivers, lagoons and swamps. Cuero y Salado is one of the most important habitats for the endangered **West Indian manatee** in Central America. Other denizens include crocodiles, caimans, turtles, howler and white-faced monkeys, agoutis, kinkajous, sloths, jaguars, ocelots, iguanas, boa constrictors, 200 species of birds and scores of freshwater fish species.

About 15 river basins, including a couple that flow through nearby Pico Bonito National Park, empty into Cuero y Salado. The 13,000-hectare park was named as a protected area in 1986. Getting to the park is quite an adventure in itself. Any of the local tour operators in La Ceiba will take you to the park. If you choose to go on your own, you'll need to contact the FUCSA office ahead of time.

The only way to get into the park, other than by boat, is along the railroad tracks from La Unión to a place called **Salado Barra**. This is the only remaining section of the railroad that was built in 1908 by the Standard Fruit Company. The Honduran government gave millions of acres of land to Standard Fruit in exchange for their building a railroad. But the only track that was ever laid led from the banana plantations to the seaport, and they later abandoned most of that. So this little stretch of railway is the only lasting benefit the people of Honduras ever received in exchange for all that land.

A small railcar runs throughout the day beginning at 7am, and takes about 45 minutes to get to Salado Barra. There seems to be no fixed schedule – they leave as soon as there enough visitors to fill the car. The ride costs $5 per person in groups of two or more. For even more adventure, you can have a local take you in a *burra* – a small hand-powered railcar like the ones you see in old Westerns.

A FUCSA guide will meet you at the visitors' center, and take you by boat on one of several itineraries through the mangroves. There's a nice beach where you can cool off in the Caribbean afterwards. *Info:* The park is administered by the **Cuero and Salado Foundation** (**FUCSA**), www.cueroysalado.org; Tel. 440-1990. Their office is in Barrio La Merced, Calle 15, in the Edificio Daytona, La Ceiba. The visitors' center at Salado Barra has a small gift shop, rest rooms and some *very basic* cabins for overnight stays. The entrance fee to the refuge is about $10.

Buses for La Unión leave from the San José bus terminal in La Ceiba, about every hour starting at 6:30 am. The ride takes about an hour and a half. To drive to La Unión, take the highway towards Tela to km 169 and take a right.

PUERTO CORTÉS

This is the largest seaport in Honduras, and one of the most important in Central America. It was founded in 1524, but for most of its history was just another sleepy seaside town. It began to grow into a major port during the banana years, but really started to explode when it was designated a **Free Trade Zone** in 1976. A four-lane highway to San Pedro Sula was built in 1996, connecting the port to the thriving *máquilas* (factories) of Honduras's main industrial region.

A typical bustling, dirty port town, Puerto Cortés has nothing in particular to interest the tourist. Just east of town however, are the Garífuna communities of **Travesia** and **Bajamar**, where you'll find a lively cultural scene and some beautiful beaches. Bajamar's annual Garífuna dance festival is a highlight.

West of Puerto Cortés is the village of **Cieneguita**, which has some very nice beaches (packed with locals on weekends, almost deserted during the week).

Going to Belize?

There is a boat from **Puerto Cortés** to **Big Creek**, **Placencia** and **Belize City** that leaves every Monday at 10am. Schedules may be erratic, so call in advance: Tel. 665-5556 or 655-1200.

OMOA

Omoa is the last major town as you head west on the North Coast towards Guatemala. A historic city with a classic **Spanish fort**, it's an increasingly popular stop on the backpacker circuit. The area is very picturesque, with the forest-clad **Merendon Mountains** rising rapidly from the coast with its funky little villages.

Omoa was one of the earliest settlements in Honduras. In the 1500s when British **privateers, buccaneers and freebooters** of various kinds used to prey on Spanish shipping, Omoa was a strategic point between the British strongholds of Belize and the Bay Islands, so the Spanish built a fortress here. By the time the huge fort was completed, the pirate era was winding down, so it never saw much action. Now **San Fernando de Omoa** is a National Monument, and a fascinating history lesson.

The nearby mountains have excellent hiking opportunities, including some nice trails along the river, with spectacular waterfalls and nice peaceful places to swim. **Cusuco National Park** is not far away (see *Chapter 6*).

The nearby town of **Masca** is worth a visit, a quaint little Garífuna community with several possibilities for hikes in the area. There are a couple of hotels in town.

Going to Guatemala?

The border crossing to Guatemala is at **Corinto**. Several buses a day leave from Puerto Cortés or Omoa (about 2.5 hours from Puerto Cortés to Corinto). Once in Corinto, you'll need to catch a pickup truck to **Arizona** in Guatemala. You can make arrangements at a small store called **Pulpería Arnold**.

When you arrive in Omoa, stop in at **Roli's Place** (see *Best Sleeps*) for the latest info on activities in the area, and crossing to **Guatemala**. *Info:* San Fernando de Omoa is open Mon-Fri, 8am-4pm; Sat-Sun 9am-5pm. Small entrance fee. Guided tours available.

CAYOS COCHINOS MARINE RESERVE

Cayos Cochinos (Hog Keys) are a group of tiny islands just a few miles off the coast, uninhabitated except for a dive lodge called **Plantation Beach Resort**. The islands are a UNESCO World Heritage site and a protected marine reserve. The Honduran Coral Reef Foundation administers the park, and has a research station there (not open to the public). *Info:* www.cayoscochinos.org.

Destinos de Exito (www.destinosdeexito.com) runs full-day tours of the keys from La Ceiba, with snorkeling, a hike and a stop at Plantation Beach for lunch.

TRUJILLO

Traveling east along the North Coast, Trujillo is the last major town before you enter the trackless wild of La Moskitia. This is one of the most historic towns in Honduras. **Christopher Columbus** landed near here in 1502, his first landing on the American mainland.

Trujillo's excellent harbor made it an important port, and for years it was the capital of Honduras. Its strategic location made it a battleground between the Spanish and the British, who mounted raids on the Spanish colonies from their bases on the

Bay Islands and in the Moskitia. In 1550, the Spanish built the **Fortress of Santa Barbara** to defend the town, but the town was captured and sacked so many times that the Spanish were almost forced to abandon it, before finally making peace with the British. In 1860, the adventurer **William Walker** was captured and executed here in Trujillo. You can visit his tomb in the municipal cemetery.

Today, the main attractions are the fort, in the center of town overlooking the bay, and the **beaches**. The beach right in town is fairly pleasant, and has several waterfront restaurants and bars. However, the **beach by the airstrip**, just a few minutes east of town, is nicer. Here you'll find the **Hotel Christopher Columbus** (see *Best Sleeps*) and a couple of other pleasant beach restaurants. **Team Marin Travel Services** (www.teammarintravel.com; Tel. 441-2091 or 987-0875) operates a pleasant ferry between Trujillo and Guanaja. It runs a couple times per week and costs $30 per person. *Info:* Fortaleza de Santa Bárbara (El Castillo) is open daily 8am-noon and 1-4pm. Entry is about $5. There's some information about the town at www.trujillohonduras.com.

CAPIRO Y CALENTURA NATIONAL PARK

This seldom-visited park protects a mountainous, stream-crossed expanse of broadleaf rain forest that rises behind the town of Trujillo to the peak of Calentura (1,220m). Along the Río Negro are many impressive waterfalls. The forest is particularly lush, and is inhabitated by all the usual animals. The park is especially known for its large numbers of howler monkeys and scarlet macaws.

The park has several trails, most branching off the dirt road that runs past the hotel **Villa Brinkley** (see *Best Sleeps*). A 45-minute hike up the river will take you to the park's highest waterfall. The hardy can hike all the way up to **Calentura**, and will be rewarded with a bit of cloud forest and a panoramic view – on a clear day you can even see the Bay Islands. Spelunkers, ask your guides about the **Cuyamel Caves**.

Turtle Tours (www.turtletours.de), located at the Villa Brinkley, does 3-day/2-night tours of the park.

LAGUNA GUAIMORETO WILDLIFE RESERVE

East of Trujillo is the **Guaimoreto Lagoon**, a large brackish lagoon lined by mangrove wetlands. You can only get here by boat. If you do, you'll see vast flocks of waterbirds, crocodiles and caimans, and maybe a dolphin or manatee dropping in from the ocean. *Info:* Capiro y Calentura and Laguna Guaimoreto are administered by a non-profit foundation called FUCAGUA. Their office is located on the second floor of the library, on Trujillo's central plaza. Stop in for current information or to arrange a tour. Turtle Tours runs tours of both parks.

6. COPÁN & THE WEST

The **Mayan Ruins of Copán** are Honduras's second-most visited attraction, after the Bay Islands. The exotic sculptures and other art treasures make it arguably the most interesting of all the world's Mayan sites. The quaint village of **Copán Ruinas** is a tourist hub, with all sorts of attractions in the area.

But this region has much more to offer. High in the jungle-clad mountains, you'll find a couple of the country's **best nature reserves**, and several **small colonial towns** that see few foreign visitors.

ONE GREAT DAY IN COPÁN

Copán is one of the few places in Honduras where tourist facilities are quite well developed. You should have little trouble dropping in for a day. There are plenty of bus (and now, air) connections to other parts of the country. Plan ahead with a local tour operator, and you can see the highlights of the ruins in a day.

Morning
The Mayan Ruins of Copán are one of the most important cultural monuments in the world. One of the largest excavated Mayan sites, Copán was a **cultural capital**, and is richer in sculptures, hieroglyphics and art treasures than any other known Mayan site.

To get the most from your visit, I recommend taking a guided tour, which you can arrange at the visitors' center. The **Copán Guide Association** (Tel. 651-4018) offers tours of the ruins, starting at $20. *Info:* Entry to the park is $10, which also includes the Sepulturas archaeological site. Entry to the Museum of Mayan Sculpture is $5. The park and the Sculpture Museum are open daily 8am-4pm.

As you explore the sights of Copán, your guide will tell you the fascinating story of the highly advanced Mayan civilization and the ceremonial site of Copán.

Stelae

A *stele* (plural: *stelae*) is a standing stone slab, generally erected to commemorate an event such as the reign of a ruler. Mayan stelae feature images and glyphs carved in relief. Most were originally painted with bright colors.

The **Great Plaza** features elaborately-carved stelae and altars featuring images of Mayan rulers and gods, with hieroglyphic inscriptions. Back in the golden age of the Maya (300-900 AD), the stelae,

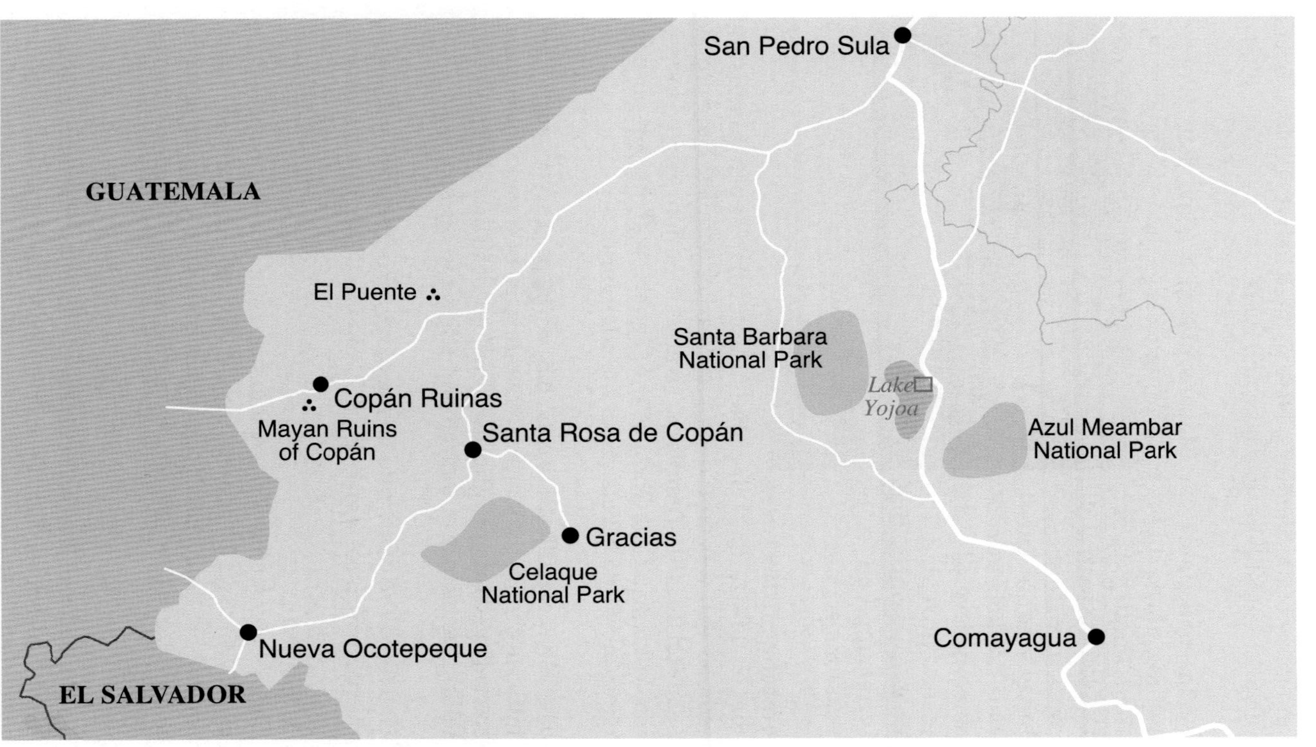
San Pedro Sula
GUATEMALA
El Puente
Santa Barbara
National Park
Lake
Yojoa
Copán Ruinas
Mayan Ruins
of Copán
Santa Rosa de Copán
Azul Meambar
National Park
Gracias
Celaque
National Park
Comayagua
Nueva Ocotepeque
EL SALVADOR

and many of the buildings, were painted in bright colors, traces of which can still be seen here and there.

At the **Ball Court**, the Mayans played a game that involved putting a hard rubber ball through a stone hoop without using their hands. Apparently they took it almost as seriously as today's Latin Americans do their soccer – some believe that the losers provided the human sacrifices that were supposed to appease the gods.

Towering 100 feet over the Great Plaza, the **Acropolis** is a large complex of pyramids and temples that was built over many earlier temples. Here are the beautiful **Rosalila Temple**, or Temple of the Sun, painted in rose-lilac colors, and the **Plaza of the Jaguars**, with its rich carvings depicting Maya beliefs about the afterworld.

The **Hieroglyphic Stairway** has 63 steps, carved with 1,500 intricate glyphs, the longest known text left by the ancient Mayans. It is believed to be an official chronology of all the rulers of Copán, telling the history of their great battles and deeds.

Unless you're really into archaeology, skip the optional visit to the **tunnels**. It costs an extra $12, and is only slightly interesting.

Afternoon

There's a cafeteria-style restaurant right on site, but it serves exactly the sort of generic tourist feed you'd expect of a place squarely in the center of the beaten path. However, we're trying to see a lot in one day, so we'll refuel with an overpriced burger for now.

The **Museum of Mayan Sculpture**, adjacent to the ruins, costs an extra five bucks, but it's worth every Lempira. Many of the original art treasures of Copán are displayed here in the museum, protected from the elements, while the *in situ* versions are actually clever replicas. Surprise!

The centerpiece of the museum is a life-size replica of the Rosalila Temple, in all its original pink splendor. The collection of Mayan sculpture is the finest in the world.

If there's time, have another stroll through the ruins after you've seen the museum. I think you'll find it quite interesting to take a second look now that you know a bit about the history of the city.

A FANTASTIC COPÁN WEEKEND

There are plenty of interesting sights around Copán. A weekend gives you just enough time to devote a good solid day to the ruins, **hike in the beautiful countryside**, and spend some time hanging out in the town of **Copán Ruinas**. But beware – once you get a taste of how much there is to do around here, you'll wish you had more time!

Friday
We'll show up in Copán Ruinas Friday evening and scope out the scene. Our first stop is the **Tunkul Bar and Restaurant**, for a cold beer and a chat with the staff about what's going on in the area. The in-house **Go Native Tours** (Tel. 651-4410) is only one of a dozen tour operators in town, offering trips to Mayan sites, cloud forests, coffee farms, Lenca villages and all sorts of other fascinating sights in the region. Another option is **Yaragua Tours** (www.yaragua.com; Tel. 651-4147). For our tour of the ruins tomorrow morning, we'll simply call the **Copán Guide Association** at the park (Tel. 651-4018).

With our plans for tomorrow all sorted, let's think about dinner. Copán Ruinas has several very nice possibilities, including healthy and delicious fare at **Twisted Tanya's**, or hearty grilled meats with a nice river view at **Carnitas Nía Lola** (see *Best Eats*).

Copán Ruinas goes to bed pretty early, and so will we, because we're going to get up bright and early for our visit to the ruins. There are good lodging options in all price ranges, from the elegant **Hotel Marina Copán** to the cozy **Casa de Café**.

Saturday

After a breakfast of sweet and juicy tropical fruit and rich Honduran coffee, we'll head to the park in plenty of time to be the first through the gates at 8am, so we'll have an hour or two to enjoy the ruins in relative peace, before the flood of day-trippers arrives. Early birds may see deer grazing among the ancient palaces in the morning mist. By late morning, the sun has burned off the mist, and the deer are replaced by herds of gringos with their ball caps, t-shirts and water bottles.

The Mayan Ruins of Copán are one of the most important cultural monuments in the world, and have been designated a UNESCO World Heritage Site. Copán is one of the three largest and most famous excavated Mayan sites. Copán was a **cultural capital**, and is richer in sculptures, hieroglyphics and art treasures than any other known Mayan site.

It has also been the subject of more research than any other Mayan city. Because of the wealth of hieroglyphics, Copán has been an invaluable source of information for scientists researching the ancient Mayan civilization.

During their golden age (300-900 AD) the Mayan empire extended from southern Mexico through Guatemala, Belize and El Salvador to western Honduras. The Mayans developed a highly advanced civilization – their calendar and their knowledge of astronomy were unequalled until modern times.

Copán's golden age began in 553 with the ruler **Moon Jaguar**, who built the spectacular Rosalila Temple. Other prominent potentates were **Smoke Imix**, who built many stelae and temples, **18 Rabbit**, who built the Great Plaza and the Ball Court, **SmokeShell**, who built the famous Hieroglyphic Stairway, and **Yax Pac**, who built Altar Q, which depicts all of Copán's rulers up to that point.

Sometime during the 9th century AD, the grand city of Copán was abandoned. While it sounds romantic to say that "no one knows why," in fact modern scientists have a pretty good idea of why the Mayan civilization collapsed.

The ancient Mayans cleared large areas of forest for agriculture, but the soil proved surprisingly poor for growing crops, so as the population grew, they kept clearing more and more land. The **deforestation** led to erosion, making the land even less able to support decent crop yields. In the end they simply couldn't grow enough food to feed themselves, and the population went into a long decline, until the Maya had dwindled to scattered bands of hunter-gatherers and farmers.

Unfortunately, history is currently repeating itself in Honduras. In many parts of the country, **slash-and-burn agriculture** has denuded whole regions, leaving the poor subsistence farmers unable to make a living. Forced to leave their homes, they move into more remote areas and repeat the process there. The Honduran government is making a valiant effort to conserve some of the rain forest, but they simply don't have the resources to stop the destruction.

It's food for thought as we explore the sights of Copán. The **Great Plaza** is a large open space dotted with stelae and altars featuring bas-relief statues of Mayan rulers and gods, with hieroglyphic inscriptions. Back in the day, the stelae, and many of the buildings, were painted in bright colors, traces of which can still be seen here and there. Most of the stelae in the Great Plaza are believed to have been built around AD 710-740 by the ruler 18 Rabbit.

South of the Great Plaza is the **Ball Court**, decorated with images of macaws, which were sacred birds. Here the Mayans played a game that involved putting a hard rubber ball through a stone hoop without using their hands. Some believe that the losers provided the human sacrifices that were supposed to appease the gods.

Towering 100 feet over the Great Plaza, the **Acropolis** is a large complex of pyramids and temples that was built over many earlier temples. Here are the beautiful **Rosalila Temple**, or Temple of the Sun, painted in rose-lilac colors, and the **Plaza of the Jaguars**, with its rich carvings depicting Maya beliefs about the afterworld.

The tallest structure at the site is the **Hieroglyphic Stairway**, built in AD 749 by the ruler Smoke Shell. The 63 steps are carved with 1,500 glyphs, the longest known text left by the ancient Mayans. It is believed to be a chronology of all the rulers of Copán, telling the history of their great battles and deeds. The stairway has provided archaeologists with some important missing links in the city's history.

One of the most interesting artworks at Copán is **Altar Q**, which was built by one of the city's last leaders, Yax Pac. It depicts all 16 of Copán's rulers up to that point, with Yax K'uk'Mo' handing the symbolic baton of kingship over to Yax Pac.

The archaeologists have dug a network of **tunnels** under the site, and two are open to the public for an extra $12. Everybody talks about them, but most visitors find them only slightly interesting.

Late morning is when the main site begins to get crowded with day trippers, so let's leave it to them for a while, and head a couple of kilometers down the road to **Las Sepulturas Archaeological Site**. The main site of Copán was a government and ceremonial center, but Las Sepulturas was where the local upper class lived. It's one of the few Mayan residential areas that have been found, and provides a fascinating look at the everyday life of the people.

After an hour or so at Las Sepulturas, it's time to think about lunch. We could take a short taxi ride back to the town of Copán Ruinas, and eat in a nice restaurant, but we still have a lot to see today, so it might be better just to brave the tourist hordes and have an overpriced and generic (but quick) lunch at the cafeteria here at the park.

After lunch, we'll visit the **Museum of Mayan Sculpture**, adjacent to the ruins. The museum costs an extra five bucks, but it's well worth it. Many of the original art treasures of Copán are displayed here in the museum, protected from the elements, while the *in situ* versions are actually clever replicas.

The centerpiece of the museum is a life-sized reproduction of the Rosalila Temple, in all its original pink splendor. The weathered gray stones that we see at Mayan sites today are in fact only shadows of their original beauty, when they were painted in bright colors.

Here you'll find the finest collection of Mayan sculpture in the world, over 3,000 pieces, many of them mounted in the facades of six reconstructed buildings. Highlights include four of the most beautiful stelae from the site, the original facade of the Ball Court, and the original Altar Q, with its relief depicting the 16 kings of Copán.

By the time we've explored the museum, it will be late in the afternoon, and the day-tripping hordes will be thinning out, but we still have time for another stroll through the ruins. I think you'll find it quite interesting to take a second look after you've seen the museum and learned a bit about the history of the city. *Info:* Entry to the park is $10, which also includes the Sepulturas archaeological site. Entry to the Museum of Mayan Sculpture is $5. The park and the Sculpture Museum are open daily 8am-4pm.

The **Copán Guide Association** offers tours of the Copán Ruins, starting at $20. You can arrange a tour on the spot at the park entrance, but it's wiser to reserve ahead. Tel. 651-4018.

We've spent a long day soaking up culture, and done a lot of walking, so in the evening we'll reward ourselves with a cold drink and a nice dinner in **Copán Ruinas**, a charming colonial village of cobblestone streets and adobe buildings with cheerful tile roofs.

The **Tunkul Restaurant and Bar** (see *Best Eats*) is one of the main hangouts in town. The owners are friendly locals who also run tours in the area. It's a capital place to get the latest local gossip, and compare notes with other hip travelers (the square tourists rushed through the ruins, then blew out of town this afternoon, without even noticing the quaint village, much less stopping for a beer and a chat with the locals).

Sunday

Rise and shine! This morning, we're going to hike through some of the most beautiful countryside in Honduras, up to **Los Sapos**, a minor Mayan site on a hill overlooking the valley of Copán. The carvings are pretty worn down, and aren't terribly interesting, but the view up here is splendid, and it's a good excuse for a moderate hike through the forest. Los Sapos is on the grounds of a very nice resort hotel called **Hacienda San Lucas** (see *Best Sleeps*). We could also get here by taxi or on horseback.

We can also visit a couple of the **Mayan stelae** that are scattered around the valley. There are at least a half-dozen individual stelae in the area, similar to the ones we saw yesterday in the Great Plaza. The best-known is called **La Pintada**, because it still bears traces of the original red paint. It's higher up the mountain from Los Sapos and has spectacular views.

Just before lunchtime, we'll head for the **Macaw Mountain Bird Park**, one of the area's most popular attractions. Scarlet macaws, parrots and toucans in a rainbow of colors flit about in large walk-in aviaries. The park is also a working coffee plantation, and you may spot many species of wild birds.

ALTERNATE PLAN

If you're **traveling with kids**, you may find that their interest in the ancient Maya is limited. Smaller children may not be up for long hikes. Take them to the **kids' museum** in Copán Ruinas (see below), then divide your day between **Macaw Mountain** and the **hot springs**.

They have a nice little riverside café here, where we'll have lunch and a cup of world-class coffee from their high-altitude coffee farm, Finca Miramundo. There's lots to see here (kids will especially like it), so let's make an afternoon of it. *Info:* www.macawmountain.com; Tel. 651-4245. Open daily 9am-5pm. Entry $10.

After a long day of walking through the forests, a nice soak in hot water is just what the doctor ordered. By the time you've been in Copán Ruinas ten minutes, you'll have heard about **Agua Caliente**, the local *balneario* or hot springs – every other person in town seems to be offering to take you there. The hot water from the springs mixes with the cool river water, and there are two pools where you can soak your tired joints, while enjoying the lovely green surroundings. *Info:* Open daily 8am-8pm. Entrance fee about $3.

A WEEKEND CLOUD FOREST ADVENTURE

Western Honduras has some of the country's finest national parks and nature reserves. The best one to visit on a weekend trip is **Celaque National Park**, where jungle rivers rush down from a mile-high cloud forest.

Friday Evening

The gateway to Celaque is the town of **Gracias**, just a couple of hours by car or bus from Copán Ruinas. Gracias is a well-preserved colonial town that has only recently begun to see a few tourists.

Guancascos Hotel and Restaurant (www.guancascos.com; Tel. 656-1219) is a local hangout for visitors heading for Celaque, so let's stop in there for the latest info. We're going to visit the park with a local guide. Not only will this be much safer and more convenient than wandering about on our own, but we'll have a better chance of spotting some wildlife. We're also going to contribute a few dollars to the local economy, which we hope will encourage the locals to preserve their rain forest instead of clear-cutting it for farms.

The helpful folks at Guancascos can put us in touch with a local guide, or we can arrange things through one of two well-known tour operators located in San Pedro Sula: **Maya Tropic Tours** (www.mtthonduras.com; Tel. 557-7071); and **Explore Honduras**, (www.explorehonduras.com; Tel. 552-6242).

We'll stay in comfort here in Gracias, either at Guancascos or just around the corner at the Hotel Patricia (see *Best Sleeps*), and get up bright and early for the 9-km ride up to the park.

ALTERNATE PLAN

Even if you're not up for a strenuous hike or camping out in the jungle, you can still enjoy Celaque. There are several **nice trails for day hikers**, including one that leads up the Rio Arcagual and through an organic coffee farm, and a longer one that brings you to a lookout point where you can see a huge waterfall cascading down the sheer mountainside.

Saturday

Any time you visit one of Honduras's wilderness areas, you want to be there as early in the morning as possible, because that's when birds and other wildlife are most active. The best plan is to camp out within the park, so that you can arise at dawn deep in the forest, far from other travelers. That's just what we're going to do. We've got our sleeping bags and rain gear, as well as food and water that we scored in Gracias yesterday. The guide is bringing along any other camping equipment we'll need.

The spectacular topography of this 266-square-kilometer park includes Honduras's highest point, the 2,870-meter **Cerro Las Minas** (El Castillo to the locals), as well as a high plateau where eleven rivers originate. This is the country's largest and highest cloud forest. Other ecosystems include pine forest and high-altitude savannah.

An easy afternoon's hike from the visitors' center brings us to the first base camp, **Campamento Don Tomas**, which consists of a small tin-roofed shack and an outhouse. Here we'll eat some of our provisions and pitch our sleeping bags for the night.

What is a Cloud Forest?

When moisture-filled warm air blows in from the ocean to meet the barrier of a high mountain range, it condenses to form a standing mass of clouds. The 100% humidity and nearly constant rain support an incredibly lush flora. Visitors see a thick forest mysteriously shrouded in fog, with damp-loving lichens and mosses covering every square inch of available space. Trees are draped with epiphytes (plants that grow in trees, such as **bromeliads** and **orchids**), creating an entire ecosystem high in the forest canopy. Many species of animals spend their entire lives up here, and you won't see them from the ground.

The next morning, we'll ascend the sheer side of the mesa. It's about three hours up a steep and strenuous trail to reach the 2,500-meter-high plateau and the edge of the cloud forest. Now our muddy, sweaty scrabble up the trail is rewarded – we can wander through a vast unspoiled cloud forest, and the hiking is easy – little undergrowth and fairly level country.

The **cloud forest** is a unique ecosystem, shrouded in mist and dripping wet at all times. Every square inch of space is covered with vegetation: moss, ferns, vines and epiphytes such as orchids and bromeliads.

There are over **150 bird species**, including the usual toucans, parrots, hummingbirds and hawks, and some birds that are rare elsewhere – the fabled quetzal and trogon are common here. We may well see deer, white-faced monkeys, sloths and *pizotes*, but don't forget to look down at the forest floor, where soldier ants and other insects go about their daily business.

Real adventurers can hike all the way up to the peak of Cerro de las Minas – some even claim to have made the round trip in one day. But we're here on a weekend trip, and one night of roughing it is plenty for us. Early in the afternoon, we'll start to make our leisurely way back down to **Gracias**, where a cold beer and a hot shower await us.

Whether you make a short or a long trip, take great care. It's always wet and muddy, often raining, and can sometimes get surprisingly cold. Choose a reputable local guide and you'll be safe enough.

A WONDERFUL WEEK IN THE WEST

With a week to spare, we'll have time to explore the Mayan ruins of **Copán** and the other attractions nearby, and to roam Honduras's largest and highest cloud forest in **Celaque National Park**. We'll spend another day or two wandering around the lovely mountain villages along the **Lenca Trail**.

RECOMMENDED PLAN: Copán Ruinas has by far the best selection of hotels and tourist facilities in the region, so you may want to make it your base for a few days. You can make day trips to the picturesque **Lenca villages** from there. For visits to **Celaque National Park**, it's best to spend the night in Gracias. Give the big bad city of San Pedro Sula a wide berth if at all possible.

COPÁN RUINAS

Many of the thousands who visit the archaeological park each year zip in and out without even stopping in the nearby town. They're missing a real treat. **Copán Ruinas** is a charming colonial village of cobblestone streets and adobe buildings with cheerful tile roofs.

As the center of tourism in the area, Copán Ruinas has a good selection of hotels and restaurants, and plenty of facilities for travelers, including three banks and several internet cafés. Although it's usually bustling with tourists, most of them are fairly hip tourists, here to enjoy the local ambience for a few days - most of the t-shirt-and-ice-cream-cone crowd make a day trip to the ruins, then rush to Roatan.

Don't Miss ...

Copán - once the bustling capital of the highly advanced Mayan civilization

Copán Ruinas - don't blow right by this quaint and friendly colonial town

The Villages of the Lenca Trail - perfect climate, classic colonial architecture, and the finest handicrafts in Honduras

Celaque National Park - easy to visit, boasting spectacular mountain landscapes and a chance to see the legendary quetzal

A few small museums on the main square are each worth a quick visit. The **Maya Archaeology Museum** has a collection of artifacts from the Copán site, including some nice ceramic and jade artworks. *Info:* Open Mon-Sat 8am-noon and 1-4pm. Entry about $2.

A new museum called **Casa K'inich** (House of the Sun) is aimed at children, with a variety of interactive exhibits about the ancient Maya. Local teachers guide kids through some fun activities - they'll learn not only about the history of the Maya, but a little about languages as well, as all the signs are in English, Spanish and Chortí Maya. *Info:* Open Mon-Sat 8am-noon and 1-5pm. Free.

There's an **airstrip** just a few minutes from the town of Copán Ruinas, which is served by charter flights. A company called **La Estanzuela Tours** was running a scheduled flight every Thursday between Copán and Roatan, but they seem to have gone belly-up. Inquire with a local tour operator for the latest.

Hedman Alas runs first-class air-conditioned **buses** three times a day from/to San Pedro Sula, with connections to Tegucigalpa and La Ceiba.

For more information about Copán

There are any number of books about Copán and the Maya available, and *National Geographic* magazine has published several excellent articles over the years.

Also check out these web sites:

- www.copanhonduras.org
- www.copanmayafoundation.com
- www.copanruinas.com
- www.asociacioncopan.org
- www.mayaruins.com
- www.mayan-world.com

THE MAYAN RUINS OF COPÁN

The **Copán Ruins Archaeological Park** is a pleasant 15-minute walk from the town of Copán Ruinas. If at all possible, be there right at 8am when the gates open.

Early morning mist rises from the jungle, revealing the huge stone heads of long-dead kings. Ceiba roots entwine the stones, flocks of colorful macaws flit about, and deer graze irreverently among the ancient palaces.

By late morning, the hot tropical sun has burned off the mist, and the deer are replaced by herds of irreverent gringos, each clad in ball cap and t-shirt, with an ice cream cone in one hand and a water bottle firmly clutched in the other. It's not possible to evade them altogether, but if you time your visit just right, you can avoid the midday rush.

The Mayan Ruins of Copán are one of the most important cultural monuments in the world, and have been designated a UNESCO **World Heritage Site**. With Chichen Itza in Mexico and Tikal in Guatemala, Copán is one of the three largest and most famous excavated Mayan sites. Copán was a cultural capital, **home to the most skilled stone carvers in the Mayan empire**, and it's richer

in sculptures, hieroglyphics and art treasures than any other known Mayan site.

Copán has also been the subject of more research than any other Mayan city. Because of the wealth of hieroglyphics, the site has been an invaluable source of information for scientists researching the ancient Mayan civilization. Thousands of smaller sites are scattered around the surrounding hills, by no means all of them excavated.

During their **golden age (300-900 AD)**, the Mayan empire extended from southern Mexico through Guatemala, Belize and El Salvador to western Honduras. The Mayans developed a highly advanced civilization - their calendar and their knowledge of astronomy were unequalled until modern times. Their monumental ceremonial sites, many of them astronomically aligned, were once the scenes of elaborate rituals, some of which included human sacrifice.

The History of Copán

In its heyday, Copán is thought to have had a population of over 20,000. Copán was at the southeastern end of the Mayan empire, but like other Mayan cities, it had no fortifications. The exact purposes of many of the structures remain unknown, but it's believed that many, particularly the trademark pyramids, had ceremonial functions.

The Maya had a custom of building new temples on top of old ones, making things difficult for historians. However, excavation of the site has revealed hieroglyphic inscriptions that tell the story of the city's ruling dynasty and their wars and conquests.

The city is believed to have been founded around 100 AD, but its recorded history begins in 426, when the ruler Yax K'uk'Mo' (or **Sun-faced Quetzal Macaw**) took the throne. Copán's golden age began in 553 with the ruler **Moon Jaguar**, who built the spectacular Rosalila Temple. Other prominent potentates were **Smoke Imix**, **18 Rabbit**, who built the Great Plaza and the Ball Court, **Smoke Shell**, who built the famous Hieroglyphic Stairway, and **Yax Pac**, one of the city's last rulers.

The conquistador Diego García de Palacio "discovered" Copán in 1576, but the site came to the attention of the modern world thanks to a book called *Incidents of Travel in Central America, Chiapas and Yucatan*, by John Lloyd Stephens, a travelogue of the region that was published in 1841. In the 1880s, archaeologists began excavating the site, and excavation and research continue to the present.

Your guide may say, with a suitably melodramatic mien, that "no one knows why this once-proud civilization disappeared without a trace," or words to that effect. While that certainly sounds romantic, in fact modern scientists have a pretty good idea of why the Mayan civilization collapsed.

The ancient Mayans proved poor stewards of their environment. They cleared large areas of forest for agriculture, not realizing that the soil that supports the lush rain forest is surprisingly poor for crops. As the population grew, they cleared more and more land, and moved into more marginal areas. The **deforestation** led to erosion, making the land even less able to support decent crop yields, and leading to cycles of droughts and floods. In the end they simply couldn't grow enough food to feed themselves, and the population went into a long decline, until the Maya had dwindled to scattered bands of hunter-gatherers and subsistence farmers. You can read a fascinating discussion of the topic in the book *Collapse*, by Jared Diamond, which examines the decline and fall of various historical civilizations around the world.

The ruins of Copán are not only interesting for their own sake – the story they tell is very relevant to our lives today. Unfortunately, history is currently repeating itself in Honduras. In several parts of the country, **slash-and-burn agriculture** has denuded whole regions, leaving the poor subsistence farmers unable to make a living. Forced to leave their homes, they are steadily moving into more remote areas and repeating the process there. The Honduran government makes a valiant effort to conserve the rain forest, but they simply don't have the resources to stop the destruction.

This tragedy of the commons is playing out on a global scale. **Rain forests** have been called "the lungs of the planet," for the role they play in turning carbon dioxide into life-giving oxygen. Honduras also has extensive **coral reefs**, the rain forests of the sea, providing habitat for thousands of important fish species. Both are steadily being destroyed by development, pollution and climate change. Unless a miracle happens, Earth's rain forests and coral reefs will be gone within our lifetimes, with unknown consequences for our climate and food supply.

The Sights of Copán

The **Great Plaza** is a large open space dotted with stelae featuring bas-relief statues of Mayan rulers, with hieroglyphic inscriptions. Some call it the Forest of the Kings. Back in the day, the stelae, and many of the buildings, were painted in bright colors, traces of which can still be seen here and there. Most of the stelae in the Great Plaza are believed to have been built around AD 710-740 by the 13th ruler, who is known as 18 Rabbit (I know, it's not the most awe-inspiring name for a bloodthirsty warrior king).

The **Ball Court** is similar to those found at other sites such as Chichen Itza, but far more beautifully decorated, with bas-reliefs of macaws. Here the Mayans played a game that involved putting a hard rubber ball through a stone hoop without using their hands. Apparently they took it almost as seriously as today's Latin Americans do their soccer – some believe that the losers provided the human sacrifices that were supposed to appease the gods.

Towering 100 feet over the Great Plaza, the **Acropolis** is a large complex of pyramids and temples that was built over many earlier temples. Here are the beautiful **Rosalila Temple**, or Temple of the Sun, painted in rose-lilac colors, and the **Plaza of the Jaguars**, with its rich carvings depicting Maya beliefs about the afterworld.

The tallest structure at the site is the **Hieroglyphic Stairway**, built in AD 749 by the ruler Smoke Shell. The pyramid has 63 steps, carved with 1,500 intricate glyphs, which represent the longest known text left by the ancient Mayans. It is believed to be an official chronology of all the rulers of Copán, telling the history of their great battles and deeds. Mayan rulers often destroyed monuments of previous rulers, so the stairway has provided archaeologists with some important missing links in the city's history. Nowadays, the temple is covered by an incongruous huge tarpaulin to protect it from the elements.

One of the most interesting artworks at Copán is **Altar Q**, which was built by one of the city's last leaders, Yax Pac. It depicts all 16 of Copán's rulers up to that point, with Yax K'uk'Mo' handing the symbolic baton of kingship over to Yax Pac.

Over the years, the Copán River has eroded away much of the east side of the Acropolis, leaving a 180-foot **vertical cut** exposed. Here you can see a fascinating cross-section of the city's history, showing how the Mayans built new monuments on top of the old ones.

The archaeologists have dug a network of **tunnels** under the site, allowing them to examine earlier structures and tombs that were built over by later inhabitants. Two of these tunnels are open to the public. One leads under the Rosalila Temple, and the other gives access to several ancient tombs. It costs an extra $12 to visit the tunnels. Although the local guides crow about them, most visitors find them only slightly interesting.

Tourist legend has it that somewhere down here is a certain stone that, if you press it just the right way, will open a hidden passageway leading to a secret tunnel full o' gold. Considering the number of scientists and tourists that clamber over the ruins on a daily basis, it seems unlikely that such a thing could have remained undiscovered, but go ahead and have a look around! *Info:* Entry to the park is $10, which also includes the Sepulturas archaeological site. Entry to the Museum of Mayan Sculpture is $5. The park and the Sculpture Museum are open daily 8am-4pm. The **Copán Guide Association** offers tours of the ruins, starting at $20, as well as horseback riding, caving, birding and other tours. You can arrange a tour on the spot at the park entrance, but it's wiser to reserve ahead. Tel. 651-4018.

Las Sepulturas

The main site of Copán was a government and ceremonial center, but Las Sepulturas was where the local upper class lived. It's one of the few Mayan residential areas that have been found, and it provides a fascinating look at the everyday life of the people. This site, a couple of kilometers down the road from the main park, includes about 40 residential complexes, where the aristocracy of Copán slept on hard stone beds, as well as some tombs.

To really appreciate the site, I recommend taking a guided tour, which you can arrange at the visitors' center at the main park. Las Sepulturas is a peaceful wooded area with some nice walking trails, a splendid place for birding, especially early in the morning.

The Museum of Mayan Sculpture

While it may seem a bit of a shame that Copán's art treasures can't be left in their original positions, they would crumble away out

there in the punishing jungle elements, so some of the most impressive sculptures have been gathered here in the museum to protect them for future generations.

The museum costs an extra five bucks, but it's worth every Lempira. Many of the original art treasures of Copán are displayed here in the museum, protected from the elements, while the *in situ* versions are actually clever replicas.

You enter the museum, most of which is underground, through the jaws of a huge snake, representing the mythological serpent that spoke to Copán's rulers in the voices of their dead ancestors. Passing through a tunnel, you are transported a thousand years back in time, to the Golden Age of the Maya.

The centerpiece of the museum is a **life-sized replica of the Rosalila Temple**, in all its original pink splendor. The weathered gray stones that we see at Mayan sites today are in fact only shadows of their original beauty - once they were painted in bright colors.

Here you'll find **the finest collection of Mayan sculpture in the world** - over 3,000 pieces, many of them mounted in the facades of six reconstructed buildings. Highlights include the original facade of the Ball Court and the original Altar Q, with its relief depicting the 16 kings of Copán.

By the time we've explored the museum, it will be about three in the afternoon, time for the day-tripping hordes to head back to their tour bus, or catch a plane back to their cruise ship and rush on to the next port. That gives us an hour to have another stroll through the ruins. I think you'll find it quite interesting to take a second look after you've seen the museum and learned a bit about the history of the city.

LOS SAPOS & OTHER MAYAN SITES

The minor Mayan site of **Los Sapos** is up in the hills overlooking the valley of Copán and the main ruins. It's called "the birthing place," because many believe that the ancient Mayan women used to come here to give birth to their offspring. The carvings are pretty worn down by the elements, and aren't terribly interesting, but the view at the site is splendid, and it's a good excuse for a moderate hike through the forest. Horseback riding is another way to get up here – it's easy to arrange for horses through any of the local tour agencies.

You don't have to walk at all if you don't want to. Los Sapos is on the grounds of a very nice resort hotel called **Hacienda San Lucas** (non-guests pay a $2 entrance fee). Take a taxi up here or better yet, spend the night. The Hacienda is a lovely place to stay, a country inn loaded with character (see *Best Sleeps*).

If you're up for more hiking (or just driving around and checking out nice views), you can visit a couple of the **Mayan stelae** that are scattered around the valley. The ruler known as Butz Hunab K'awil, or Smoke Imix, erected these stelae, which are similar to the ones in the Great Plaza. The best-known is called **La Pintada**, because it still bears traces of the original red paint. It's higher up the mountain from Los Sapos and has spectacular views. There are at least a half-dozen more of these individual stelae around, some easy to find, some not.

El Puente is the second most important Maya site in Honduras, but compared to its sister city of Copán, it's hardly known to visitors. It's a pretty big site, with over 200 structures, including a 12-meter pyramid, but most of it remains unexcavated.

The visitors' center has a small museum with some nice artworks in stone and jade, as well as rest rooms and a small café. The site on a river surrounded by lush forest, a fine place for bird watching. *Info:* El Puente is about an hour from Copán Ruinas, just before the town of La Entrada. It's easily accessible by a paved road. Open daily 8am-4pm. Entry $5.

MACAW MOUNTAIN BIRD PARK

At this well-designed park, you can see some of the lovely avian inhabitants of Honduras in comfort. Scarlet macaws, toucans and parrots of all colors cavort in large cages and walk-in aviaries. There are also lots of wild native and migrant birds hanging around.

The park is a working coffee plantation, set in a beautiful nine-acre tract of old growth forest with a river and freshwater springs. Spectacular trees and tropical foliage make it a mini-botanical garden. Butterflies flit about the lovely network of trails and the elevated viewing decks in the forest canopy.

There's a nice little riverside café where you can have lunch and a cup of the local brew, roasted on the spot. There's also a swimming spot in the river, where you can have a cooling dip after walking about the grounds in the tropical sun.

The same company operates a high-altitude coffee farm called **Finca Miramundo** (see below). *Info:* www.macawmountain.com; Tel. 651-4245. Open daily 9am-5pm. Entry $10.

FINCA MIRAMUNDO

The coffee plantation of **Finca Miramundo** is an excellent trip, a must-do if you have the time. The tour of their facilities is informative and entertaining, and the location, 1,250 meters above Copán in the lush green mountains, is spectacular. It's about a 50-minute ride by 4WD truck, with fabulous views all the way.

Have you ever wondered about where your morning cuppa comes from? Perhaps you should, because the coffee you choose to buy can have consequences for the people and wildlife in countries such as Honduras.

Coffee is the world's second-most traded commodity (after oil). The coffee trade is important not only for local communities, but also for the global environment, as rain forest is often cleared to make space for coffee plantations.

Finca Miramundo produces **estate coffee**, which means that it is grown, roasted and packaged all on a single plantation or "estate," and never blended with beans from other farms. An estate coffee is analogous to a fine wine, which bears the name of the village it comes from.

Miramundo is **shade-grown coffee**. This means that instead of clearing rain forest for the coffee trees, they left some of the tall trees in place, so the coffee grows under the partial shade of high canopy. This is far friendlier to the local animals and birds, and produces better coffee. Growing fine shade-grown is also better for the local humans than growing the cheap stuff. Less of the rain forest is cleared and, because much of the crop is sold directly to consumers, the farmers get to keep more of the money.

After a morning tour, you can have lunch at the *finca* house. It's beautiful up here, and you could certainly make a day of it if you like. There are some moderate hiking trails and a waterfall pool for swimming. The area is an **excellent place for birding**. Shade-grown coffee plantations attract an amazing number of bird species, and they are easy to spot because of the cleared areas. The coffee plantations are surrounded by a protected forest area that extends all the way up to the peak of Mt. Miramundo.

You can buy sacks of the fine coffee here or at the sister establishment, **Macaw Mountain Bird Park** (see above). *Info:* Arrange a tour with the folks at Macaw Mountain, or one of the operators in Copán Ruinas. www.cafemiramundo.com.

AGUA CALIENTE

By the time you've been in Copán Ruinas ten minutes, you'll have heard about **Agua Caliente**, the local *balneario* or hot springs – every other person in town seems to be offering to take you there. The springs are the perfect place to be after a long hike or a day trudging around the ruins. The hot water from the springs mixes with the cool river water, and there are two pools where you can soak your tired joints, while enjoying the lovely green surroundings. There are changing facilities, bathrooms and a basic snack bar.

I'd give the place a miss on the weekends, when it's absolutely mobbed with locals. *Info:* Open daily 8am-8pm. Entrance fee $3.

TO & FROM GUATEMALA

Copán is just 12 km from the Guatemalan border, and the road that passes Copán is the main route between the two countries. A side trip to Guatemala isn't very feasible – there's nothing of particular touristic interest near the border. If you're traveling overland to or from **Guatemala City** however, this is the route you'll take.

It's 7-8 hours by bus between Guatemala City and Copán Ruinas. The border is open daily 7am-5pm. *Info:* **Monarcas Travel** (www.angelfire.com/mt/monarcastravel; Tel. 502/7832-1939 in Guatemala) and **Atitrans** (www.atitrans.com; Tel. 502/7832-3371 or 502/7831-0184 in Guatemala) each offer minivan service to Antigua and Guatemala City for about $30-37.

THE LENCA TRAIL

The **Lenca** people are the largest of Honduras's indigenous groups, spread throughout the western part of the country. The national hero **Lempira** united the various Lenca tribes and made a valiant stand against the Spanish back in the 1500s. Today, the Lenca are more or less assimilated with the dominant *mestizo* culture, and their language survives only in a few place names and local words. Some of their traditional ways live on, however.

These villages, tucked into the rugged mountain terrain, are some of the oldest and most picturesque in Honduras, with ornate colonial churches, cobblestone streets, white walls and red-tiled roofs. Here you'll find the best local handicrafts in the country. A particularly nice town is **Belén Gualcho**, with its Sunday morning street market that attracts people from all over the region.

The best way to see the sights is with **Lenca Land Trails**, located at the **Hotel Elvir** (see *Best Sleeps*. www.Lenca-Honduras.com; Tel. 662-1375 or 662-0805). Bilingual guide Max Elvir has an encyclopedic knowledge of the local landscape and culture, and can arrange a tour to anywhere you'd like to go in the region.

SANTA ROSA DE COPÁN

The large town (or small city) of **Santa Rosa** is the main commercial and transportation hub of the Copán region.

The downtown area features picturesque cobblestone streets and restored colonial buildings, including the splendid **Cathedral of Santa Rosa**. The climate is very pleasant and the surrounding mountains are luxuriant. Despite its attractions, Santa Rosa sees fairly few tourists.

Santa Rosa has been a center for tobacco production since 1765, when the Spanish chose the town as the administrative center for the royal monopoly of the evil weed. Today, you can visit the **Flor de Copán cigar factory**, where well-known brands such as Santa Rosa, Davidoff and Zino are rolled by hand, just the way it's been done for centuries. *Info:* Open Mon-Fri 8am-4pm; Sat 8-11am. Guided tours (in Spanish) cost about $2.

If you prefer caffeine to nicotine, drop in at **Beneficio Maya** for a fascinating look at how coffee gets from the farm to your cup. Beneficio Maya produces high-quality shade-grown coffee from beans purchased directly from small local growers. It's liveliest during coffee harvest season (Oct-Feb) but worth a visit any time. The easiest way to get there is by taxi, which should cost no more than a buck or two. *Info:* www.cafecopan.com; Tel. 662-1665.

GRACIAS

Most travelers use **Gracias** as a way station for visits to **Celaque National Park**, but it's a well-preserved colonial town that's worth a visit in its own right. During the colonial era, Gracias was an important political center, but most of the 19th and 20th centuries passed it by. Only recently has it started to see a few visitors.

The main tourist highlights are **three large colonial churches**, the oldest of which dates from the 1600s, and the **Castillo de San Cristobal** high above the city, with its old Spanish cannons. It's a steep hike up to the fort, but worth it for the spectacular view of the churches and the mountain of Celaque.

Gracias would also make a fine base for day trips along the Lenca Trail. Notable nearby villages include **La Campa**, a great place to buy some of the fine Lenca ceramic pots and cookware, and **San Manuel Colohete**, with one of the finest colonial churches in the country and a fantastic view.

Just outside of town are some very nice **hot springs**, located on a nice jungle river. On weekends, the springs are mobbed with locals but (unlike at Agua Caliente near Copán Ruinas) you'll see few gringos. *Info:* Open daily until dusk. Entry about $2. There are rest rooms and a basic snack bar.

CELAQUE NATIONAL PARK

This vast expanse of highlands includes Honduras's highest point, the 2,870-meter **Cerro Las Minas** (El Castillo to the locals). The topography of the park is spectacular – a high plateau covered with cloud forest. Eleven rivers originate on this plateau, and one plunges over the cliff edge in a fabulous waterfall. Celaque means "box of water" in the local Lenca language.

Celaque has **several nice trails for day hikers**, but adventurers who don't mind some strenuous hiking and a night or two camping in the jungle will be rewarded with a huge expanse of unspoiled cloud forest.

The 266-square-kilometer park includes Honduras's largest and highest cloud forest, several other ecosystems including pine forest and high-altitude savanna, watered by rushing mountain rivers with waterfalls and hot springs.

Visit the park with a local guide. It's much safer and more convenient, you'll have a better chance of spotting wildlife, and supporting the local tourist industry encourages the locals to preserve their rain forest instead of clear-cutting it for farms. **Guancascos Hotel and Restaurant** (www.guancascos.com; Tel. 656-1219) in Gracias is a local hangout for visitors heading for Celaque, so stop in there for the latest info. The helpful folks there can help find a local guide, or you can arrange things through one of two well-known tour operators located in San Pedro Sula: **Maya Tropic Tours** (www.mtthonduras.com; Tel. 557-7071); and **Explore Honduras** (www.explorehonduras.com; Tel. 552-6242).

You have several lodging options, depending on how much time you have and how serious you are about spotting wildlife and birds. You can stay in comfort in Gracias, at Guancascos or just around the corner at the nice **Hotel Patricia** (see *Best Sleeps*), and get up bright and early for the 9-km ride up to the park. Or, to be there early for the best birding, you can sacrifice some comfort and sleep at one of the very basic lodgings at the edge of the park.

The **visitors' center** has some basic bunk beds available for four or five bucks, and is run by a friendly family who can cook meals on request. Guancascos also has a small and basic cabin for rent up there. There's no electricity, so bring a flashlight as well as a sleeping bag and basic camping supplies.

From the visitors' center, a well-marked trail leads up the **Río Arcagual** and through an organic coffee farm – it's a fine place for an easy day hike. Another trail leads to an overlook with a view of an awesome waterfall pouring off of the plateau.

About a three-hour hike up from the visitors' center is the first base camp, **Campamento Don Tomas**, which consists of a small tin-roofed shack and an outhouse. It's another three hours up a steep and strenuous trail to reach the 2,500-meter-high plateau and the edge of the cloud forest. Here is **Campamento Naranjo**, even more basic than the first camp – which means basically just a flat spot to pitch a tent.

This vast cloud forest is a unique ecosystem, shrouded in mist and dripping wet at all times. Tall trees block out the sun, and the forest floor is clear of undergrowth. Every square inch of space is covered with vegetation: moss, ferns, vines and epiphytes such as orchids and bromeliads.

There are over **150 bird species**, including the usual toucans, parrots, hummingbirds and hawks, and some birds that are rare elsewhere – the fabled quetzal and trogon are common here. You may well see deer, white-faced monkeys, sloths and *pizotes*, and the fortunate may even get a glimpse of the elusive jaguar, puma, ocelot or Baird's tapir.

You can hike all the way up to the peak of **Cerro de las Minas** in another two to three hours. While some hardcore hikers have made the round trip from the visitors' center to the peak in one day, most ecotourists will choose to camp for the night at Campamento Don Tomas, Naranjo or both.

For the real trail-blazing adventurer, there are other trails up to the cloud forest that have seldom been trodden by foreigners, but that you can take in the company of a machete-wielding local guide. There are a couple of possible routes from **San Manuel Colohete**, and another from **Belén Gualcho**.

Take great care on Celaque. It's always wet and muddy, often raining, and can sometimes get surprisingly cold. It's easy to get disoriented up in the cloud forest. Hikers, both locals and tourists, have gotten lost and died up here, so be sure to check in at the visitors' center, and bring all appropriate clothing and equipment.

Other places to get info about local guides and current conditions are the forestry services (**COHDEFOR**) office in Castillo de San Cristóbal (Tel. 656-1362) and **Proyecto Celaque** in Santa Rosa de Copán (Tel. 662-1459), a German-funded conservation project.

NUEVA OCOTEPEQUE

Nueva Ocotepeque is high in the mountains in the southwest corner of the country, near the **borders with El Salvador and Guatemala**. A flood destroyed the old colonial village of Ocotepeque in 1934, and the new town was built in an unattractive modern style. The main landmark is a huge bus station. A typical border town, there's little to see here, but there's a decent selection of shops, banks, internet cafés and such basic tourist facilities, as well as a couple of budget lodgings (see *Best Sleeps*).

SAN PEDRO SULA

This sprawling city in the north of Honduras is the country's economic capital. Founded in 1536, it was a sleepy colonial town until the 19th century, when the banana industry took off and **San Pedro Sula** began to grow into a major commercial center. Today it's one of the fastest-growing cities in Central America, supported by an ever-increasing number of *máquilas*, where men, women and children slave away to produce cheap clothing for sale in the North American market.

There's almost nothing to interest a tourist in this dysfunctional metropolis. Whatever beautiful old colonial buildings there were have long since been torn down or crumbled. Sorry *suleños*, but Tegucigalpa is much more interesting. SPS boasts the **highest crime rate in the country** and the highest AIDS rate in Central America.

Most travelers use San Pedro as a pit stop on the way to more interesting locales. However, if you are forced to spend a night here, you'll find plenty of shopping and a wide selection of hotels and restaurants. If you plan your trip well, this won't happen: although you may fly into San Pedro, you can catch a connecting flight to La Ceiba or the Bay Islands, or an express bus to Copán. If you're traveling by bus in the western part of the country, you may well have to change buses here, which can be a hassle,

Getting Around Town

San Pedro Sula is laid out in a typical Latin American grid pattern. *Calles* (streets) run perpendicular to *avenidas* (avenues), and the city is divided into four quarters: NE (northeast), NO (northwest), SE (southeast) and SO (southwest). Few buildings have street addresses as such. Instead, locations are described as "on the corner of..." or "in between..." particular streets.

because buses for different destinations leave from different terminals. In other words, you may have to get off one bus, get a taxi to the other station (do not walk around the dodgy bus station neighborhoods) and get on another bus. Travel adventure!

One of the few sights of interest is the **Museum of Anthropology and History**. Located a few blocks from Central Park, this is one of Honduras's largest museums. Exhibits cover the history of the Sula Valley from Pre-Columbian times to the present, and include a large collection of Mayan artifacts. *Info:* 3 Avenida between 3 and 4 Calles NO. Open 9am-4pm, closed Tuesday. Entry $2.

The **Central Park** and the **Cathedral** are worth a quick look. The Parque Central has recently been renovated. Busy and well-lit, it's safe enough for a stroll and a bit of people-watching. Check out the moneychangers and street vendors, then have a seat at one of the sidewalk cafés bordering the park for a rich coffee and a sickly-sweet pastry.

Guamilito Market, between 8 and 9 Avenidas and 6 and 7 Calles NO, is the country's largest handicraft market. Here is a wide variety of ceramics, wood carvings, hammocks, woven clothing, baskets, rugs and wall hangings, as well as fresh vegetables and flowers, rum, cigars and the usual tourist junk. Have fun bargaining with the merchants, but watch your pockets!

EL CUSUCO NATIONAL CLOUD FOREST PARK

Located in the spectacular **Merendón Mountain Range**, this park has better tourist infrastructure than most, and it's just a few miles from San Pedro Sula, so it sees a fair number of visitors, especially locals. However, it's not exactly easy to get here on your own. You can take a tour from San Pedro or Copán, most of which include a night in the park.

Maya Tropic Tours (www.mtthonduras.com; Tel. 557-7071), a local operator that's been in business for 30 years, does a two-day trip to Cusuco for around $230 per person (2 person minimum), including transport and lodging. They'll take you up to the park in a 4WD truck, and you'll spend the night in a small cottage – basically like camping, as there's no electricity or running water, but there is a toilet and a place for cooking.

The park, the 2,000-meter mountain and the river that flows from it, all take their names from the *cusuco*, which is the local name for an armadillo. Familiar to residents of the southern US as road kill, they are endangered in Central America, where some of the locals eat them. Their shell is also used to make the *charango*, a stringed instrument similar to a (small) guitar.

Although the area was heavily logged before the park was created, it still includes a few small areas of primary forest. The highest peak in the park is **Cerro Jilinco** (2,240 meters). Due to the huge difference in elevation, the park contains many different ecosystems, from tropical pine and broadleaf forests to cloud forest at the top.

Visitors will see giant ferns and gorgeous waterfalls, the highest 165 feet. You may also encounter monkeys, *pizotes*, agoutis or sloths. Hiding out in remote recesses are tapirs and all five species of pussycats – jaguar, puma, ocelot, margay and jaguarundi.

Over **300 bird species** have been spotted here, including the quetzal with its impressive long tail feathers. Beauty can be both a blessing and a curse – the quetzal is rare nowadays because of over-hunting. *Info:* The visitors' center is a 2-3 hour drive from San Pedro Sula. Take the highway towards **Copán**, then head for **Cofradía** and then **Buenos Aires**. The road to the park is very basic and very steep. It's passable only with 4WD, and perhaps not at all during the rainy season. Buses go only as far as Cofradía.

The visitors' center is well equipped, with maps and displays of the flora and fauna in the park. There are pretty good camping facilities, including showers and rest rooms. The park is open daily 6am-5pm. Entry is $15.

The **Hector Rodrigo Pastor Fasquelle Ecological Foundation** operates several educational programs and conservation projects in Cusuco, and runs a basic inn in Buenos Aires, where you can stay if you want to be in the park early for the best birding. *Info:* in San Pedro, at the corner of 1 Calle and 7 Ave NO.

DEEPER IN THE JUNGLE

The parks and reserves we've discussed are the ones that are reasonably easy to visit, but western Honduras has several others that are visited only by the hardiest of adventurers.

Pico Píjol, with its 2,280-meter high namesake, is an important watershed for the surrounding region, and includes four different types of tropical and subtropical forests with amazing biodiversity. It has no tourist facilities of any kind, but you can find a local guide by inquiring at the office of **AECOPIJOL**, a local conservation group, located in Morazán (Tel. 691-0412; Email aecopijol@yahoo.es).

On either side of Lake Yojoa, Honduras's largest natural lake, are two national parks, **Santa Bárbara** and **Cerro Azul Meambar**. The region is one of the most biologically diverse in the country. 17 individual ecosystems are home to over 400 bird species and dozens of types of orchids, bromeliads, ferns and other plants, including a few that are found nowhere else in the world. Both parks are hard to get to, with almost no facilities, but you can find a local guide through the tourist information center in Santa Bárbara (Tel. 643-2910).

7. LA MOSKITIA

The fabled **"Mosquito Coast"** is the most remote and sparsely populated section of Honduras, a vast expanse of jungles and swamps far away from civilization. **No roads lead to the region**, and the only inhabitants are indigenous people living in a few small fishing villages. Undisturbed wildlife and fascinating cultural encounters await travelers with the patience and sense of adventure to visit.

It isn't feasible to visit this remote region on a day trip, so this chapter features just three trips: a four-day trip, a weeklong trip and a two-week expedition. It takes most of a day just to get here, and it's not a region where anything happens quickly. Thanks to **regular air connections from La Ceiba**, the area is far more accessible than it was in the past, but a 4-day/3-night trip is about the shortest that makes sense.

RECOMMENDED PLAN: Take a tour of **La Ruta Moskitia**, starting with the Miskito communities located along the coast, and enjoy the beach and the lagoons. If you have more time, take a boat up the **Río Plátano** to Las Marias for a visit to the **Pech people** and a hike in the rain forest with the howler monkeys.

Don't Miss ...

Beaches & Lagoons - Swim on wild deserted beaches and see vast flocks of birds in mangrove-lined lagoons

The Río Plátano - Take a dugout canoe up the river into the deep jungle

Nighttime Boat Rides - Cruise the lagoons at night to see crocodiles, nocturnal animals and a sky filled with stars

The vast and sparsely-inhabited eastern region of Honduras encompasses **the largest remaining tract of primary forest in the country**, which has been called "the last lungs of Central America." The region includes **six protected areas**: the Río Plátano Biosphere Reserve, Patuca National Park, Laguna de Caratasca Biological Reserve, Rio Kruta Biological Reserve, Rus Rus Biological Reserve, and the Tawahka Anthropologic Reserve.

Along most of the coast, a narrow, sandy coastal strip separates the Caribbean Sea from large lagoons that are surrounded by mangrove wetlands. Further inland are tropical broadleaf rainforest and pine savannah.

The region has 2,000 species of plants, 377 species of birds, 200 reptiles and amphibians, and 39 mammals, including several rare or endangered species such as the giant anteater, Baird's tapir, white-lipped peccary, harpy eagle and several species of jungle cats. Manatees paddle around the lagoons, white-faced and howler monkeys frolic in the trees and jaguars prowl below. The beaches provide nesting grounds for four species of endangered sea turtles.

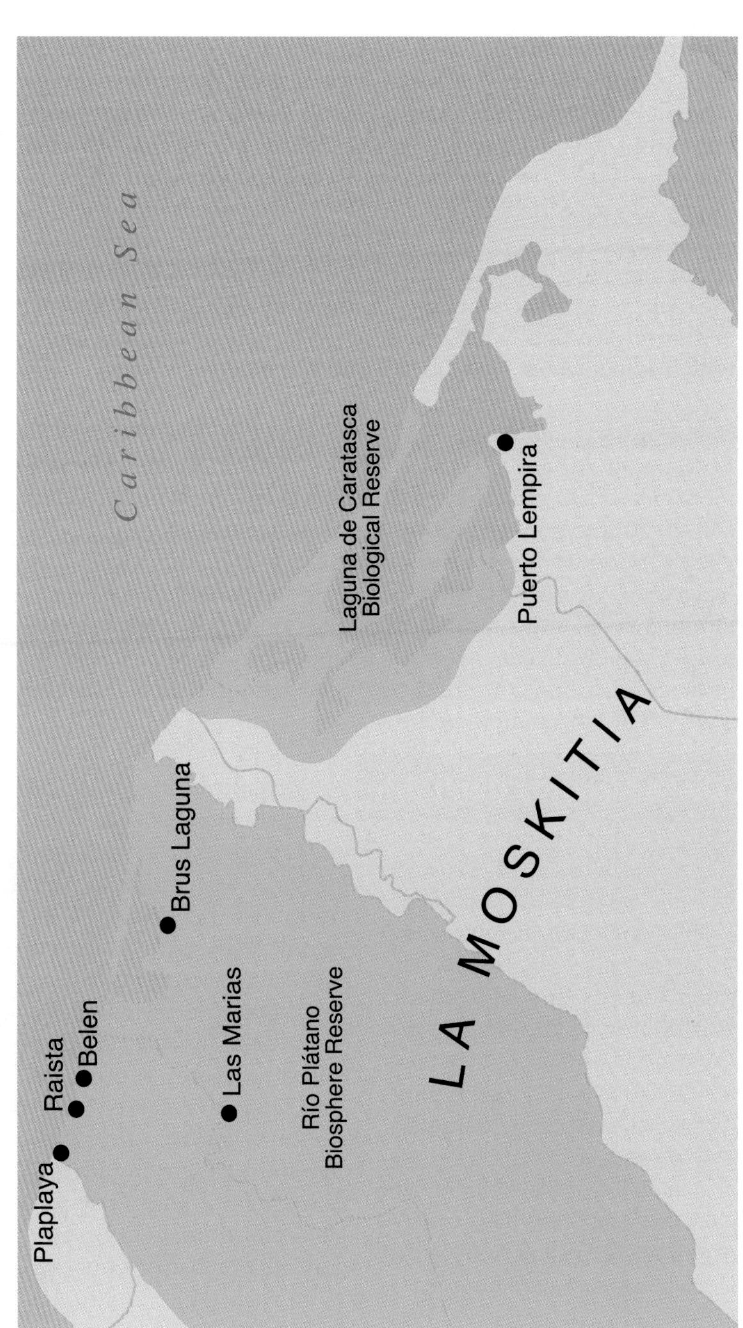
Caribbean Sea
Laguna de Caratasca
Biological Reserve
Puerto Lempira
LA MOSKITIA
Brus Laguna
Las Marias
Río Plátano
Biosphere Reserve
Plaplaya
Raista
Belen

La Moskitia is home to endangered people as well – the Miskito, Pech, Garífuna, and Tawahka – each with their own unique languages, cultures, and traditions, which they are struggling to hold onto as the modern world slowly encroaches on their domains. They are very poor but very friendly, and most are happy to guide visitors.

Along the river, you'll see petroglyphs, strange designs carved in the rocks by unknown people a millennium ago. Some are said to be signposts pointing to a legendary White City (Cuidad Blanca), which some believe lies hidden out in the dense jungle.

A new project (launched in February 2006) called **La Ruta Moskitia Ecotourism Alliance** (**LARUMO**) has made it much easier and more pleasant to visit La Moskitia. With help from an international conservation group called **Rare** (www.rareconservation.org), local people in six indigenous communities within the Rio Plátano Reserve have formed an alliance to upgrade their tourist services – lodging, food, transportation, guided tours – to *norteamericano* tourist standard. They've also created a professional marketing package, including a web site (www.larutamoskitia.com) that has a wealth of information on the region.

These Miskitos Don't Bite

The Moskitia region takes its name not from the pesky little bugs that swarm there, but from the far more pleasant human inhabitants, **the indigenous Miskitos**. Traditionally, the Spanish language does not use the letter K, so the typical Spanish spelling is Mosquitia. The letter K (or X) in a place name tells you that it's an Indian name. You'll see the name of this region spelled both ways – La Moskitia or La Mosquitia.

La Moskitia used to be a place where even seasoned adventure travelers had little choice but to go with a package tour, and even the tour operators couldn't be sure what you were going to find when you got there. Now the villages on La Ruta Moskitia (The Moskitia Route) are organized and ready to receive visitors. La Ruta Moskitia offers package tours of varying lengths. You can also take a trip with one of the tour operators from La Ceiba, or visit on your own.

This is ecotourism at its best. The indigenous people are making money by preserving their natural treasures instead of destroying them, and because LARUMO markets directly to tourists, the locals get to keep most of the dough. LARUMO trains residents as nature guides and park rangers, and supports various locally-managed conservation projects.

Projects such as LARUMO are badly needed, for the **Rio Plátano Biosphere Reserve** faces many threats to its existence. In 1996, UNESCO added the reserve to its List of World Heritage Sites in Danger. In the west, the forest is steadily shrinking as small farmers and cattle ranchers clear forest for agricultural land. Deforestation leads to increased sedimentation, harming the delicate wetlands. Uncontrolled logging, commercial hunting, and fishing with gill nets go on throughout the area, undisturbed by the tiny park staff, who simply don't have the resources to manage the 5,250-square-km preserve.

Two airlines serve the region: **Sami** and **Sosa**. Both are small airlines with unpredictable schedules. Call for the latest information.

La Realidad

If you're expecting an untouched wilderness with noble savages living in peace and plenty, the reality of environmental damage and poverty in La Moskitia may be a shock. Along the lower Rio Plátano, ranchers have cleared large areas of forest, and gill-netters have cleared the rivers of fish.

The people out here are very poor, and they know little of modern hygiene. Near settlements, the natural beauty is marred by trash and sewage. Locals pilot their *pipantes* through floating garbage and plastic bags without a second thought. The indigenous peoples' way of life is under threat from the demands of the modern economy. Fortunately, enlightened NGOs such as Rare and MOPAWI are teaching locals sustainable ways of generating income.

Don't let the few problems get you down. The wilderness is still beautiful, and the local people are unbelievably friendly.

Sosa (www.laceibaonline.net/aerososa; Tel. 443-1399) flies from La Ceiba to Brus Laguna three times a week. **Sami** (Tel. 442-2565) flies from La Ceiba to Brus Laguna and Belen, with connecting flights to Puerto Lempira, Ahuas, and Wampusirpi.

The airstrip in Palacios (which doubled as the town soccer field) is closed, and no one knows when or if it will reopen. Brus Laguna and Puerto Lempira are currently the only ways to fly into La Moskitia.

An overland trip to La Moskitia can be done in a single day from La Ceiba, but it's a long hot and dusty day, a route for true adventure travelers only. From La Ceiba, take a bus to the town of Tocoa, then catch a *paila* (pickup truck) to Batalla. From here you'll take a *collectivo* boat to Raista/Belen. Great patience and flexibility, as well as decent Spanish language skills, are essential. It's probably not possible during the rainy season.

Once you are in La Moskitia, the classic mode of travel is the *pipante,* a small dugout canoe with an outboard motor on the back. There are two kinds of boat service. An *expreso* boat is like a taxi: you pay for the whole boat. A *collectivo* waits to depart until a full load of passengers shows up. Obviously, the latter is the cheaper option, but all boat travel in La Moskitia is expensive, as gasoline has to be brought in by boat from the nearest outpost of civilization.

It's easy to hire local guides here in the region, but some are better than others. The locals here speak their own Miskito language. Local guides may have a limited command of Spanish, much

Cash is King

The only kind of money that's going to do you any good out here is **Honduran Lempiras,** preferably in small bills. The local businesses are not able to accept dollars or, in most cases, even to make change for notes larger than 100 Lempira. **None of the businesses along La Ruta Moskitia accept credit cards.** There's a bank with an ATM in Puerto Lempira, but that's about the extent of banking facilities in the region.

less English. Not all are well-trained in the finer points of ecotourism. We heard a story from one hapless traveler whose guides ignored him once they got out in the bush, and shot and roasted a couple of endangered species of birds! If you travel to La Ruta Moskitia, or take a tour with an experienced tour operator, you'll have local guides who have been trained to cater for North American guests and to make minimal impact on the forest.

Be Prepared!

Come prepared when traveling here. You'll need a proper pair of hiking boots for the mud and the snakes, long-sleeved (but light) pants and shirt for the mosquitoes, and a light raincoat and a hat for the weather. Lodging places are very basic out here, so bring a sleeping bag and a towel. Most places have no electricity, and it gets *really* dark, so bring a flashlight. Do not forget insect repellent with DEET and strong sunblock. And, oh yes – pack light!

Companies running tours to the region include **Omega Tours** (www.omegatours.hn; Tel. 440-0334 or 965-5815), **La Moskitia Eco-Aventuras** (www.honduras.com/moskitia; Tel. 440-2124 or 965-7742), **Garífuna Tours** (www.garifunatours.com; Tel. 448-1069 or 440-3252), and **Turtle Tours** (www.turtletours.de).

FOUR DAYS ON LA RUTA MOSKITIA

Thanks to LARUMO, it's feasible to have a safe and comfortable visit to this remote region, even on a short trip. We're going to do some **spectacular birding** and have some fun with the **friendly Miskito people**.

Day One

It takes about an hour to fly from La Ceiba to **Brus Laguna**. This one-time pirate hideout is a grungy little settlement, but we aren't staying. We'll take a *pipante* through the maze of creeks and lagoons, upriver into the **Great Pine Savannah**. Keep your eyes open for flycatchers, meadowlarks and white-tailed hawks. We'll spend the night at **Yamari Savannah Cabañas**, on the banks of a clear little river. Like all the lodging places along La Ruta Moskitia, the cabañas are nothing fancy, but they're clean and comfortable enough, and they have mosquito nets!

After dark we'll take a boat ride around the waterways and look for nocturnal wildlife such as crocodiles and caimans. Above, we see a vast spread of stars – we're far from the nearest city lights out here.

Day Two

The best time for birding is early morning, so we'll get up with the sun for a short boat ride before breakfast. We'll see vast flocks of water birds. Anhingas, herons and egrets are commonplace, and we may well get a glimpse of a rare green ibis.

The locals offer various types of tours and activities. You can go tubing or kayaking on the river, or go out with one of the local fishermen and learn to fish in the traditional Miskito way.

Later we'll take a boat ride to our next stop, the beachfront village of **Belen**. We'll roam the beach in the afternoon, then spend the night at **Pawanka Beach Cabañas**. These thatched beachfront huts are the nicest of the accommodations along La Ruta Moskitia. The local folks will turn out to fete us with a bonfire on the beach. As we feast on fresh lobster and fish, a local group will present some traditional Miskito singing and dancing.

Day Three

The next morning, we'll head a short way up the coast to **Raista**. Raista is probably the "touristiest" spot in La Moskitia, although that isn't saying much.

Most all the tour companies bring their guests to Raista (a couple dozen visitors a week).

Raista has a butterfly farm where you can see some of the local species, and some good hiking trails, with a couple of troops of white-face and howler monkeys living in the area. You can cool off by floating down **Paru Creek** in an inner tube. You can take a boat ride around Laguna de Ibans, a freshwater lagoon separated from the ocean by a narrow sandbar, to see an amazing variety of birds.

The most interesting thing in Raista is the **Ecocentro Raista**, a lodge on the shore of the lagoon, and the friendly Bodden Family who run it. It's a basic but comfortable place to stay, and Doña Elma Bodden serves home-cooked meals that some call the best in Honduras.

Day Four

With sand in our shoes, we take one final boat ride, back to Brus Laguna and our flight to La Ceiba.

Best Birding

For hardcore birders, the top destination has to be La Moskitia. Here you can explore both coastal ecosystems and the deep jungle, far from civilization. **You're more likely to see something really rare here than anywhere else.** In the lagoons, you may see mangrove swallows skimming the water, purple gallinules with their yellow feet and red bills, or several species of ibis, including the rare green ibis with their bright green bills and feet.

Up in the jungle, flocks of chachalacas and scarlet macaws fly overhead. You may espy toucans and toucanets, several species of hummingbirds, birds of prey such as ospreys and white-tailed hawks, three types of woodpeckers, caracaras, trogons, flycatchers, kiskadees, tanagers, grackles, oropéndolas and many more!

A WILD WEEK ON LA RUTA MOSKITIA

A week gives us time to visit all the main destinations on La Ruta Moskitia, and enjoy the beaches, the lagoons and the deep forest. We'll also visit three of the **indigenous groups** that live in La Moskitia: the Miskito, the Pech and the Garífuna.

Day One

An hour's ride from La Ceiba in a twin-engine prop plane brings us to **Brus Laguna**. This town was a notorious pirate hideout back in the days when British buccaneers lurked among the labyrinthine waterways of the Mosquito Coast and launched attacks against the Spanish treasure ships. The name of the town is believed to be a corruption of "Brewer's Lagoon," named after a particularly nasty pirate called Bloody Brewer. Today the town doesn't appear to be any more salubrious than it was then, a grungy place of wooden shacks and muddy water.

Fortunately, we aren't staying. We'll take a *pipante* through the maze of creeks and lagoons, upriver into the Great Pine Savannah. Keep your eyes open for flycatchers, meadowlarks and white-tailed hawks.

We'll spend the night at **Yamari Savannah Cabañas**. Like all the lodging places along La Ruta Moskitia, the cabañas are nothing fancy, but they are clean and comfortable enough, and they have mosquito nets! On the banks of a clear little river, there are some pleasant swimming places around.

After dark we'll take a boat ride around the waterways. The night time is the right time to see nocturnal wildlife. We're guaranteed to see lots of crocodiles and caimans. But it's worth taking the trip just to look at the stars – everyone who comes here remembers them. Far away from urban light pollution, you can see the whole Milky Way sprawling across the sky. If you're patient (and if the mosquitoes will leave you alone) you'll see shooting stars, which are meteors burning up as they enter the atmosphere, as well as man-made satellites making their way across the sky.

Day Two

The best time for birding is early morning, so we'll get up with the sun for a short boat ride before breakfast. We'll see vast flocks of water birds. Anhingas, herons and egrets are commonplace, and we may well get a glimpse of a rare green ibis.

The locals offer various types of tours and activities. You can go tubing or kayaking on the river, or go out with one of the local fishermen and learn to fish in the traditional Miskito way.

Later we'll take a boat ride to our next stop, the beachfront village of **Belen**. We can spend the afternoon riding horses on the beach, or visiting some of the **nearby Miskito villages**. We'll spend the night at Pawanka Beach Cabañas. These romantic little thatched huts, right on the beach, are the nicest of the accommodations along La Ruta.

Belen is no Daytona Beach, but it can offer fine dining and interesting nightlife, even though there are no restaurants as such, and not much in the way of electricity. The local people are a friendly lot, and they're happy to have us, so they'll all turn out to fete us with a bonfire on the beach. As we feast on fresh lobster and fish, a local women's group will present some traditional Miskito singing and dancing.

Day Three

The next morning, we'll take a boat ride a short way up the coast to **Raista**. Raista is probably the "touristiest" spot in La Moskitia, although that isn't saying much. Most all the tour companies bring their guests to Raista (a couple dozen visitors a week).

There are several cool things to do here. There's a butterfly farm where you can see some of the local species and learn about the life cycles of these most colorful of insects. There are a couple of good hiking trails, with a couple of troops of white-face and howler monkeys living in the area. You can cool off by **floating down Paru Creek in an inner tube**. You can take a boat ride around Laguna de Ibans, a freshwater lagoon separated from the ocean by a narrow sandbar, to see an amazing variety of birds. Nearby **Banaka Creek** has some ancient petroglyphs.

But it may be that the main attraction in Raista is the **Ecocentro Raista**, a basic but comfortable lodge on the shore of the lagoon, and the friendly Bodden Family who run it. The Boddens have been welcoming guests for many years, some of the first in La Moskitia to do so. Old William carves wooden oars on the beach, and his wife serves up home-cooked meals. Everyone who visits raves about the fine vittles served up in Doña Elma's kitchen. Son Eddy arranges tours throughout the area.

Day Four

Let's take a day trip from Raista a little further up the coast, and visit the easternmost of Honduras's Garífuna villages, **Plaplaya**. This little beach village is really in the middle of nowhere, so it offers an authentic look at Garíf culture. If we're lucky, we might hear a local drum and dance group laying down that hypnotic *punta* rhythm.

Between April and August, we can visit the **Plaplaya Sea Turtle Conservation Project**. This is the only place in Honduras where sea turtles are protected during their yearly nesting ritual. Female sea turtles return year after year to the beaches

ALTERNATE PLAN

Birds and monkeys aren't the only wildlife that thrive in La Moskitia. This region offers some very fine fishing. The lagoons are thick with tarpon and four species of snook. Offshore snapper, grouper, barrucuda and shark are waiting. **Team Marin Honduras Fishing** offers complete fishing tours from two to eight days. They put you up at the basic **Hotel Paradise** in Brus Laguna and you fish, fish, fish! *Info:* www.teammarinhondurasfishing.com; Tel. 434-3261, 434-3421 or 987-0875.

where they were born, and lay their eggs in the sand. When the babies hatch, they scamper to the sea *en masse*. Elsewhere in Honduras, the nesting sea turtles have been hunted to extinction, both for their meat and for their eggs. Without the vigilant volunteers of the PSTCP, poachers would dig up every last egg to sell to simpletons for their supposed aphrodisiac properties.

There are a couple of basic *hospedajes* in Plaplaya, but we'll head back to Raista in the evening, because we want to catch a boat up the river first thing in the morning. Besides, it would be a shame not to have another one of Doña Elma's dinners.

Day Five

Raista is the gateway to the Río Plátano, as it's the most reliable place to get a boat up the river to Las Marias (and beyond). We've already arranged for a boat, so we'll head out of town bright and early.

The **Río Plátano** is a large river that serves as highway, aqueduct, plumbing and communications lifeline to the people living in the region. As we head upriver, we pass long dugout *pipantes* loaded to the gunwales with yucca, corn, plantains and coconuts, and the smaller canoes called *cayucos* with whole families piled in. Children interrupt their swimming and diving games to wave as we go by. Women glance up from doing their laundry along the shore. Turtles, iguanas and the occasional caiman or crocodile splash into the water at our passage, and we're beginning to see jungle birds such as parrots and toucans.

About 10 km up the river we arrive at **Las Marias**, a village of bamboo shacks inhabited by Miskito and Pech people, La Moskitia's best-known ecotourism destination.

The Pech are one of the smallest indigenous tribes in Honduras. There are only a couple thousand of them left, and their language is spoken by only a few old-timers.

The local folks are quite welcoming and happy to show us around, though they don't speak English (some don't speak terribly good Spanish). There's a local system of rotation for tour guides, so whoever is next in line will be hired to show us the local attractions. If your Spanish is up to it, you'll learn a bit about the plants that the locals use for food, medicine, building materials and almost every other necessity.

There are several trails from the village, of varying lengths and levels of difficulty. You can take a short afternoon hike, or spend two days trekking up to the summit of **Pico Baltimore** – it's not a terribly high hill, but it offers views of the surrounding jungle and the Caribbean. Your chances of seeing wildlife are excellent. Some of the trails lead to enigmatic petroglyphs, strange carvings in the rocks. They are known to be around 1,000 years old, but little or nothing is known about the people who made them.

There's a choice of a half-dozen little *hospedajes* to sleep at. These are the most rustic of the lodgings on La Ruta, which is very rustic indeed. The cuisine here is not like Doña Elma's. I'll bet you rice and beans are on the menu tonight (unless it's beans and rice for a change).

Day Six

Today we're going to push farther up the river, this time in a tiny *cayuco* poled by two sweating guides. With no motor, we glide

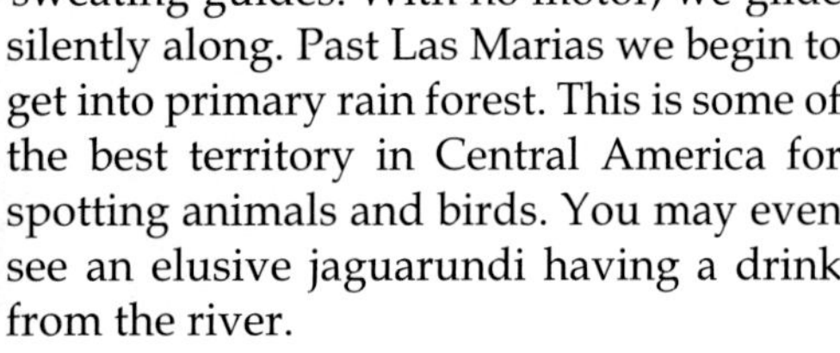

silently along. Past Las Marias we begin to get into primary rain forest. This is some of the best territory in Central America for spotting animals and birds. You may even see an elusive jaguarundi having a drink from the river.

Our destination is the site of the **Walpaulban Sirpi petroglyph**. We'll take a short hike in the rain forest, then cool off with a swim in the river. Oh, the crocodiles? They don't tend to hang out this far up the river, where the water is fast-flowing. Just keep your eyes open. In the afternoon, we'll head back downriver for another night in Las Marias.

Day Seven

We'll take our last boat ride, down the river to Brus Laguna to meet our flight to La Ceiba and (sniff!) home.

TWO WEEKS DOWN THE RÍO PLATANO

Now this is a trip for **true adventure travelers only**. Omega Tours is going to take us on a two-week trip through the wildest and most remote region of Honduras. We'll be **camping out in the wilderness** and traveling by foot, mule, 4WD truck, inflatable raft, dugout canoe, boat and small plane. Along the way, we'll shoot some rapids, catch some fish, see mysterious petroglyphs and meet indigenous people. This may be the best trip for seeing wildlife and birds in all of Central America.

Day One

Our guides take us in a 4WD truck to **Catacamas**, in the wild and lawless province of Olancho. The hotel where we spend the night is nothing fancy, but it's the last we'll be sleeping in for a couple of weeks.

Day Two

We pass through **Dulce Nombre De Culmi** on a dirt road that gets worse and worse until it peters out into a muddy forest trail. This is *bandito* country: the Honduran government is only a distant rumor out here, and the locals walk around with six-guns strapped to their hips. Most guidebooks tell you to avoid this region, with good reason. I wouldn't dream of coming up here on my own, but our guides know their way around and are equipped with everything we need to be self-sufficient (including, I assume, their own "peacemakers").

After a long and grueling day of travel, we arrive in **Bonanza**, the last outpost of civilization. No nightlife here, folks. In fact, there's no electricity, no hotels, nothing but a few cattle ranchers slashing and burning grazing land out of the rain forest. We'll stay with a local family or pitch our tents.

Day Three

The next morning, we leave our truck behind, load our equipment onto mules and set out towards the river. At first we see large areas that have been cleared for cattle (a little sad but ideal for spotting birds), but by evening we're walking through primary rain forest. We set up camp and cook dinner over a wood fire.

Day Four

Breakfast is rice, beans and coffee cooked on the campfire. After a moderate day's trek with the mules, we reach the point where Río Blanco and Río Guarasca meet to form the **Río Platano**. Here we pump up our inflatable raft and prepare for the weeklong trip down the river.

Days Five-Eleven

A solid week of adventure is ahead of us. At some points, we run class II and class III rapids, but most of the time we're floating lazily down the river, keeping our eyes open for animals, of which we see plenty. This is **primary rain forest**, far from any other humans.

On Day Eight, we'll reach **El Subterraneo**. Here the entire river disappears into an underground passage. We'll have to portage the raft several times, an ordeal that will take most of the day.

On our trip down the river, we'll see several **petroglyphs**, the mysterious rock carvings left here by unknown ancient people. Some of these are supposed to be signposts pointing the way to

the legendary *Ciudad Blanca* (White City). Somewhere in this area are said to be the ruins of a pre-Columbian city that's bigger and cooler than Copán, Tikal and Chichen Itza all rolled into one. Over the years, a few Indiana Jones-style adventurers have dared to brave the jungle to find this hidden Shangri-La. None have returned.

On Day Eleven, we'll reach **Las Marias**. This tiny Miskito/Pech village is the most remote point that most visitors to La Moskitia will reach. For us it represents a return to civilization, our first contact with other humans in a week. After another dinner of our favorite dish, we'll bed down in one of the very basic *hospedajes* in town.

Day Twelve

We deflate our trusty raft, and load it and all our other stuff on a *pipante* for the trip down to the coast. In **Raista**, we may have time for a visit to the butterfly farm and a stroll on the beach before bedding down at the Boddens' Ecolodge. Doña Elma's home cooking is world-famous, and it seems like the meal of a lifetime to us. After all these days in the wilderness, Raista seems like a bustling tourist town, although it seems like the ends of the earth to most of the visitors, who came from the other direction.

Day Thirteen

The plane from Brus Laguna to La Ceiba only flies three days a week, so if it's one of those days, we'll be flying back to La Ceiba. If not, we'll continue by water up the coast to Batalla – from there it's (usually) possible to take a 4WD truck along the coast back to civilization. Back in La Ceiba, we'll spend a night at Omega Tours' home base and lodge on the Cangrejal River (see *Chapter 5*).

PUERTO LEMPIRA

Puerto Lempira, at the far eastern end of Honduras, is the largest town in La Moskitia, and the most "civilized," with an airstrip, several hotels and restaurants, and even a bank (at last report, the ATM was still working!).

Puerto Lempira has the feel of a frontier trading post. It's the commercial hub for the region, and lots of people from the surrounding countryside come in every day to shop or visit the local health clinic.

What Price Adventure?

Traveling to La Moskitia isn't that cheap. Although lodging and food cost next to nothing, the high price of gas makes boat transportation pricey. Tour prices vary depending on the number of people in your group, with much lower per-person prices for larger groups. A four-day trip should cost around $500-700 per person double occupancy, or $350-500 per person with a group of four. A weeklong trip runs $800-1400 per person double or $550-900 with a group of four. Omega Tours' 13-day expedition runs $2,335 per person double, or $1,530 with a group of four.

This area sees very few foreign tourists. Most of the tour companies take their guests to the Río Plátano region, far west of here. But if you're a seasoned adventure traveler, you can take a plane from La Ceiba, and stay in one of the cheap *hospedajes* in town – I guarantee it will be a trip to remember, far off the tourist trail.

Puerto Lempira is on the banks of the largest lagoon in La Moskitia, most of which is a protected biological reserve. **Laguna de Caratasca** teems with tarpon and snook, barely disturbed by anglers. It's easy to arrange a fishing trip with a local guide.

The birding in the fresh water Tansing Lagoon and the rain forest up the clear Mocoron River are said to be splendid.

A Word about MOPAWI

MOPAWI stands for *MOskitia PAWIsa apiska,* which means Moskitia Development Agency in the local Miskito language. This non-governmental organization is helping the indigenous people of La Moskitia to replace destructive agricultural practices with more sustainable ones. They provide loans to local entrepreneurs for such things as small cacao and cashew farms.

The Honduran government is pretty much non-existent in this region, so for many local people, MOPAWI is the infrastructure of La Moskitia – the telephone company, the bank and the post office. *Info*: www.mopawi.org.

8. TEGUCIGALPA & SOUTHERN HONDURAS

Honduras's capital is a chaotic but fascinating metropolis, with some **lovely colonial architecture** and the country's finest art museums. Tegucigalpa's altitude of 975 meters gives it a consistently pleasant climate, dry and cool for most of the year.

Among the surrounding mountains are several **picturesque towns and villages** where you can shop for wonderful **handicrafts** and enjoy magnificent mountain views. **La Tigra National Park** is a lush cloud forest within easy day-trip range of the city.

ONE GREAT DAY IN TEGUCIGALPA

We'll spend the morning seeing the sights in the **historic old city**, then head up to **El Picacho** for a panoramic view of the capital in its rugged valley.

Morning

Most of Tegucigalpa's sights are in the historic downtown area, which centers on the Central Park (also known as the **Plaza Morazán**). Here you'll find some gracious old colonial buildings and interesting art museums.

Honduras has a long tradition of fine painters and sculptors. Here in Tegucigalpa are a set of small museums where you can see the best of their work. Our first stop is the **National Art Gallery** (Galería Nacional de Arte), located just off the central park. Honduras's most prestigious museum has a collection of paintings, sculpture and *objets d'art* that covers the country's entire history. They are arranged in chronological order, from prehistoric cave paintings to ancient Mayan works to paintings from the country's most famous artists, including Sierra, Figueroa and Velásquez.

The building itself is a lovely example of classic colonial architecture. In fact, it's one of the oldest in the city, built in 1654. *Info:* Open Mon-Fri 9am-4pm; Sat 9am-noon. Tel. 237-7989.

Not far away on Avenida Cervantes, the **Museum of the Honduran Man** (Museo del Hombre Hondureño) has a nice selection of works from Honduran artists, mostly contemporary paintings, also housed in an interesting historic building.

Skip the Villa Roy

Everyone will tell you to see the **Villa Roy Museum**, but unless you're a real history buff, it's just not that exciting. The museum, housed in a former presidential palace, has a mix of exhibits on Honduran history. Most are pretty dry, and the descriptions are in Spanish only.

Two large downtown banks have art exhibits that are worth a look. On Boulevard Miraflores, the main building of the **Banco Atlantida** has a small but excellent display of pre-Columbian artifacts and some contemporary Honduran paintings. *Info:* Open Mon-Fri 9am-3pm. Free.

A couple blocks south of the Central Plaza is the **Arturo Medrano Art Gallery**, a very fine collection of Honduran paintings. *Info:* Open Mon-Fri 9am-4pm. Free.

On the main square, the recently renovated **San Miguel Cathedral** is worth a look. Its twin towers are typical of Spanish colonial churches, but the mermaid pillars are quite distinctive, and the interior is impressive, with an ornate Baroque-style altar, gold and silver decorations and paintings.

Once we've soaked up as much culture as we can stand, we'll take a short stroll through the Plaza Morazán, and sit down at one of the cafés ringing the square for a nice cup of Honduran coffee and a spot of people-watching. To the west of the square is a pedestrian street (*peatonal*), clogged with street vendors, a colorful place to observe the daily life of the *capitalinos*.

After lunch, we'll catch a cab at the square and take a ride up to Picacho for a panoramic view of the city. You can't miss **El Picacho Cristo**. The 20-meter high statue of Christ can be seen

① Plaza Morazán
② National Art Gallery
③ Museum of the Honduran Man
④ San Isidro Market
⑤ Hedman Alas Bus Station
⑥ Multiplaza Mall
⑦ Plaza San Martín Hotel District
← Cristo Picacho
Avenida La Paz
Colonia Palmira
Boulevard Morazán
Comayagüela
Estadio Nacional
Tegucigalpa
Parque La Paz
Boulevard Suyapa
6a Avenida
1a Avenida
← Airport
Santuario Nacional →

from all over the city. It's the centerpiece of the pleasant **United Nations Park**, from which you can enjoy a birds-eye view of Tegucigalpa sprawling chaotically through its serpentine valley.

Also up here is the **Tegucigalpa Metropolitan Zoo**, the only sizable zoo in Honduras. Here are 310 species of Honduran animals and birds, including jaguars, monkeys and tropical birds. There's also a bit of a botanical garden and some replicas of Mayan ruins. Unfortunately, like most Central American zoos, it's old-fashioned and poorly maintained, with the animals in small and dirty enclosures. The entry fee is almost nothing, so have a quick look. It's a good "teachable moment" for kids. *Info:* Open daily 8am-3pm.

It's easy enough to explore Tegucigalpa by taxi, but if you'd like to take a guided tour, there are several options. **Arrecife Tours** (www.arrecifetours.com; Tel. 231-3526 or 231-3527) offers a half-day city tour for about $35 (in groups of two or more), plus trips to other attractions in the region. Other local operators are **Destinos de Éxito** (www.destinosdeexito.com; Tel. 236-9651 or 236-9704) and **Gray Line Tours** (www.graylinehonduras.com; Tel. 220-1552 or 220-7257).

A WONDERFUL WEEKEND AROUND TEGUCIGALPA

With a weekend to spare, we can tour the historic center, pay a visit to the bustling city market in **Comayagüela**, then head up into the mountains to visit a **quaint colonial town** and **La Tigra National Park**.

Friday Evening

We've made a reservation in advance at our hotel, so their van will meet us at the airport, and we'll get checked in with no hassle. Any of the upscale hotels will be glad to arrange a guided tour of La Tigra National Park for Sunday (or call one of the tour companies listed above). You can also book a guided tour of downtown Tegucigalpa if you like, but I think we can get around well enough by taxi to see what we want to see.

Saturday

Honduras has a long tradition of fine painters and sculptors. Here in Tegucigalpa are a set of small museums where you can see the best of their work. The main museums are open only until noon on Saturdays, so first thing in the morning, we'll take a taxi straight to the **National Art Gallery** (Galería Nacional de Arte), located just off the central park.

Honduras's most prestigious museum has a collection of paintings, sculpture and *objets d'art* that covers the country's entire history. They are arranged in chronological order, from prehistoric cave paintings to ancient Mayan works to paintings from the country's most famous artists, including Sierra, Figueroa and Velásquez.

The building is a lovely example of classic colonial architecture. In fact, it's one of the oldest in the city, built in 1654. *Info:* Open Mon-Fri 9am-4pm; Sat 9am-noon. Written guides available in English, but guided tours only in Spanish. The entry fee is no more than a couple of bucks. Tel. 237-7989.

Not far away on Avenida Cervantes, the **Museum of the Honduran Man** (Museo del Hombre Hondureño) has a nice selection of works from Honduran artists, mostly contemporary paintings, also housed in an interesting historic building.

Two large downtown banks have art exhibits that are worth a look (they're closed on Saturdays, so if you're an art buff, you may want to plan your museum excursion for a weekday). On Boulevard Miraflores, the main building of the **Banco Atlantida** has a small but excellent display of pre-Columbian artifacts and some contemporary Honduran paintings. *Info:* Open Mon-Fri 9am-3pm. Free.

Take a Taxi!

Tegucigalpa is not a safe place to wander around on foot. After dark, a taxi is the only safe way to travel, and many areas, including Comayagüela, are dodgy even during the day.

A couple blocks south of the Central Plaza is the **Arturo**

Medrano Art Gallery, a very fine collection of Honduran paintings. *Info:* Open Mon-Fri 9am-4pm. Free.

Everyone's been telling us to see the **Villa Roy Museum**, but I think we'll skip it. The most interesting exhibit is a small collection of antique cars that the Honduran president used to ride in - not the sort of thing I came to Central America to see.

There are two old colonial churches in the downtown area that are worth a quick look. On the square is the **San Miguel Cathedral**, which has recently been renovated. Its twin towers are typical of Spanish colonial churches, but the mermaid pillars are quite distinctive, and the interior is very impressive, with a vast vaulted ceiling, an ornate Baroque-style altar, gold and silver decorations and paintings. A few blocks away is the **Iglesia de San Francisco** (Church of St Francis), Tegucigalpa's oldest church, built in the 16th century.

Once we've soaked up as much culture as we can stand, we'll take a short stroll through the Plaza Morazán, and sit down at one of the cafés ringing the square for a nice cup of Honduran coffee and a spot of people-watching. To the west of the square is a pedestrian street (*peatonal*), clogged with street vendors, a colorful place to observe the daily life of the *capitalinos*.

Is it Morazán?

You're sure to hear the story that the **statue of Morazán** in the Central Square is actually a second-hand statue of one of Napoleon's generals. Supposedly the government officials who were sent to Paris to buy the statue drank and gambled the money away, and ended up settling for the cheapest statue they could find. Truth or urban legend? Take a good look and judge for yourself!

Are you up for a little adventure? Then after lunch, let's take a taxi across the river to Comayagüela, where the **San Isidro Market** is located. The city's largest market spills out of a huge building into surrounding streets. This is no quaint flowers-and-handicrafts tourist market, but rather a place where locals go to buy their daily necessities. It's a bustling, noisy scene that will give us a fascinating look at the real Central America. Take this opportunity to buy anything you might need at a rock-bottom price, but keep your hand on your wallet!

After a visit to the market, get right back in a taxi for a ride up to Picacho. You can't miss **El Picacho Cristo**. The 20-meter high statue of Christ is reminiscent of the more famous one in Rio de Janeiro. Perched high on a hill, it can be seen from all over the city. It's the centerpiece of the pleasant United Nations Park, from which you can enjoy a birds-eye view of Tegucigalpa sprawling chaotically through its serpentine valley.

Also up here is the **Tegucigalpa Metropolitan Zoo**, the only sizable zoo in Honduras. Here are 310 species of Honduran animals and birds, including jaguars, monkeys and lots of colorful birds. There's also a bit of a botanical garden and some replicas of Mayan ruins. Unfortunately, the whole park is poorly maintained and run-down. I find it depressing to see the animals in their small and dirty enclosures, but this is probably the only sight of a jaguar that we'll get, so let's have a quick look. *Info:* Open daily 8am-3pm. Entry fee is a few Lempira.

It's still the middle of the afternoon, so let's visit the lovely town of **Santa Lucia**. Just a 20-minute drive from Tegucigalpa, Santa Lucia is a typical colonial village of cobblestone streets, white-washed walls and red tile roofs, perched on a mountainside with a spectacular view.

Santa Lucia has some **nice handicraft shops**, as well as **colorful gardens** where the locals cultivate flowers to be sold in the markets of Tegucigalpa. Santa Lucia and the other old mining towns in the area form a popular tourist circuit, and there are several pleasant little places to eat.

Take a look inside the 18th-century church, which is full of beautiful paintings and statues, including a famous figure of Christ that was given to the town by King Philip II of Spain in 1574.

We can have dinner here before heading back to our hotel in Tegucigalpa and early bed, to rest up for the rain forest tomorrow.

Sunday

The Honduran rain forest is simply not to be missed, so we'll get up bright and early and visit **La Tigra National Park**. Located 11 km from Tegucigalpa, the park is easy to get to and easy to visit, with a well-maintained network of trails. High up in the mountains above the city (1,800 meters), the mountain streams and waterfalls of this lush cloud forest provide much of the region's drinking water.

La Tigra has two visitors' centers, both with access to several trails. We'll head for the **Jutiapa Visitor Center**, which is closer to Tegucigalpa, and has access to the easiest hikes. The easiest trail is Las Granadillas, just over a half kilometer long with gentle grades. It runs alongside a stream and leads to a wooden observation platform. For a longer hike, take the Bosque Nublado Trail through the cloud forest, or the moderate Jucuara Trail that leads through pine and broadleaf forest to a spring. The Cascada Trail leads to the park's highest waterfall (60 meters high), about 4 km from the Jutiapa Visitor Center. *Info:* La Tigra is managed by Fundación Amigos de La Tigra

ALTERNATIVE PLAN

If handicrafts are your passion, then spend less time in Tegucigalpa, and visit **Valle de Ángeles**, another 20 minutes or so past Santa Lucia, which has more and better craft shops (see later in this chapter).

(AMITIGRA), www.nps.gov/centralamerica/honduras/home.html; Tel. 235-8494. Their office in Tegucigalpa is open Mon-Fri, 8am-noon and 2-5pm. The park is open Tue-Sun, 8am-5pm (no visitors admitted after 2pm). Admission is $10 adults, $5 for kids under 12.

A FANTASTIC WEEK IN SOUTHERN HONDURAS

The capital is the most interesting large city in the country. Several nearby villages offer quaint colonial architecture and wonderful crafts. Few tourists visit the **southern coastal area**, but if you do, you'll find **black sand beaches** and wonderful fresh seafood.

RECOMMENDED PLAN: Sleep in Tegucigalpa or one of the nearby villages. One day is plenty to see the sights of the capital city. Spend a day exploring the **mountain villages** (maybe two if you're a real handicrafts buff). Spend a couple of nights up at **La Tigra**, so you can have a full day with the trees and the birds. If you have more time, and you want to get off the beaten path, head down south and take a boat out to **Isla Del Tigre**.

TEGUCIGALPA

A visit to Honduras's capital will open your eyes to the reality of the Third World. The city is a chaotic, noisy, bustling sprawl that nevertheless has a certain dignity of its own. Here you can see the incredible gulf between rich and poor that afflicts Honduras and the world. Downtown, gleaming shopping malls and luxury hotels serve foreign business people and the tiny Honduran elite. On the outskirts, vast slums of hastily-built shacks of cardboard and corrugated tin creep ever higher into the surrounding mountains.

According to the textbooks used in Honduran schools, the city's name means "Silver Hills" in the language of the indigenous

Don't Miss ...

Tegucigalpa Art Museums - Honduras's finest museums, displaying the country's rich tradition of visual art

La Tigra National Park - well-maintained trails take you through a lush cloud forest crisscrossed by mountain streams and waterfalls

Colonial Villages - old mining villages with spectacular mountain scenery, picturesque colonial architecture, and interesting crafts

Nahuatl. Some historians have pointed out that this doesn't make much sense, as the Nahuatl never mined for silver. So who knows?

History & Layout

Tegucigalpa was founded in 1578 as a center of silver and gold mining. During the years after independence, the capital of Honduras alternated several times between Tegucigalpa and the rival city of Comayagua until 1880, when Tegucigalpa was permanently chosen as the capital. Depending on who's telling the story, this was either because the *comayagüeños* snubbed President Marco Aurelio Soto's wife, or because Tegucigalpa was a more important economic center.

Tegus (as locals call it) was definitely no planned city. It grew up around the gold and silver mines, slowly filling up a narrow and serpentine valley. Thanks to the difficult topography, Tegucigalpa does not have the orderly street grid of most other Central American cities. Also unlike other Honduran cities, Tegucigalpa has never suffered a major flood, earthquake or other disaster, so many of the old colonial-style buildings remain.

Most of these are to be seen in the historical center, which centers on the Central Park or **Plaza Morazán**. The main commercial district is along the **Boulevard Morazán**. Across the Choluteca River is the sister city **Comayagüela**, which was originally a separate municipality, but has been gobbled up by the growing metropolitan area.

Sights

Tegucigalpa's most interesting sights are the museums and old colonial buildings in the area around the Central Park. Also called the Plaza Morazán, the city's main square is shady and pleasant enough, ringed with cafés. To the west of the square is a pedestrian street (*peatonal*), clogged with street vendors, a colorful place to observe the daily life of the *capitalinos*.

The **National Art Gallery** (Galeria Nacional de Arte), located just off the central park, is Honduras's finest museum, with a collection of paintings, sculpture and *objets d'art* that covers the country's entire history. They are arranged in chronological order, from prehistoric cave paintings to ancient Mayan works to works from the country's long tradition of fine visual artists, including locally famous names such as Sierra, Figueroa and Velásquez.

The building is a lovely example of classic colonial architecture. In fact, it's one of the oldest in the city, built in 1654. *Info:* Open Mon-Fri 9am-4pm; Sat 9am-noon. Written guides available in English, but guided tours only in Spanish. The entry fee is no more than two Dollars. Tel. 237-7989.

Not far away on Avenida Cervantes, the **Museum of the Honduran Man** (Museo del Hombre Hondureño) has a nice selection of works from Honduran artists, mostly contemporary paintings, also housed in an interesting historic building.

Two large downtown banks have art exhibits that are worth a look. On Boulevard Miraflores, the main building of the **Banco Atlantida** has a small but excellent display of pre-Columbian artifacts and some contemporary Honduran paintings. *Info:* Open Mon-Fri 9am-3pm. Free.

A couple blocks south of the Central Plaza is the **Arturo Medrano Art Gallery**, a very fine collection of Honduran paintings. *Info:* Open Mon-Fri 9am-4pm. Free.

Everyone will tell you to see the **Villa Roy Museum**, but it's probably the least interesting of the major museums, with some pretty dry exhibits on Honduran history, and a small collection of antique cars that the Honduran president used to ride in.

There are three old colonial churches in the downtown area that are worth a quick look. On the square is the **San Miguel Cathedral**, which has recently been renovated. Its twin towers are typical of Spanish colonial churches, but the mermaid pillars are quite distinctive, and the interior is very impressive, with a vast vaulted ceiling, an ornate Baroque-style altar, gold and silver decorations and paintings.

The **Iglesia de San Francisco** (Church of St Francis), near the Central Park, is Tegucigalpa's oldest church, built in the 16th century. The enormous **Iglesia de Nuestra Señora de los Dolores** dates from 1730, and has an astounding interior, including a beautiful painted dome. Take a taxi to this one, as it's several blocks away from the Central Park.

You can't miss **El Picacho Cristo**. The 20-meter high statue of Christ is reminiscent of the more famous one in Rio de Janeiro. Perched high on a hill, it can be seen from all over the city. It's the centerpiece of the pleasant United Nations Park, from which you can enjoy a birds-eye view of Tegucigalpa sprawling chaotically through its serpentine valley.

Also up here is the **Tegucigalpa Metropolitan Zoo**, the only sizable zoo in Honduras. Here are 310 species of Honduran animals and birds, including jaguars, monkeys, parrots. There's also a bit of a botanical garden and some replicas of Mayan ruins. Unfortunately, like most Central American zoos, it's old-fashioned and poorly maintained, with the animals in small and dirty enclosures. *Info:* Open daily 8am-3pm. Entry fee a few Lempiras.

In an eastern suburb of Tegucigalpa, a huge church called the **Santuario Nacional** is perched on a hill with a fine view of the valley. Nearby, the much smaller and plainer **Basílica de Suyapa** houses the Virgin of Suyapa, a tiny statue that represents the patron saint of Honduras. When the Santuario Nacional was built in the 1950s, the virgin was moved there, but according to the locals, she didn't approve of the grand new church, and miraculously reappeared inside the old one, where she remains.

One of Tegucigalpa's modern landmarks is the **Mall Multiplaza**, a huge US-style shopping mall. Expatriate businessmen and the few well-heeled locals find all the familiar *norteamericano* brands, including US fast-food joints. The shops are clean and pleasant, but overpriced.

For a much more Honduran shopping experience, take a taxi across the river to Comayagüela and the **San Isidro Market**. The city's largest market is no quaint flowers-and-handicrafts tourist market, but rather a place where locals go to buy their daily necessities. It's a bustling, noisy scene that will give us a fascinating look at the real Central America. Take this opportunity to buy anything you might need at a rock-bottom price. This is one of the worst parts of town, so keep a firm hand on your wallet!

SANTA LUCIA

Several small and picturesque old mining towns in the region are well worth visiting for their splendid mountain views, quaint colonial architecture and nice handicraft shops. Santa Lucia, Valle de Ángeles and San Juancito lie just north of Tegucigalpa, in and around La Tigra National Park. Any of them would make a good day trip from Tegucigalpa, and you could make the whole circuit in one long day.

Santa Lucia is the closest of the villages to Tegucigalpa, just about 20 minutes north of the city. At 5,000 feet above sea level, and surrounded by pine forests, this small town is steadily growing into a fashionable suburb of Tegus. Santa Lucia's main claim to fame is her **18th-century church**, which is full of beautiful paintings and statues, including a famous figure of Christ that was given to the town by King Philip II of Spain in 1574.

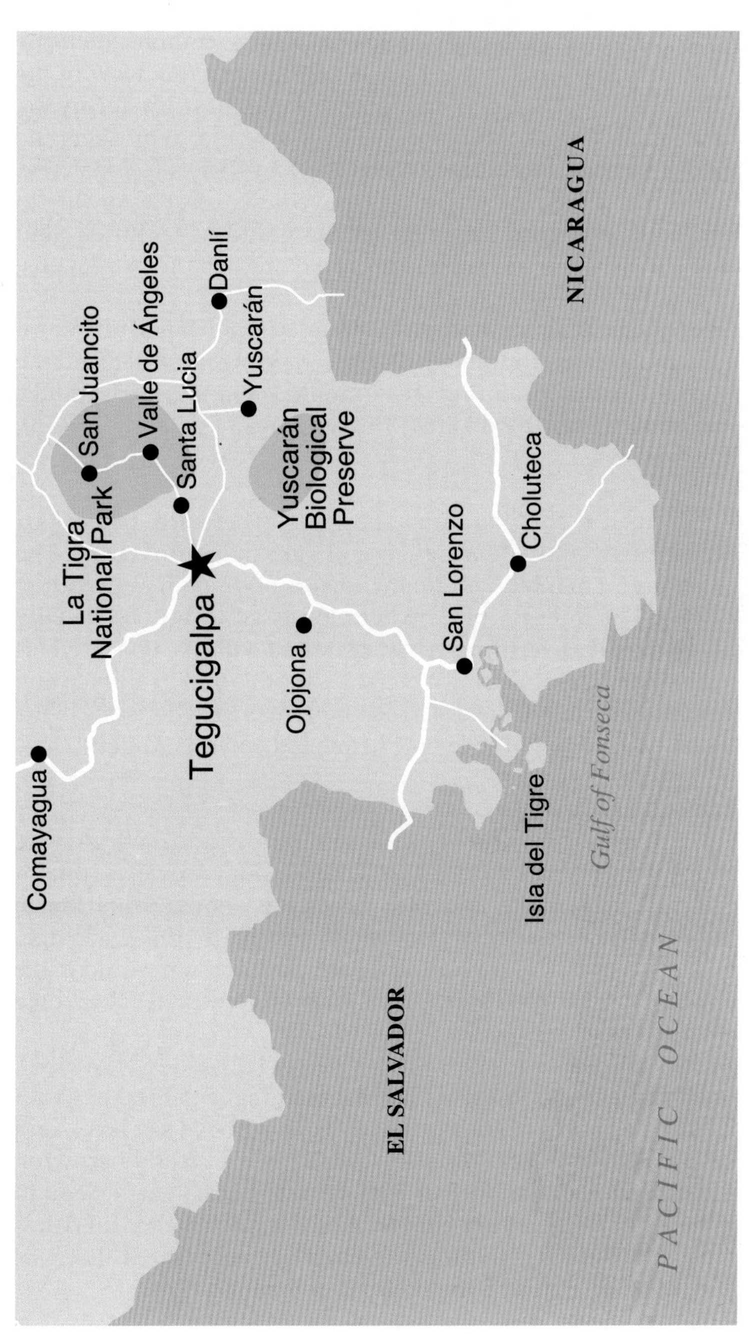
NICARAGUA
Danlí
Yuscarán
San Juancito
Valle de Ángeles
Santa Lucia
La Tigra
National Park
Yuscarán
Biological
Preserve
Tegucigalpa
Ojojona
Choluteca
San Lorenzo
Comayagua
Isla del Tigre
Gulf of Fonseca
EL SALVADOR
PACIFIC OCEAN

There are also some nice handicraft shops, as well as colorful gardens where the locals cultivate flowers to be sold in the markets of Tegucigalpa.

Santa Lucia is the Honduran headquarters of the **US Peace Corps**. Volunteers are trained here before being sent on the Corps' social and conservation programs all over the country.

If you like snakes, don't miss the **Santa Lucia Serpentarium**, located on the outskirts of town. *Info:* open daily 9am-4pm.

VALLE DE ÁNGELES

Continuing along the road from Tegucigalpa, we come to one of the finest towns in Honduras for local handicrafts. **Valle de Ángeles** is especially noted for its wood carvings. It's a little bigger and a little more touristy than Santa Lucia, especially lively on weekends.

Most of the action is around the **Municipal Craft Market** (Mercado Municipal de Artesanías), conveniently next to the bus stop. Here, in several large covered halls, you'll find a wide selection of handmade items, many produced right here in the area. Also at the market is a school that teaches native crafts. If you're lucky, you may get to watch some of the local artisans making the famous mahogany boxes, furniture and animal carvings. You'll also find lovely pieces in silver, pewter, leather and ceramics, as well as paintings, tapestries, traditional clothing and hammocks. Across the street from the craft market is **Lesandra Leather**, a local maker of fine leather products. Tourist souvenirs such as t-shirts, cigars and rum are not lacking.

If you'd prefer to stay in a peaceful little town, rather than in noisy, smoggy Tegus, consider using Valle de Ángeles as your base in the region. **La Posada De Las Nubes** is one of several basic but comfortable little inns. There are several pleasant little places to eat. **La Casa de las Abuelas** (Grandmothers' House) is famous around the country for homestyle typical dishes such as *pupusas, tamales, frijolitos* and *anafre* (see *Best Sleeps and Eats*).

SAN JUANCITO

The next stop on the circuit is this funky little town, 34 km northeast of Tegucigalpa, in the middle of **La Tigra National Park**.

San Juancito was a bustling gold and silver mining center until the **Rosario Mining Company** pulled up stakes in 1950, leaving much of the town abandoned. The old mining facilities, plantation-style homes and graveyard lend a bit of Wild West atmosphere.

Today, the village is picturesque enough, with some humble colonial houses and a handicraft studio where local artisans make a variety of items.

San Juancito is one of the gateways to La Tigra National Park. Just up the road at the **El Rosario visitors' center**, there's an "eco-hostel" that offers basic-clean-and-cheap lodging at the edge of the rainforest (see below).

LA TIGRA NATIONAL PARK

Situated 11 km from Tegucigalpa, this park is easy to get to and easy to visit, with a well-maintained network of trails. High up in the mountains above the city, the mountain streams and waterfalls of this lush cloud forest provide much of the region's drinking water. At an altitude of about 1,800 meters, the park has a pleasant climate year-round.

Mining has been going on in the area of the park since 1580. From 1879 through 1954, the New York-based Rosario Mining Company conducted heavy mining, with their main plant at El Rosario. Heavy logging also went on during this time, so the park has little or no primary forest today. In 1980, La Tigra became Honduras's first national park.

La Tigra has two visitors' centers, both with access to several trails. If you want to visit on a day trip from Tegus, head for the Jutiapa Visitor Center, which is closer and has access to the easiest trails. The easiest trail is **Las Granadillas**, just over a half kilometer long with gentle grades. It runs alongside a stream and leads to a wood observation platform. For a longer hike, take the **Bosque Nublado Trail** through the namesake broadleaf cloud forest, or the moderate **Jucuara Trail** that leads through pine and the broadleaf forest to a spring. The **Cascada Trail** leads to the park's highest waterfall (60 meters high), about equidistant from Jutiapa and El Rosario.

The **Jutiapa visitors' center** is a 22-kilometer drive from Tegus – take the road towards El Hatillo. Buses for Los Planes (1.5 km from Jutiapa) leave from Herrera Park in Tegucigalpa, first bus at 7am. There's a small and basic lodging that costs about $15 per person, or you can camp for $5.

The **El Rosario visitors' center**, near San Juancito, has a larger lodge, public bathrooms and a small cafetería. Buses for San Juancito leave from the San Pablo Market in Tegucigalpa at 3pm on weekdays, 8am on Sat and Sun. *Info:* La Tigra is managed by Fundación Amigos de La Tigra (AMITIGRA), www.nps.gov/centralamerica/honduras/home.html; Tel. 235-8494. Their office in Tegucigalpa is open Mon-Fri, 8am-noon and 2-5pm. The park is open Tue-Sun, 8am-5pm (no visitors are admitted after 2pm). Admission is $10 adults, $5 for kids under 12, seniors and disabled. For guided tours, or to stay at the ecolodge, you must make reservations with AMITIGRA.

OJOJONA

In the other direction, about 44 km south of Tegucigalpa, lies yet another picturesque mountain village of white adobe, red tile and grey cobblestones. **Ojojona** was established in the 17th century, and is now a National Heritage Site, renowned for its three beautiful colonial churches. Ojojona is also famous for its handicrafts, especially brightly colored ceramic pots, jars and figurines.

COMAYAGUA

Heading northwest of Tegucigalpa on the road to San Pedro Sula brings us to this historic city, founded in 1537. Comayagua's strategic location made it the political and cultural center of the district. After independence, it was the capital of Honduras for many years, before losing that distinction to Tegucigalpa.

Comayagua has some of the finest colonial architecture in the country. Many of the historic buildings around the central **Plaza La Merced** have recently been renovated and cleaned up for tourists. If you're traveling by car between San Pedro and Tegus, don't fail to make a stop here.

Sights include **Comayagua Cathedral**, the churches of **La Merced**, **La Caridad**, **San Francisco** and **San Sebastian**, as well as the home of national hero **Francisco Morazán**. The **Museum of Archaeology** is worth a short visit.

You'll see lots of gringos in Comayagua, many of them military personnel from nearby Palmerola, a US air base.

About 18 km east of Comayagua is **Montaña de Comayagua National Park**. Unfortunately, it has been badly deforested, but it still contains some pristine areas, including a bit of cloud forest the higher elevations. The park is home to monkeys, white-tailed deer and ocelots, as well as a variety of birds including toucans, quetzals and chachalacas. There are a couple of impressive waterfalls, as well as caves and ancient petroglyphs. To get here, go to the village of Río Negro, from whence a couple of trails lead into the park. Basic lodging is available in the village. *Info:* The park is administered by **ECOSIMCO** (Tel. 772-4681). Call them to arrange a guided tour, or inquire at the public school in Río Negro.

YUSCARÁN

About 65 km east of Tegucigalpa is **one of the best-preserved colonial towns** in Honduras. A major mining center in the 18th and 19th centuries, today Yuscarán is a quaint but sleepy little town with winding cobblestone roads and magnificent mountain vistas.

The entire village is a national historic site. On the small central park you'll find a lovely colonial church and the Casa Fortín, which houses a small history museum.

Yuscarán is famous throughout Honduras for the local brand of *guaro*. *Guaro* (short for *aguardiente*, or "firewater") is a very cheap, strong liquor made from sugarcane. The distillery is open to the public on weekdays, and offers free tours.

Towering over the town is the mountain of Montserrat, much of which is (theoretically) protected as the **Yuscarán Biological Reserve**. The reserve includes several waterfalls, cloud forest at the top and a variety of animals and birds. At last report, there were few or no facilities for visitors, but a local conservation group has been working on some hiking trails, so inquire in town for the latest information.

DANLÍ

This pretty little town, 100 km east of Tegucigalpa, is a center for tobacco cultivation. There's a small history museum and a huge, crumbling colonial church that are each worth a short visit.

LA MURALLA NATIONAL PARK

This park, known as the **Pride of Olancho**, is far off the beaten tourist path. It's not difficult to visit - on the contrary, it has a good infrastructure, with a visitors' center and several well-maintained paths. However, it's in a remote area, 200 km north of Tegucigalpa in the wild and lawless province of Olancho, so it's a destination for adventure travelers only.

La Muralla is near the town of **La Union**, about 31/2-hours from Tegucigalpa, along a small highway that leads from Tegus north to La Ceiba. The ride is spectacularly scenic, but dangerous. Armed bandits have held up both buses and private cars and robbed travelers at gunpoint. It's probably best to visit this park only with an organized tour.

Hardy travelers who make it to La Muralla will get to see lots of bright jungle flowers and mushrooms, and may get a glimpse of three-toed sloths, howler monkeys, white-tailed deer, tapirs, or porcupines. Hundreds of bird species live in the park, and it's one of the best places to spot the legendary quetzal, the sacred bird of the Mayans.

The nearby town of La Union has a couple of very basic lodgings, **Hotel La Muralla** and **Hotel Karol**. Each has rooms with shared bath for about $5. *Info:* The park is administered by the COHDEFOR office in La Union, which is open Mon-Fri 8am-5pm. Register with them before visiting. Entry $5.

SIERRA DE AGALTA

Another remote destination for serious eco-adventurers, this is one of the largest and most diverse protected areas in the country. This very large park (400 square km) has large areas of primary forest, and encompasses several different ecosystems, including cloud forest and tropical dry forest. Hidden away in the deep forests are archaeological sites, caves and waterfalls.

There are a few trails, and basic camping facilities, but almost no visitors. *Info:* The park is accessible from Juticalpa, Catacamas and Gualaco, all of which have some basic lodging places.

SAN LORENZO

San Lorenzo is a busy commercial city on the south coast, home to the port of Henecán, Honduras's only major port on the Pacific. Most tourists come here only to change buses on the way to Coyolito and the ferry to the Isla del Tigre.

San Lorenzo is a major center for seafood packing plants serving the shrimp and fish farms in the region. If you come around mealtime, it's worth stopping long enough to eat in one of the local restaurants, which are famous for seafood – check out the area around the waterfront **Hotel Miramar** (see *Best Eats*).

CHOLUTECA

Honduras's fourth-largest city (population 100,000) is very historic, with some well-preserved colonial architecture in the downtown area around the Parque Central. See the 17th-century cathedral and home of **José Cecilio del Valle**, a hero of the 1821 Central American independence movement.

Southern Discomfort

I really hate to dismiss an entire region of the country, but the fact is that there are good reasons why very few tourists visit the south coast of Honduras.

First of all, it's the **hottest part of the country**, a low coastal plain pounded by relentless sun during the dry season and torrential rains during the wet season. Second, much of the region is an **environmental disaster zone**. Slash-and-burn agriculture has deforested vast areas, and some are now in advanced stages of desertification. Along the coast, shrimp farms have devastated the mangrove wetlands that once provided habitat for land and sea life. The final kicker is that there just isn't a lot to see.

If you love adventure travel, far from other tourists, spend a couple of days on the **Isla del Tigre**. Otherwise, enjoy the old colonial towns in the cool and scenic mountains around Tegucigalpa, and save your beach activities for the North Coast.

CEDEÑO

The closest beach town to Tegucigalpa, **Cedeño** swarms with *capitalinos* on weekends and holidays. It's a pretty grubby little place, but there are some striking beaches of black volcanic sand – the best are outside of town. There are a few beach *champas* for food and drink.

ISLA DEL TIGRE

This small volcanic island in the Gulf of Fonseca has a distinctive conical shape which you may recognize from the two-Lempira bill.

The name comes from the pumas (locally called *tigres*) that once inhabitated the island. About three hours from Tegucigalpa, the islands' beaches are a popular weekend destination for *capitalinos*. The beaches (some black sand, some white) are mobbed with locals on weekends, but generally deserted during the week.

Getting here involves taking a bus from San Lorenzo or Choluteca to Coyolito, where you can catch a boat to the island. The boat is a sort of *collectivo*: they leave as soon as they have a full load of passengers. Expect an interesting, but not quick, journey. The ride to the island takes about half an hour, and costs no more than a couple of bucks.

The town of **Amapala** was Honduras's main port on the Pacific until the mainland port of Henecán replaced it in the 1950s, and the lively commercial town faded into today's sleepy sun-baked village. The town's colorful old buildings have a certain dilapidated brand of charm.

The beaches don't compare with those on the Bay Islands and the North Coast. They lack the Caribbean vibe, but some have volcanic black sand, and most are deserted during the week. Some are cleaner than others.

The most popular is **Playa Grande**, about 40 minutes' walk from town. It's a pretty black sand beach with nice waves and several beach *champas* serving food and drink, but it's mobbed on the weekends and none too clean. Farther around the island is **Playa Negra**, also exotic black sand with a view of the mountain in the background. All the way on the other side of the island is the most isolated and nicest beach, **Playa Gualora**.

Hikers can trek up a dirt road to the top of the cone for a panoramic view of the Gulf of Fonseca and the three countries on its shores.

The **Mirador de Amapala** is about the only decent hotel on the island. Another lodging option is to stay at one of several private homes that have recently set up as bed and breakfasts. The local people are famous for their hospitality, and this would be a good way to go far beyond the usual tourist experience (see *Best Sleeps*).

There's a small tourist office right by the dock in Amapala, with information on activities and lodging on the island.

9. TWO GREAT WEEKS IN HONDURAS

This country has an awful lot to see and do - coral reefs, beaches, cloud forests, mangrove wetlands, Mayan ruins, quaint colonial villages. In two weeks, we'll just have time for a taste of each, while leaving a little time for relaxing in the sun.

RECOMMENDED PLAN: Plan your trip around **La Ceiba**, because it's the main travel hub for most of the interesting parts of the country. La Ceiba is the center of the ecotourism scene on the North Coast. It also has plane and ferry connections to the **Bay Islands**, and flights to **La Moskitia**. **Copán** is a two-hour bus ride away. Fly into La Ceiba, then spend a few days in each of these areas.

Day One – La Ceiba

We're staying at one of the **jungle lodges** in the area, either the first-class **Lodge at Pico Bonito** or the bargain-priced **Omega Lodge** (see *Best Sleeps*).

We've made all our arrangements beforehand, so the staff from our lodge will meet us at the airport, ferry terminal or bus station, and whisk us straight to our cozy rain forest hideaway. We'll have time to take a short stroll in the forest, then cool off in the pool with a cold beer before dinner.

We'll make arrangements for a local English-speaking guide to accompany us to the rain forest tomorrow, so we'll learn some interesting stuff about the region and have a good chance of seeing some wildlife, as we support the local economy. See *Practical Matters* for a list of tour operators throughout the country.

Day Two – Pico Bonito National Park

Morning is always the best time to spot wildlife, so we'll head into the forest early. **Pico Bonito** is the third-largest protected area in Honduras, and has the greatest difference in altitude. Nine impressive mountain peaks are drained by 19 major rivers, with hundreds of magnificent waterfalls. There are eight distinct ecosystems, including tropical broadleaf and pine forests, and true cloud forest at the higher elevations.

Don't Miss ...

Pico Bonito National Park – hike in the mountain cloud forest and go rafting on the Cangrejal

Tela Parks – coastal lagoons teem with colorful birds; visit Punta Sal, Punta Izopo and Lancetilla Botanical Gardens

The Mayan Ruins of Copán – cultural capital of the pre-Columbian world

Dive/Snorkel in the Bay Islands – explore some of the world's finest coral reefs

Alternate Plan: The Mosquito Coast – Honduras's isolated eastern region has pristine jungle rivers and friendly indigenous people living a simple lifestyle

If we're lucky, we may see *pizotes*, agoutis, tapirs, anteaters, wild boars, white-faced and spider monkeys, genets, sloths, jaguars, pumas and ocelots. Over 300 species of birds have been observed in the park. Naturally, orchids, bromeliads and other resplendent flowers are common, especially in the high cloud forest. Colorful butterflies and hummingbirds flit about.

The **Río Zacate** has a series of waterfalls, some with nice pools for swimming. The 130-foot-high La Ruidosa is about an hour walk up the river, along a well-maintained trail through the lush rain forest. The trail offers spectacular views of the jungle and the Caribbean Sea below, as well as a good possibility of seeing some monkeys or other jungle denizens.

Day Three – The Cangrejal River

The **Cangrejal River**, on the eastern border of the park, offers some of the best whitewater river rafting in the world, with class III and IV rapids, and it's runnable year-round. It's a double adventure to navigate the rapids while racing through the extravagant vegetation of the rain forest.

If you've never rafted before, don't worry – we'll be riding in an

inflatable rubber raft with a guide, and wearing a helmet and life jacket. Our trip begins with a short warm-up, floating through some very mild rapids, and an instruction session with our bilingual guide.

Now that we have a clue what to do, we're ready to run the class III and IV rapids, with steep drops, waterfalls and narrow gorges with rocks towering hundreds of feet overhead. At some point, we'll leave the rafts and have a swim in a crystal-clear waterfall pool, surrounded by the lush green jungle.

A half-day rafting trip takes around four hours, and will cost you $50-70 per person, including transportation and a light picnic lunch. Experienced rafters can take a full-day trip, starting further up the river, with more intense rapids and technical whitewater.

The two main rafting tour operators, **Omega Tours** and **Jungle River Lodge**, each have basic but comfortable lodges right on the river. They can also pick you up from any of the lodges in the area. At the end of the day, soaking wet, tired and maybe just a little bit sore, but happy, we head back to our jungle lodge for an ice-cold beer and a hearty dinner. We go to sleep to the sounds of the jungle, to wake up and have yet another adventure in the morning.

See *Best Activities* for more details of rafting trips.

Day Four - Tela

It's time to change our base of operations. From La Ceiba, we'll take a bus or a van an hour west to Tela, where we'll check into a beachfront resort such as **Villas Telamar**, or perhaps the economical B&B **Maya Vista**. We'll line up a tour of **Punta Sal** for tomorrow morning, then pay a visit to **Lancetilla Botanical Garden**.

The largest botanical garden in Central America, Lancetilla has over 1,200 species of tropical plants in its **arboretum** and the adjacent **Lancetilla Nature Reserve**.

We'll see not only native Central American plants, but **exotic fruits from all over the world**, including mangosteens, keppel fruits, durians, rambutans and carambolas from Malaysia, pili nuts from the Philippines, Barbados cherries, and jaboticabas from Brazil. Towering bamboo, fragrant jasmine, rustling palms and all the other wonders of the tropics are here in leafy profusion. Flower lovers will delight in the **National Collection of Orchids**, with over 1,000 varieties of exotic flowers.

Over 200 species of birds have been identified in the park, including some that are very rare elsewhere. You may see several varieties of trogons, motmots, harpies, oropéndolas and toucans, to say nothing of swarms of hummingirds and butterflies.

After a couple of hours of walking around the park, we'll cool off with a swim in the **Lancetilla River**, then head back to our hotel for a cold beer and a nice dinner. Tomorrow we're up early for a visit to the coast.

Day Five – Jeanette Kawas National Park

This diverse park on the western end of the Bay of Tela was formerly named Punta Sal, but was renamed for murdered environmental activist **Jeanette Kawas**. Most of the park is a vast area of **mangrove wetlands**, a labyrinth of estuaries, lagoons, canals and flooded forests. A tour of the park makes for an action-packed day and provides a good contrast to mountainous Pico Bonito.

Several local tour operators offer trips to Punta Sal (as most locals still call it). Perhaps the best known is **Garífuna Tours** (www.garifunatours.com). Their office is near the central park in Tela, and they run daily boat tours that showcase the diversity of

the area. **Coco Tours** (www.hondurascoco.com) is another possibility.

First thing in the morning, we'll take a half-hour boat ride across Tela Bay, to the peninsula of Punta Sal, quite possibly seeing enormous pods of porpoises on the way.

Now we hike across the peninsula, passing out of the mangrove forest and into tropical broadleaf rain forest. If we're lucky, we'll see some white-faced and howler monkeys. If nothing else, we're certain to hear the howlers in the distance, sounding like a bunch of big dogs barking.

On the other side of the peninsula is **Playa Cocolito**, a classic Caribbean beach with snow-white sand and turquoise water. There's a bit of coral reef just offshore, and most visitors do some snorkeling at this point, but there's nothing here to compare with the scene on the Bay Islands, where we'll be in a few days, so we'll skip the snorkeling in favor of a boat tour to the **Micos Lagoon**, the best place to spot birds - over 350 species have been sighted here.

It will take us most of the day to see all this, so it will be dinnertime by the time we make our stop in **Miami**, one of the most picturesque of the Garífuna villages. There are a couple of small *champa* restaurants here - one of them will serve us a plate of fresh grilled fish with rice and beans and fried plantains.

Day Six - Copán Ruinas

Now it's time to leave the coast and head into the interior of the country, the cool western highlands. We'll take one of the first-class air-conditioned buses of the **Hedman Alas** line (www.hedmanalas.com) to Copán. We'll have to change at their terminal in San Pedro Sula, but other than that it's a straight shot. There's nothing to detain us in noisy and dirty San Pedro.

There's a bus from Tela at 6:30am that would get us to Copán in time for a late lunch, but that's way too early for us, especially after staying up late last night, dancing to *punta* music in the Zona Viva. We'll have an early lunch in Tela, and take the 12:45pm bus. We make a leisurely entrance in Copán Ruinas in the late afternoon. The most character-filled lodging in the area is a nice little inn called **Hacienda San Lucas**, on a hill overlooking the valley of Copán (see *Best Sleeps*). If you'd prefer an upscale place right in town, the **Hotel Marina Copán** can't be beat.

After checking in at our lodging, we'll head over to the **Tunkul Bar and Restaurant**, for a cold beer and a chat with the staff about what's going on in the area. The in-house **Go Native Tours** (Tel. 651-4410) will try to tempt us with trips to Mayan sites, cloud forests, coffee farms, Lenca villages and all sorts of other fascinating sights in the region, but we already know where we're going tomorrow morning. We can arrange a tour of the ruins here, or simply call the **Copán Guide Association** at the park (Tel. 651-4018).

Copán Ruinas has several very nice possibilities for dinner, including healthy and delicious fare at **Twisted Tanya's**, or hearty grilled meats with a nice river view at **Carnitas Nía Lola** (see *Best Eats*). This is a good place to recover from Tela – the town goes to bed pretty early, and so will we, because we're going to get up bright and early for our visit to the ruins.

Day Seven – The Ruins of Copán

After a breakfast of sweet and juicy tropical fruit and rich Honduran coffee, we'll head to the park in plenty of time to be the first through the gates at 8am, so we'll have an hour or two to enjoy the ruins in relative peace, before the flood of day-trippers arrives with their ball caps, fanny packs and water bottles.

The Mayan city of Copán was a cultural capital, and is richer in sculptures, hieroglyphics and art treasures than any other known Mayan site. During their golden age (300-900 AD) the Mayans had a highly advanced civilization that extended from Mexico to western Honduras. Their calendar and their knowledge of astronomy were unequalled until modern times.

Sometime during the 9th century AD, the grand city of Copán was abandoned. While it sounds romantic to say that "no one knows why," in fact modern scientists have a pretty good idea of why the Mayan civilization collapsed.

The Mayans cleared large areas of forest for agriculture, but the soil proved poor for growing crops, so as the population grew, they kept clearing more and more land. The **deforestation** led to erosion, making the land even less able to support decent crop yields. In the end they simply couldn't grow enough food to feed themselves, and the population went into a long decline.

Unfortunately, history is currently repeating itself in Honduras. In many parts of the country, **slash-and-burn agriculture** has denuded whole regions, leaving the poor subsistence farmers unable to make a living. Forced to leave their homes, they move into more remote areas and repeat the process there.

Food for thought as we explore the sights of Copán. The **Great Plaza** is a large open space dotted with stelae and altars featuring bas-relief statues of Mayan rulers and gods, with hieroglyphic inscriptions. Back in the day, the stelae, and many of the buildings, were painted in bright colors, traces of which can still be seen here and there.

The **Ball Court** is decorated with images of macaws, which were sacred birds. Here the Mayans played a game that involved putting a hard rubber ball through a stone hoop without using their hands. Some believe that the losers provided the human sacrifices that were supposed to appease the gods.

Towering 100 feet over the Great Plaza, the **Acropolis** is a large complex of pyramids and temples that was built over many earlier temples. Here are the beautiful **Rosalila Temple**, or Temple of the Sun, painted in rose-lilac colors, as well as the **Plaza of the Jaguars**, with its rich carvings depicting Maya beliefs about the afterworld.

The 63 steps of the **Hieroglyphic Stairway** are carved with 1,500 glyphs, the longest known text left by the ancient Mayans. It is believed to be a chronology of all the rulers of Copán, telling the history of their great battles and deeds.

Late morning is when the main site begins to get crowded with day trippers, so let's leave it to them for a while, and head a couple of kilometers down the road to **Las Sepulturas Archaeological Site**. Las Sepulturas is one of the few Mayan residential areas that have been found, and provides a look at the everyday life of the people.

After lunch, we'll visit the **Museum of Mayan Sculpture**, adjacent to the ruins. Many of the original art treasures of Copán are displayed here in the museum, protected from the elements, while the *in situ* versions are actually clever replicas.

Here you'll find the finest collection of Mayan sculpture in the world, over 3,000 pieces, many of them mounted in the facades of six reconstructed buildings. Highlights include four of the most beautiful stelae from the site, the original facade of the Ball Court, and the original Altar Q, with its relief depicting the 16 kings of Copán.

We've spent a long day soaking up culture, and done quite a bit of walking, so in the evening we'll reward ourselves with a cold drink and a nice dinner in Copán Ruinas. After dinner, why don't we check out one of the local gathering spots for a chat with some fellow travelers, the better to plan tomorrow's tour of the region?

Day Eight - The Lenca Trail

The region around Copán has much more to see, including spectacular mountains, picturesque colonial villages with great shopping for local handicrafts, and coffee plantations that are great spots for birding. The climate up here in the mountains is consistently pleasant year-round.

Santa Rosa de Copán, the main commercial and transportation hub of the Copán region, has a picturesque downtown, with cobblestone streets around the restored Cathedral of Santa Rosa. Here we can also visit the Flor de Copán cigar factory, or the Beneficio Maya coffee farm.

Other well-preserved colonial towns include **Gracias** with its three large churches and the fortress of San Cristobal perched high above the town; **San Manuel Colohete**, with one of the finest colonial churches in the country; and Belén Gualcho, with its Sunday morning street market. Throughout the region, we'll see lovely local crafts on sale.

If you really want to learn about the region, then let's take a tour with **Lenca Land Trails** (www.Lenca-Honduras.com; Tel. 662-1375 or 662-0805). They'll pick us up in the morning and take us wherever we want to go. In the evening, they'll deposit us back at our hotel in Copán Ruinas, where we'll make an early evening of it. We're heading for the Bay Islands tomorrow, and it will be a long travel day.

Day Nine - The Bay Islands

We've left the most popular region of Honduras until last. This will be the only really grueling travel day on our itinerary. We'll take a Hedman Alas express bus to La Ceiba (changing buses in San Pedro Sula), then take a flight or a (cheaper but slower) ferry to Roatan or Utila.

ALTERNATE EXTREME ECO-PLAN

If you really want the rain forest experience, you could take the bold step of skipping Copán altogether, and instead making a four-day trip to **La Moskitia**, Honduras's most remote region (see *Chapter 7*). It's easy enough to fly out there from La Ceiba.

ALTERNATE ECO-PLAN
If you're the kind of traveler that likes to get off the beaten tourist path, and you haven't seen enough of the rain forest, then spend a day (or more) at **Celaque National Park**, not far from Copán, where waterfalls launch themselves from the high rocky plateau covered in cloud forest. On a day hike or an overnight camping trip, you're likely to see some of the local forest dwellers (see *Chapter 6*).

There is an airstrip at Copán Ruinas, so it might be possible to take a charter flight directly to Roatan. A company called **La Estanzuela Tours** was running a scheduled flight every Thursday between Copán and Roatan, but they seem to have disappeared. Inquire with a local tour operator to see if flights are available, because that would save us a lot of travel hassle.

It would also give us another whole morning in the Copán region! We could visit **Macaw Mountain Bird Park**, to see a rainbow of scarlet macaws, parrots and toucans, and have a splendid lunch at their nice little riverside café.

We've already chosen a place to stay in the islands. All three islands have spectacular diving, fishing and beaches, but **Roatan** is the largest, and has far more tourist infrastructure and "things to do" than smaller **Utila** and **Guanaja**. If you want to be where the action is, then let's go to Roatan, where we'll stay at the beautiful **Paya Bay Beach Resort**, the elegant **Lily Pond House B&B**, or the budget-priced **Reef House Resort**. If you want a more laid-back island with a bit of a youth scene and the world's cheapest diving, then we'll head for Utila and stay at the **Mango Inn**, which has a couple of price options, or at **Deep Blue**, a totally relaxed resort with an awesome beach.

Wherever we plan to stay, by the time we get there this evening, we'll be ready for a cold drink, a hot meal and a relaxing swim, with a minimum of delay. Therefore, as usual, we've called ahead and arranged for our resort to send someone to meet us right at the airport or ferry dock, and whisk us to the bar and the beach *muy pronto.*

Days 10-14 - The Bay Islands

We have four days of dream vacation ahead of us, as we explore some of the most beautiful coral reefs and beaches in the world. The only real question is, how much diving and/or snorkeling do you want to squeeze in?

Gung-ho divers can get in three or even more dives per day, but most of us will be content to do two tanks in the morning, then spend a leisurely afternoon swimming and sipping umbrella drinks in the shade of the swaying palms. Eat an enormous amount of fish and seafood, including conch fritters at every meal.

If you can tear yourself away from the diving, go fishing for a day. You can spend the morning stalking bonefish on the flats, then troll offshore for wahoo and billfish in the afternoon. See *Best Activities* for details of the spectacular diving and fishing opportunities in the islands.

On Day Fourteen, it's boo-hoo time. There are a few direct flights from Roatan to the US. The other option is to change planes in SPS or Tegus. Whichever way you go, be sure there's a little sand in your shoes when you tearfully board the plane. That means you'll be back!

10. BEST SLEEPS & EATS

In the heavily-touristed Bay Islands, and in the large cities of Tegucigalpa and San Pedro Sula, you'll find **a full range of lodgings**, from luxurious resort complexes to funky backpacker crash pads. There are a few upscale lodgings dotted elsewhere in the country, but most areas of Honduras are still comparatively untouristed, and the level of available lodgings stops well short of posh.

What local lodgings lack in luxury however, they often compensate for in character. You'll find **wonderfully laid-back bungalows amid lush greenery**, where you wake up to the magical sound of palm fronds rustling in the breeze, and you'll meet colorful expatriate innkeepers. In most areas, you should have no problem finding a comfortable and clean room with the usual amenities, and you may be pleasantly surprised at the prices.

HOTELS

There's a 16% tax added to all hotel rooms, which is sometimes but not always included in quoted prices. Some hotels expect you to pay a deposit (or even the whole price!) up-front when making your reservation. When booking online, read cancellation policies carefully.

Lodging Prices

$ Backpacker: $10 or less
$$ Budget: $10-30
$$$ Midrange: $30-60
$$$$ First-class: $60-110
$$$$$ Luxury: $110 and up

Prices quoted are for one double room.

Upscale hotels accept major credit cards, but most cheap local places do not. Most upper-end hotels will gladly arrange transportation to and from the nearest airport, which is well worth it for the extra safety and convenience.

EATING OUT

Like her people, Honduras's cuisine reflects a mix of influences. The indigenous people, the Spanish, the Afro-Caribbeans and the Americans have all left their culinary mark.

In most of the country, "typical" food follows the Latin American tradition: lots of beans and rice, big hunks of meat and overcooked vegetables. What the Hondurans call a *plato típico* consists of a big piece of meat or fish, one or more vegetables (often a fried plantain and a pile of chopped cabbage), and a large helping of rice and beans. Some travelers give *comida típica* the thumbs-down, because the beans and rice, served at all meals, can get boring, and because cooks tend to go heavy on the lard and the salt.

Tortillas are a major staple. *Baleadas* are flour tortillas filled with beans and/or meat and cheese, the Honduran equivalent of a taco or burrito. *Tamales,* corn flour steamed in a corn husk with a pork filling, are everywhere. Some traditional spots serve variations on the corny theme such as *pupusas, montucas, ticucos, atoles* or *chilates.* A uniquely Honduran dish is *anafre,* a sort of bean dip served in a small ceramic container to keep it warm.

The Garífuna of the North Coast are famous for their grilled fish (which tastes best in a thatched *champa* on the beach at night) and for their coconut bread. **Fresh fish and seafood** are the main attraction along both coasts and in the Bay Islands, where it's served with a Caribbean seasoning. Seafood is on upscale menus throughout the country, but alas, away from the coast, you are likely to be presented with an unspectacular frozen fish or shrimp.

Tegucigalpa, San Pedro and, to a lesser extent, other cities, feature a range of restaurants including **French**, **Italian**, **Chinese**, **Mexican** and other worldwide favorites. Eateries in tourist areas serve American favorites such as **burgers**, **chicken wings** and **pizza**. The results can be very good, or they can be lame and overpriced.

Honduran **coffee** is excellent. In some areas, you can visit a coffee farm and buy top-quality estate coffee right from the source. I like a *café con leche*, which tends to be about half milk. If you want black coffee, ask for *café negro*.

Beer (*cerveza*) is brewed in the Germanic lager tradition. The local brands Salva Vida, Port Royal and Imperial are all good. Wine is, of course, not produced in the tropics, so most Hondurans aren't big wine drinkers. A limited selection of imported wine (often from Chile) is available at upscale restaurants.

Rum (*ron*), distilled from sugar, is the typical tropical liquor. There's a variety of brands available, ranging from cheap rotgut to fine dark sipping rum. Some of the locals drink *guaro*, a clear liquor distilled from sugarcane. Similar to moonshine or to Jamaican "overproof" rum, *guaro* is very cheap and very strong. You have been warned.

Whatever you eat in Honduras, do not neglect to sample some of whatever **fruits** are in

Where to Eat?

A *comedor* is a small local café serving cheap and hearty fare. A *champa* is literally a thatched hut: it often means a beachfront restaurant or bar. A *pulpería* is a small store that sells groceries and every little thing.

season. The mangos, pineapples, papayas, bananas, citrus and other tropical delights that grow down here are simply different fruits from the ones you buy at the supermarket back home: sweet, juicy and cheap. Quench your thirst with a *pipa,* a chilled green coconut with a straw inserted so you can sip the sweet milk. Kids love to chew a stalk of sugar cane. Fresh-squeezed **juices** from a rainbow of exotic fruits are available everywhere. Don't be afraid to experiment.

THE BAY ISLANDS

The Bay Islands are a major tourist destination with a huge choice of places to stay. Budget travelers and wealthy globetrotters will find a good selection of hotels, resorts and vacation rentals. Most are on the beach. Almost all cater to divers, and offer a vacation package of bed, meals, diving and bar action. Your first choice is to decide between the bright lights of tourism on **Roatan** or the more laid-back lifestyles offered on the small islands of **Utila** and **Guanaja**. There are no true luxury resorts, but some of the smaller properties and B&Bs are quite elegant.

BEST SLEEPS ON ROATAN

Roatan is about 30 miles long, with only a few small villages. Resorts, hotels, B&Bs and dive lodges are scattered around randomly, most outside of these metropolises.

Anthony's Key Resort $$$$$

Anthony's is the most famous Bay Island resort. Some guests love it and others find it impersonal and "touristy." Some find little reason to leave, as Anthony's offers just about every type of tour and activity available on Roatan. There are no phones or TVs in the rooms, but most have AC. *Info:* Sandy Bay. www.anthonyskey.com; Tel. 445-3003 or 800/227-3483 US.

Paya Bay Beach Resort $$$$$

This is one of the most beautiful resorts in the Bay Islands. On the northeast corner of the island, immediately next to two great white sand beaches, Paya Bay is small and quiet, perfect if you just want to dive and be mellow. It's an hour's taxi ride from the airport, remote from the cruise ship day-trippers. The 10 rooms have AC but no phones or TV. No problem – you can stay connected with the wireless internet. *Info:* www.payabay.com; Tel. 435-2139.

Luna Beach Resort $$$$

With 19 suites and some four-bedroom houses, this resort is on 33 acres with a freshwater pool, dive shop, restaurant, bars, game room, and all the usual beach toys. The owner, Mr. Chuck, lives on the premises and helps make guests feel like they have a friend helping them enjoy their holiday. The dive shop has all the goodies, with PADI and SSI certification programs. *Info:* West End. www.lunabeachresort.com; Tel. 445-4025.

Bananarama Dive Beach Resort $$$$

Owner Ron Smith has been busy updating the 13 cabins with new mattresses, hardwood floors, etc. This is a good thing, as in the past some guests have found the accommodations on the rustic side. AC costs $10 extra, and is only available for a few hours every day. The resort is not directly on the beach, but it's less than 100 feet away from one of the finest beaches in the world. Snorkeling is great directly in front of the resort. The dive operation has an excellent reputation and they have all the usual water sports equipment handy. *Info:* www.bananaramadive.com; Tel. 445-5005 or 727/564-9058 US.

Bay Island Beach Resort $$$$

This resort has a comprehensive dive operation that visits the best dive spots on all the Bay Islands. The beach in front of the resort is lovely and there is excellent snorkeling right here. In fact, there's an interesting snorkeling trail beginning just a few feet away from the beach with labels identifying typical sea life. Groups from the cruise ships love it. *Info:* www.bibr.com; Tel. 445-3020 or 800/4-ROATAN US.

Fantasy Island $$$$
This is a mass-tourism-oriented diving and beach resort on its own little island, an all-inclusive cattle operation with wonderful snorkeling and water sports but unremarkable rooms and food. The rooms have AC and TV. Extensive amenities include a pool, tennis courts, marina, kayaks, windsurfing gear, and on and on. The dive program is extensive, with PADI training at all levels including children's classes. *Info:* www.fantasyislandresort.com; Tel. 455-7499 or 800/676-2826 US.

Half Moon Bay $$$$
These 14 bungalows have balconies and hammocks overlooking the sea. Some units have AC. Lunch at the restaurant is one of life's great experiences. It's not a fancy place – the clientele runs from tourists to down-at-heel gringos going to seed in the tropics, drunk at 11am. The fish, shrimp and lobster have been gently lifted from the sea yards from where you are sitting. The fish sandwiches are so juicy it drips off your elbow as you take your fist bite. *Info:* www.halfmoonbaycabins.com; Tel. 445-4047 or 800/989-9970 US.

CoCo View Resort $$$
Informed divers consider the dive operation at this resort to be one of the best. There is excellent diving directly in front of the resort, including a monumental wall and the wreck Prince Albert. The list of PADI courses goes on and on. CoCo View has 26 rooms and eight beachfront rental houses, including some romantic bungalows over the water at the end of long walkways. Some of the cheaper rooms are on the run-down side. Local musicians entertain in the bar. *Info:* French Cay. www.cocoviewresort.com; Tel. 455-7502 or 800/510-8164 US.

BEST EATS ON ROATAN

Most resorts do all-inclusive packages with rooms, diving and three meals a day included. Some have wonderful food and some are just average. Buffet dining is the usual deal. At restaurants, seafood is almost always the best thing to order. Fish, lobster and shrimp are locally caught and of excellent quality. Prices are generally slightly lower than in the US. You'll run into a few lobster bargains.

For really fine dining, **Chez Pascal,** at the Island Pearl Hotel (Tel. 445-5001), features a French cook serving up some of the best seafood in Honduras. Their lobster dishes show much more imagination than some of the funkier places on the island. Try their lobster crepes or thermidor.

A lovely seafood dinner in the village at a funky palm-roofed, open-air restaurant such as **Eagle Ray's Bar & Grill**, West End, is always a good evening. Lobster and fresh fish are what's happening here. Try the fritters. Wonderful tropical fruit drinks can fill you up so don't drink too many before dinner. Get a table on the patio so you can enjoy the view of the Caribbean.

Hole in the Wall, located in Jonesville near Oak Ridge, is famous for their Sunday all-you-can-eat dinner with lobster, shrimp, BBQ filet mignon, Harry's world-famous beans, home-baked bread, and dessert, all for about $15. The bar is on the water and you have to get there by boat.

Foster's is a good bet in the evenings for live music and rowdy crowds. The drinks are reasonable and the conch fritters are great.

BEST SLEEPS ON UTILA

A laid-back place with chickens running around in the airport parking lot, **Utila appeals to hardcore divers, anglers and the backpacker generation**. It's famous for spectacular diving, whale sharks, budget lodging and midnight trance parties on the beach. Utila has a small number of resorts, most of them dedicated to diving, diving and diving. All offer weeklong dive packages, usually including accommodations, some or all meals, transportation to and from the airport or dock and three or more dives per day.

Utila is famous for its budget accommodations and inexpensive diving. Some of the less expensive places do not require reservations, relying on walk-in traffic, but I recommend advance reservations in all circumstances. Telephone the day before you fly to confirm that your rooms will be ready and waiting for you.

Mango Inn $$$$$

Mango is one of the best-known resorts on the island, with 23 air-conditioned rooms and cabins. Located in the village, the resort is clean and comfortable, with a good bar and restaurant. Diving is coordinated through the Utila Dive Center. *Info:* www.mango-inn.com; Tel. 425-3305.

Utila Lodge $$$$

This small lodge has eight air-conditioned rooms built over the water right in the colorful village. They are nicely furnished, with private balconies and hammocks. There's a pleasant restaurant, hot tub, wireless internet and Utila's only hyperbaric pressure chamber. Owners Jim and Kristy Engel incorporate their own charm into the operations, chatting with guests at meals and organizing excursions to nearby attractions. Diving and fishing depend on outside operators, but the owners know the best ones. *Info:* Tel. 800/282-8932 US.

Deep Blue Resort $$$$

No phones, no TV, just dive, dive, dive. Deep Blue is a wonderful place to stay, an all-inclusive "diving vacation venue." You can only get here by boat, so privacy is assured. The resort is on a quiet beach with palm trees. The diving

What's Included?

It can be tricky to compare the **dive packages** offered by different resorts. Some weeklong packages are for six days, some are for seven, and a few are even for eight. Count the number of days you get to dive, not the number of nights included. Most places include three dives per day, with one or two night dives included. Many resorts also offer all the shore dives you can eat for no extra charge. Realize that, although the shore dives in front of most of the resorts are quite good, you will probably be too tired to take advantage of this after three or four boat dives daily.

nearby is great, so shore dives are definitely the thing to do. The 10 rooms have private balconies with views of the beach. Owner Jasmine does the cooking, relying on fresh local ingredients and lots of seafood. The lodging is not five-star, but the dive operation is. The PADI dive shop is one of the best in the area, with all the usual training courses and a full complement of rental equipment. *Info:* www.deepblueutila.com; Tel. 425-2015.

BEST EATS ON UTILA

Count on fantastic seafood, served at your lodge or at a variety of local palm-frond-covered eateries. Be sure to try some local specialties like *pastelitos* (stuffed pastries) or coconut bread. The **Island Café** near Coco Loco is a great spot for seafood, with fabulous fish dinners for around $6. **Susan's Restaurant**, on Suc-Suc Cay, also serves inexpensive seafood, with few meals more than $5.

The Mango Inn has the great **Mango Café,** which has a slightly more romantic atmosphere than some of the other places and, of course, seafood.

BEST SLEEPS ON GUANAJA

Guanaja is **the quietest of the three main Bay Islands**, and offers only a few lodging options. There's a paved airstrip, but no real roads – local transportation is by boat. Most visitors to this off-the-beaten-path destination are here for diving or fishing.

Unfortunately, the Posada del Sol, once the nicest place to stay on the island, is now closed.

Nautilus Resort $$$$

You'll need to hop a ride on one of the resort's boats to get to the 60 acres on a hill overlooking the long, white sand beach that are the setting for Nautilus's seven rooms. Of course, diving is the thing here and all the usual rental equipment and certification courses are available. Fishing, kayaking and most other activities can be arranged. The sea breeze keeps the sand fleas more or less under control. *Info:* Near Bonacca Town. Tel. 453-4389.

West Peak Inn $$$$

Six cabins, four rooms, a tropical bar and a pleasant restaurant. Meals are served family-style and usually include whatever seafood has been hauled in that day. There's a vast white sand beach with almost no one on it. Snorkeling is fantastic directly in front of the inn. Diving and fishing can be arranged, as can multi-day kayaking trips around the island. This is a place to chill out, rather than a full-on dive resort. *Info:* www.westpeakinn.com; Tel. 408-3072.

Hotel Rosario $$$

The Rosario is the best of the inexpensive hotels on Guanaja. You can get TV and AC but you have to pay a little more. It is on a small cay by itself, so you'll need for them to come and get you by water taxi. *Info:* Tel. 453-4240.

Island House $$$

Owner Bo offers rooms in the main lodge and two separate guesthouses. There's no AC, but louvered windows allow the sea breezes to blow gently through. The beach is one of the nicest anywhere. As the resort is small, dive trips usually include only a couple of people – no cattle boats here. The bar is at the end of a dock right over the water. Hammocks are strategically placed for your reclining pleasure. *Info:* www.bosislandhouse.com; Tel. 991-0913.

BEST EATS ON GUANAJA

Most visitors eat in their lodges, but there are lots of interesting dining experiences around the island. Budget travelers will find plenty of inexpensive options, especially if you develop a taste for the local chow.

The Pirate's Den in Bonacca has seafood and great rum drinks. **End of the World** (Tel. 991-1257), at Michael's Rock

Sand Fleas Anyone?

The Bay Islands are rife with **irritating sand fleas**, almost invisible little buggers that swarm around the beach. Many swear by Skin-So-Soft, and it is a good idea to bring some as well as the usual high-DEET mosquito repellant. Some use a local concoction called Jungle Juice. Try them all. Maybe something will work for you. Try not to scratch.

Beach has great steaks and seafood. Nearby **Casetta 2000** serves burgers and beer at a classic little beach bar with a sand floor and the breeze blowing through. The **Crazy Parrot Bar** in Sandy Bay does fried chicken, fish soup, jerk chicken, lobster fritters and umbrella drinks. **Dina's Reef House** (Tel 453-4538) in Pelican Reef has typical island seafood, a waterside dock and a great view.

SLEEPS & EATS ON CAYOS COCHINOS

Thirteen small sand islets, "cays" as they are called locally, constitute the Cayos Cochinos or Pig Islands. The cays are a couple of miles from the mainland, easily reachable by boat from Roatan or La Ceiba. The area surrounding them is a **Marine Protected Area** and offers probably the best diving in Honduras. *Info:* www.cayoscochinos.org.

Plantation Beach Resort $$$

The only resort on the Cayos, Plantation Beach offers spectacular diving, with reefs and sea life in virgin condition. There's only room for 20 divers, so there is rarely anything in the water you could call a crowd. The PADI facility offers the usual training and rental equipment. There are opportunities for windsurfing, kayaking and other non-diving activities, but diving is the primary focus. The beach is superb. *Info:* www.plantationbeachresort.com; Tel. 442-0974.

THE NORTH COAST

The four main tourist areas of the North Coast have four different vibes, and four different mixes of lodging options. All have nice beachfront lodgings, and all have low-budget places right in town, in case you want to be close to the nightlife.

La Ceiba is jungle lodge territory. **The Lodge at Pico Bonito** is one of the nicest resort hotels in all of Honduras. The newer **Las**

Cascadas is a worthy competitor. There are also nice jungle lodges for lower budgets: **Jungle River Lodge** and **Omega Jungle Lodge** are very economical, but they have access to the very same rain forest.

Tela is Honduras's up-and-coming beach capital, and it has nice beachfront hotels in several price ranges. **Trujillo** and laid-back **Omoa** are less touristed, but also have fine beaches.

BEST SLEEPS IN LA CEIBA

Jungle Lodges

The Lodge at Pico Bonito $$$$$

The only true luxury lodge on mainland Honduras, The Lodge is on the edge of **Pico Bonito National Park**. The 200-acre site lies between two rivers, with 8,000-foot Pico Bonito in the background. Several hiking trails begin on the grounds, and The Lodge has their own guides for hiking, horseback and whitewater rafting trips. It's all just 20 minutes west of La Ceiba Airport. The 22 cabins have private verandas, hammocks, beautiful wood floors, rattan furniture and local artwork. There are ceiling fans but no AC, and phones but no TVs. You won't need 'em – the altitude and the shade of the forest keep things cool, and you didn't come here to watch TV!

For upscale ecotourism, Honduras is not yet in the same league as Costa Rica and Belize, but The Lodge is a giant step in the right direction, and is already inspiring imitators. *Info:* www.picobonito.com; Tel. 440-0388, 440-0389 or 888/428-0221 US.

Las Cascadas Lodge $$$$$

This challenger to The Lodge is on the other side of the park, on the Cangrejal River. You'll go to sleep to the sound of the river, and wake up to the singing of the jungle birds. The grounds are a garden of colorful foliage, shaded by giant mahogany trees. There are only four rooms, each with a four-poster canopy bed, a nice stone-and-tile bathroom and – the *piéce de resistance* – a private screened porch overlooking the namesake waterfall. The dining is intimate and excellent – the chef is cooking for fewer than a dozen guests! *Info:* www.lascascadaslodge.com; Tel. 419-0030 or 877/556-1321 US.

Noa Noa Lodge $$
This small lodge is near The Lodge at Pico Bonito, on a beautiful site with enormous mango trees and views of the mountains. Run by a European couple, it's no luxury lodge, but it's fairly new, clean and comfortable. There are five rooms with private bath, a small pool and an outdoor restaurant and bar. *Info:* www.stealth-iss.net/noanoa/lodge.html.

Jungle River Lodge $
On the banks of the Cangrejal, this adventure lodge has basic and cheap rooms, which are usually taken by people on their whitewater rafting and rain forest tours. Owner Oscar Perez is a local who's been running the rivers of the region for 15 years. The lodge is nothing fancy, but it has a restaurant and bar, natural pools in the river for swimming, and a zipline, in case you (or your kids) wish to zip through the jungle canopy. There's a resident scarlet macaw that will keep you company at breakfast, and a friendly doberman. *Info:* www.jungleriverlodge.com; Tel. 440-1282, 440-1268 or 398-7641.

Omega Jungle Lodge $
This is another basic lodge on the river, used by Omega Tours to house their guests. Omega have been running rafting, hiking and horseback riding tours since 1992. The cabañas are basic – like screened-in porches with candles – and cheap. The nicer cabins have private bathrooms with hot showers. One is nestled among giant bamboo, and the other has a view of the El Bejuco waterfall. The grounds are like a botanic garden, with mango and orange trees, orchids, bromeliads, and plenty of opportunities to spot local birds. Restaurante La Jungla is a traditional thatched *champa*, serving typical local dishes. *Info:* www.omegatours.hn; Tel. 440-0334 or 419-0003.

Best Hotels in La Ceiba

Quinta Real Hotel and Convention Center $$$$$

On the beach in the Zona Viva, this grand Spanish-style building is the nicest of the hotels in town, with first-class facilities and pleasant rooms with ocean views. The 81 rooms and suites have AC, phone, TV, safes, irons, hair dryers and internet access. The resort has all the amenities: pool, spa, a small gym, restaurant and bar, beauty parlor, gift shop, business center, laundry service, private parking and 24-hour security. Right in the nightlife district, it isn't the quietest hotel in town, but if you're looking for a first-class hotel on the beach, this is it. *Info:* www.quintarealhotel.com; Tel. 440-3311, 440-3319 or 888/790-5264 US.

Vacation Rentals

If you plan to stay in one place for a week or more, renting a guest house may be a good alternative to staying at a hotel. Local real estate agencies have rentals available, from moderately-priced apartments to luxurious seaside villas. Use a Honduras-based search engine to find a local agent, or check out **www.travel-to-honduras.com**, which has links to rentals throughout the country (see *Web Sites*, near the end of the *Practical Matters* chapter). One caveat: what you see on a web site and what you find when you arrive may be two different things (the same applies to hotels). Ask plenty of questions, and search online for comments from other travelers who've rented through a particular agency in the past.

Coco Pando Resort Hotel $$$

This unpretentious hotel is on the beach between La Ceiba and the airport, far enough from both to be secluded. Hosts Charlie Meador and John Salzer are easy-going and helpful, and repeat guests remark on how much at home they feel here. The seven rooms have private bath, AC, ceiling fans, TV and even coffee machines. There's a very nice beach area with a barbeque, hammocks and kayaks, plus free internet access, parking and 24-hour security. The rooftop Iguana Bar and Restaurant is a local favorite, famous for homemade bread and shrimp *diablo*. *Info:* www.cocopando.com; Tel. 969-9663 or 866/463-6959 US.

Gran Hotel Paris $$$
If you need to stay in the center of town, this is the best option. Across from the Central Park, this place has recently been renovated, and offers 63 clean and comfortable rooms, each with private bath, AC, phone and TV. There's a pool, a restaurant and bar, 24-hour security and a car rental agency on-site. *Info:* www.granhotelparis.net; Tel. 443-2391 or 443-1643.

Hotel Canadien $$$
Fifteen minutes east of La Ceiba, this mid-price hotel faces a nice swimming beach that goes on for miles. The French Canadian owners are amiable and accommodating, the rooms are comfortable and the food gets rave reviews. The 40 suites have separate bedrooms and sitting rooms, AC and a view of the Caribbean. On the roof, with a panoramic ocean view, El Mirador is cooking seafood and steaks on the grill. The pool is quite nice, with a little thatched *champa* close by for a cold one. *Info:* Tel. 440-2099.

Banana Republic Guesthouse $$
This little guesthouse is run by the Jungle River Lodge folks, and many of the guests will be going on their rafting and hiking tours. It's in the finest tradition of low-priced lodgings: modest but clean and welcoming, with all the services a budget traveler needs. There are showers with plenty of hot water, laundry service, a tropical garden with hammocks, a 24 hour-watchman and an internet connection. The bar is a laid-back spot to swap stories with fellow adventurers. The breakfasts are healthy and hearty, with cappucino and tangy fruit smoothies. And here's the clincher: there's a dog *and* a cat! Grab your backpack and head for the airport! *Info:* Avenida Morazán. www.jungleriverlodge.com; Tel. 440-1282, 440-1268 or 398-7641.

There are quite a few budget lodgings around the Central Plaza and Avenida San Isidro. Some of the better ones are **Hotel VIP Siesta B&B** (Tel. 443-0968 or 443-0969), **Hotel Colonial** (Tel. 443-1953) and backpackers' favorite **Hotel San Carlos** (Tel. 443-0330).

BEST EATS IN LA CEIBA
La Ceiba has a wide range of restaurants, aimed at both locals and travelers. You can have a fancy candlelight dinner, a fresh fish at

a funky beach bar, or a cheap and filling meal at a clean and efficient cafeteria. And of course, La Ceiba has the most hopping nightlife scene in Honduras. Some very good restaurants are found in the local hotels. Having lunch or dinner in the rain forest at **The Lodge at Pico Bonito**, or on the beach at the **Coco Pando** (see above) is a great way to spend an afternoon or evening.

Ricardo's

This is the place everyone will tell you to go to. Ricardo's has won lots of awards, and several writers have called it the best restaurant in Honduras. Beef is the specialty, but the seafood and pasta dishes are also excellent. There's a good salad bar, a rarity around here (don't worry, the lettuce has been washed with purified water). *Info:* Open for lunch and dinner Mon-Sat. Avenida 14 de Julio. Tel. 442-0468.

Expatriates Bar & Grill

The name tells the story. This is the main hang for the local English-speaking posse – Americans working for Standard Fruit, British and Canadian expats. A lot of local tourist-industry workers from around the North Coast and Bay Islands hang out here too. Anglo bar fare is on the grill, the game is on the TV, and Jimmy Buffett is on the stereo. *Info:* On 12th Calle at Col. Naranjal. Open Thur-Mon from 4pm.

Cafetería Cobel

If you want to try some typical Honduran dishes, this is the place. Located in the center of town, it's cheap but clean and welcoming. *Baleadas* come stuffed with beef, chicken, eggs, beans and all the usual goodies. *Sopa de caracol* (conch soup) and other traditional dishes are well done. *Info:* 7th Calle. Open for breakfast, lunch and dinner.

El Patio

This pleasant little place also serves very good *comida típica*. Located not far from the bus station. *Info:* Avenida 15 de Septiembre. Open daily for lunch and dinner.

Restaurants and bars line 1st Calle, which runs along the beach through the Zona Viva. The fanciest is the **Meson del Puerto**, which serves fine cuisine by day and becomes a lively bar by night. Across the street is **Caribeños**, with good *típico* food, and **Mango Tango**, which has live music on weekends.

The Garífuna village of Sambo Creek, 15 minutes east of La Ceiba, has several nice beachfront eateries. At **El Mirador**, on the roof of the Hotel Canadien (see above), fish, shrimp and steaks are cooking on the grill. The **Sambo Creek Restaurant** and the thatched **Champa** are other good choices for seafood and Italian dishes. In the evening, you might see a live *punta* band.

BEST SLEEPS & EATS IN TELA

Villas Telamar $$$$

This large resort is just west of the town center. Many of the package tour operators put people up here. The rooms have all the comforts - AC, TV, phone, kitchens and small balconies. There are two nice pools – kids love the slides, and mom and dad love the Jacuzzi after a long day's hiking. There are two restaurants, a bar, tennis courts and even a nine-hole golf course. You can rent horses for a gallop on the beach, or bikes for a ride around town. The main attraction is the fine white beach, kept neat and clean and watched over by security guards (in contrast to the dirty and dangerous beach in the center of Tela). On the downside, it isn't the most peaceful spot in the area. On weekends the area fills up with locals, some of whom like to tear around on 4WD all-terrain vehicles. *Info:* www.telamar.com; Tel. 448-2196 or 800/742-4276 US.

Hotel Cesar Mariscos $$$$

This family-run hotel faces the beach in downtown Tela. Some of the 19 rooms have AC, others have a ceiling fan. All have private bath, nice beds and TV. Most have a private balcony with a view of the bay. There's a pool and Jacuzzi, a restaurant, bar and wireless internet. The open-air seafood restaurant is famous throughout Honduras, so even if you don't stay here, try to stop in for a meal.

Info: Avenida Uruguay. www.hotelcesarmariscos.com; Tel. 448-2083 or 448-1934.

Maya Vista $$$
This unique hotel is on a hilltop a couple of blocks from the central plaza and the beach. It's a crazy architectural creation with different levels connected by zigzagging staircases, like something out of a Dr Seuss book. Some rooms have terraces with lovely views and cool sea breezes. French Canadian hosts Pierre and Suzanne are super-friendly. Repeat and long-term guests note that wonderful feeling of staying at someone's house. The nine rooms are not very fancy, but they are comfortable and attractive, with private bathrooms, and most have AC. There's a lookout tower with a 360-degree view of Tela and its sweeping bay – a nice place for a sunset drink. The restaurant has a spectacular view and great food, with lobster and shrimp prominently featured. Amenities include private parking, internet access and laundry service. *Info:* www.mayavista.com; Tel. 448-1497 or 448-1928.

Caribbean Coral Inn – Triunfo $$$
This funky but friendly place is on the beach in the Garífuna village of Triunfo de la Cruz. If you're looking for the definition of a "laid-back Caribbean beach shack," this place is as good an example as any I've seen. Step out of your cabin directly onto the sand, and use one of the hammocks slung between the coconut trees, or the free snorkel gear, fishing poles and bikes. Grilled fish, seafood stew, curry chicken and other typical Caribbean favorites are on the menu. *Info:* www.caribbeancoralinn.com; Tel. 994-9806 or 957-8605.

Hotel Mango $$
This small budget lodging is a block from the Central Park, and about three from the beach. They have a bar and restaurant, a Spanish school and (as does almost every other lodging in town) a tour operation. All 10 rooms have private bath and fan. Some have AC and cable TV. *Info:* www.mangocafe.net; Tel. 448-0338.

BEST SLEEPS & EATS IN OMOA

Most visitors to Omoa are backpacker types, and this is reflected in the selection of lodgings. The nicest place is the mid-priced **Flamingo**. There are quite a few basic budget places. Two of the budget hotels in town, **Roli's Place**, run by a Swiss gentleman, and **Pia's Place**, run by a Dutch lady, have a spirited feud a-goin' on, trying to steal each other's guests and allegedly removing each other's signs and so forth. Grab yer shotgun, ma! Other options that are okay for the prices include **Bahía de Omoa, Tatiana, Río Coto** and **Geminis**.

Hotel y Restaurante Flamingo $$$

The nicest hotel in Omoa is located on the beach, where the main road intersects with the beach road. There's nothing fancy about the two-story pink concrete structure, but the rooms are clean, the location is perfect and the price is right. The 10 tile-floored, pastel-colored rooms have AC, private bath and TV. Two have ocean views. The restaurant is known for their fresh seafood, and has a nice beach view. *Info:* www.globalnet.hn/flamingo; Tel. 658-9199.

Punto Italia $$$

This fairly new place on the way into town has an elegant Italian restaurant, a small supermarket, and one mini-suite for rent, with private bath and Jacuzzi. *Info:* www.puntoitalia.net; Tel. 658-9125.

Pia's Place and Bahia de Omoa $/$$$

A Dutch/German couple runs two lodgings on the south end of the beach. **Pia's Place** has dorm beds for $3 and double rooms for $7. Next door is the more upscale option, **Bahia de Omoa**. Three double rooms have private bathrooms with hot water, for about $30. *Info:* Tel. 658-9076.

Roli's Place $

This well-known backpacker stop is a short walk from the beach. Swiss owner Roland Gassmann also runs **Yax Pac Tours** (www.yaxpactours.com), which does a variety of trips in Honduras and Guatemala. Roli is a great source of information on the area, including the latest formalities for getting to Guatemala. *Info:* Tel. 658-9082.

Omoa is no glamorous tourist hotspot. It's more of a place where expats quietly go to seed. You'll find plenty of seeds sprouting at **El Paraíso de Stanley**, the current local hangout. Another good place to hear the latest local gossip is **El Botín Suizo**, a beachfront restaurant and bar run by yet another Swiss expat.

BEST SLEEPS AROUND TRUJILLO

Christopher Columbus $$$$

The area's priciest hotel is just east of town, adjacent to the airstrip, a beach resort in green concrete. The forested mountains rise right behind the hotel. The 71 rooms have private bath, AC and TV. There's a nice little pool, a dock, tennis courts, a bar and a restaurant. The beach here is nice and clean, a wonderful place for a swim. Next door are the funky little **Bahía** and **Gringo** bars. *Info:* www.christophercolumbusbeachresort.com; Tel. 434-4966.

Villa Brinkley $$

In most tourist towns, there's one lodging that everybody talks about – savvy travelers come back year after year, and locals and expats hang out in the bar telling tall tales. In Trujillo, that place is Villa Brinkley. It also happens to have the best view in the entire area, a panorama of Trujillo Bay and, on a clear day, the Bay Islands. Hiking trails into **Capiro y Calentura National Park** begin just past the hotel (see *Chapter 5*). The interior is decorated with Mayan-themed wood carvings. The 20 spacious rooms have private bath, AC and TV. Some have large marble tubs, and several have spectacular views. The restaurant is justly famous, with fresh local dishes and a salad bar. Owner Peggy Brinkley attends to every detail. There's a pool, a small gym, a gift shop and internet access. Also here is the office of **Turtle Tours** (www.turtletours.de), which offers tours all over the North Coast. *Info:* Tel. 434-4444; Email brinkley@hondutel.hn.

Agua Caliente $$

Eight km out of town on the way to Puerto Castilla, Agua Caliente, as the name implies, is located at a natural hot spring. There's a nice spa facility out here in the forest, with steam baths, Jacuzzis and even massages on offer. The 16 tiled cabinas have private bath, AC and TV. There's a bar and restaurant. *Info:* Tel. 434-4247.

Campamento $$
Four km in the other direction, past the village of Cristales, is this isolated beach hideaway. The friendly Remaud family has eight tiled cabinas with private bath and AC. The beach is very nice, with white sand, swaying coconut palms and all that is proper. The home-cooked meals are wonderful. *Info:* Tel. 434-4244 or 991-3391.

Hotel O'Glynn $$
This midrange hotel in the center of town looks a little seedy from the outside, but the 25 rooms are clean, with private bath, AC and TV. Pool, bar and restaurant. Host Johnny Glynn is a great source of information about the area. *Info:* Tel. 434-4592.

Casa Kiwi $
On the beach six km from Trujillo, this place is a favorite stop on the backpacker circuit. The Casa is located on large grounds with a secluded and peaceful beach. There are dorm beds and private rooms with ceiling fans, and cabañas with AC and private balconies. If I told you the prices, you wouldn't believe me – it is very cheap. Every amenity a budget traveler could desire is here: bar and restaurant, internet access, hammocks, bikes for rent, book exchange, lockers, laundry service, parking and 24-hour security. The host is a friendly bloke from New Zealand who is happy to arrange tours in the area, as well as transport to and from town. *Info:* www.casakiwi.com; Tel. 434-3050 or 967-2052.

BEST EATS IN TRUJILLO

In the center of town, the beach below the Fortress of Santa Barbara is lined with *champas* (little thatched-roof restaurants and bars). The best known is **El Rincón de los Amigos**, where a mix of locals, expats and tourists eats seafood and listens to American music.

Other local watering holes are the **Gringo** and the **Bahía**, both out by the Christopher Columbus Hotel. One of the best hotel restaurants is at **Villa Brinkley**, with fresh healthy fare and an unbeatable view.

COPÁN AND THE WEST

BEST SLEEPS IN COPÁN RUINAS

Copán sees travelers of every class, from upscale ecotourists to the backpacker crowd, so there's a wide range of lodging choices. At the bus station, you'll be mobbed by hustlers offering to find you cheap hotel rooms and/or local tours.

Hotel Marina Copán $$$$

This peaceful oasis on the Central Park is the oldest hotel in town, and a major part of local history. Guests rave about the professional and personal service. The architecture is classic colonial, with lovely tile, carved wood furnishings and nice art on the walls. The 50 rooms and suites are spacious and spotless, with private bath, AC, ceiling fans, TV and phone. The most picturesque are in the older rear section. The pool is something special, charming tile surrounded by tropical greenery. There's a spa, a gift shop, free parking and free wireless internet. Glifos Restaurant is generally considered one of Copán's finest. *Info:* www.hotelmarinacopan.com; Tel. 651-4070, 651-4071 or 800/893-9131 US.

Posada Real de Copán $$$$

If you'd rather stay just out of town at a place with a grand view, this is a good choice, on a hilltop with a panoramic view of the Copán valley. The 80 rooms are quite spacious, with tile floors, pastel walls, modern bathrooms, AC, phones and TV. There's a pool and Jacuzzi, a gift shop, parking, and a hiking trail. The restaurant and bar are elegant, but the food is good, not great. *Info:* www.posadarealdecopan.com; Tel. 651-4480, 651-4481 or 651-4482.

Hacienda San Lucas $$$$

This is not just a lovely country inn with wonderful views of the Copán Valley, not just one of the most character-filled places to stay in the entire country, but a heartwarming story of sustainable tourism. The old *hacienda* (farmhouse) has been in the Cueva family for 100 years. In 2000, Flavia Cueva, a local Honduran lady who lived in the US for several years, converted the property to an ecolodge. Now, a lot of folks in Honduras call their places ecolodges, but Ms. Cueva restored the hacienda in classic style, and the contractors used only local materials and local craftsmen, with no power tools. The inn was a huge success, and has become a favorite of chic ecotourists, written up in all sorts of high-tone travel magazines.

The eight rooms have no AC, phones or TVs, nor will you miss them. Electricity is provided by a small solar-power installation, so after dark most of the light is provided by candles, which many guests find to be a wonderful part of the atmosphere. The rooms are pure rustic charm, but they are no funky shacks. The bathrooms are modern, with plenty of hot water, and the beds are comfortable. Fine woodwork and local art grace the walls. The cuisine is likewise earthy and local, featuring homemade tortillas and fresh vegetables from the farm. *Info:* www.haciendasanlucas.com; Tel. 651-4495.

La Casa de Café $$$

This cozy B&B four blocks from the Central Park gets rave reviews for the fine service and home-like atmosphere. The 10 rooms have private bath and ceiling fan. A pretty garden has hammocks and an impressive view of the valley and the mountains. True to its name, the House of Coffee serves a damn fine cup of estate coffee from local growers. Breakfasts are hot and hearty, with ham and eggs and fresh tortillas. *Info:* www.todomundo.com/casadecafe; Tel. 651-4620.

Moderately-priced hotels on the Central Park include **Hotel Los Jaguares** (Tel. 651-4451), which has 10 rooms with private bath and AC; and **Hotel Yaragua** (www.yaragua.com; Tel. 651-4147), home base for **Yaragua Tours**, which runs adventure and cultural tours in the region.

Copán has several cheap dormitory-style lodgings, a couple of which are famous stops on the backpacker circuit. **Hotel Los Gemelos** (Tel. 651-4077), a couple blocks from the Central Park, has small but clean rooms for under $10, plus an internet café. The humble but friendly **Via Via** (www.viaviacafe.com; Tel. 651-4652) has dorm beds and rooms with private bath. The restaurant has some vegetarian dishes. Another backpacker option is **Iguana Azul** (Tel. 651-4620), three blocks from the center.

BEST EATS IN COPÁN RUINAS

As one of the top tourist draws in the country, the Copán area has a wide selection of restaurants. Thanks to rich ecotourists and poor backpackers (who have more in common than you might think), you'll find more healthy and creative dining options here than elsewhere in the country. However, you can also find plenty of overpriced tourist chow, and not only at the cafeteria at the ruins site.

Several of the hotels have good restaurants, notably the pricey cuisine of **Glifos** at the Marina Copán and the roll-your-own-tamales candlelit dinners at **Hacienda San Lucas**. Inexpensive and lively restaurants cluster for a block or two around the Central Park. If you stroll around here, you won't fail to find a spot for dinner. The nightlife scene is low-key – there are nice places for a friendly drink, but no hopping discos.

Twisted Tanya's

This famous local spot has a view of the mountains and a mix of tourists, expats and locals getting twisted. The vivacious Tanya is a great source of information on travels in the area. The ever-changing menu includes an international

Coffee in Copán

The Copán area is **coffee-growing country**. Most restaurants are proud of their fresh-roasted brew. I highly recommend a visit to one of the local coffee plantations. Visit www.sweetmarias.com/coffee.central.honduras.html for more information about Honduran coffee.

variety of dishes, with an emphasis on fresh local ingredients and a dash of Bay Islands style. "If it's in the market, it's on the menu." How about conch soup, an avocado shrimp cocktail, vegetarian curry or homemade hummus? Meat lovers won't be complaining once they get a load of the huge filet mignons and ribeyes. The happy hour (4-6pm) is famous. *Info:* www.twistedtanya.com; Tel. 651-4182. Closed Sunday.

Llama del Bosque

This local classic has been around since 1975, serving up *comida típica* such as *baleadas, parrilladas* and *anafre de chorizo,* as well as tourist fare like sandwiches, salads and spaghetti. Most dishes are less than $5. *Info:* Tel. 651-4431. Open daily for breakfast, lunch and dinner.

Tunkul Restaurant and Bar

A block from the Central Park, this local institution is *the* place to meet the local posse and hear the latest travel tips. The food is a mix of Central American cuisine (*baleadas* and *quesadillas, anafres* and the infamous *Nachos Catrachos*) and international bar food (cheeseburgers, chicken wings, pasta and salads). Portions are large, and most dishes are under $6. Happy hour begins here just as it ends over at Tanya's. Occasionally there's a bit of live music. El Tunkul is home base for **Go Native Tours**, which runs tours all over the region. *Info:* Tel. 651-4410.

Carnitas Nía Lola

Another popular spot in town, with splendid views of the valley from the second floor. Famous for huge portions of grilled meats, including the namesake *carnitas* (hunks of grilled pork). Happy hour here is also lively. *Info:* Tel. 651-4196. Open daily 7am-10pm.

La Casa de Maíz

This pleasant outdoor terrace a block from the Central Park celebrates the humble Honduran staple, corn (or maize, as our British cousins call it). *Tamales,* corn flour wrapped in a corn husk and filled with meat or beans, don't get any more authentic than this. If you're feeling corny, try one of the less-familiar items such as *pupusas, montucas, ticucos, atoles* or *chilates. Info:* Tel. 651-4080. Open daily 7am-9pm.

Coffee Casita

If you love coffee, have lunch at the Macaw Mountain Bird Park (a don't-miss attraction in its own right - see *Chapter 6*). Their shade-grown estate coffee comes from their high-altitude plantation up at Finca Miramundo, is roasted right here in a quaint old Turkish roaster, and brewed up on a modern Swiss machine. Damn good cup! Damn good cup! Enjoy your cappuccino or espresso with a nice lunch at this beautiful outdoor café, overlooking a rushing mountain stream and surrounded by tropical verdure and resplendent birds. *Info:* www.macawmountain.com; Tel. 651-4245. Open daily 9am-5pm.

BEST SLEEPS IN SANTA ROSA DE COPÁN

Hotel Elvir $$$

The Elvir is the best hotel in town, and the home base of local guide Max Elvir and his tour company, **Lenca Land Trails**. Max knows all there is to know about the region, and can arrange tours to the nearby Lenca villages, or any of the other local attractions. There are 44 rooms with private bath, AC and TV, as well as a restaurant, bar and pool. *Info:* www.lenca-honduras.com; Tel. 662-1375 or 662-0805.

Other mid-price options are the colonial-style **Hotel Casa Real** (www.hotelcasarealsrc.com; Tel. 662-0801 or 662-0802) and the cozy and friendly B&B **La Posada de Juan** (Tel. 662-0254).

There are several low-budget lodgings near the central plaza, the best of which are **Hotel Rosario** (Tel. 662-0211) and **Hotel Castillo** (Tel. 662-0368), with very basic rooms for about ten bucks.

BEST SLEEPS & EATS IN GRACIAS

Hotel Guancascos $$

This is the nicest lodging in town. The 11 spacious rooms have tile floors, nice bathrooms and ceiling fans. The owner, a Dutch expat, organizes tours to **Celaque National Park** and other spots in the area. This is the place to stop in for the latest local info. They also have a rustic cabaña up at the edge of the park (see *Chapter 6*). You could stay up there before your hike, in order to be on the spot at dawn for the best birding, then check in at the Guancascos afterwards, when you're ready for a hot bath and a cold beer. *Info:* www.guancascos.com; Tel. 656-1219.

Other options include the mid-priced **Posada de Don Juan** (Tel. 656-1020), **Aparthotel Patricia** (Tel. 656-1281), and the backpacker's favorite, super-cheap **Hotel Erick** (Tel. 656-1066). The **visitors' center** at the park has a rustic lodging with seven beds, a kitchen with running water (but no electricity) and an outhouse. There are a few good places to eat. **Restaurant La Fonda**, on the central park, and **El Hogar**, near the bus station, both serve good typical dishes.

BEST SLEEPS IN SAN PEDRO SULA

If you've already read Chapter 6, then you know that I see no reason for a tourist to spend any more time in this city than is necessary to change buses. However, if you do get caught overnight here, or if you just want to stay in a first-class American-style hotel for a change, you'll have plenty of options. San Pedro's best hotels are aimed squarely at business travelers: large, centrally located, lavishly appointed and soulless. All of these have rooms with private bath, AC, phone and cable TV, and all accept credit cards.

Hotel Copantl $$$$$

The best of the high-rises has 190 rooms on eight floors, with a grand lobby and atrium. The restaurant is on the top floor, with a panoramic view of the city. The rooms are spotless and particularly well-appointed, with DVD players, safes, minibars, ironing boards and coffee makers. There's a business center, beauty salon, two restaurants and a piano bar, gift shop, laundry service, lighted parking, uniformed security, a huge outdoor swimming pool, a Jacuzzi, tennis courts, a gym, and a special kids' pool and play area. *Info:* Blvd. del Sur, across from the Mall Multi Plaza. www.copantl.com; Tel. 556-8900.

Microtel Inn & Suites $$$$

If you get stuck having to spend a night in the area, this is a good choice, outside the city center, but convenient to the airport and major highways, with clean and comfortable rooms and every amenity you could need. There's a pool, a large tropical garden, gym, business center, restaurant and bar and a kids' playground. *Info:* Boulevard al Aeropuerto. www.hotelhonduras.com; Tel. 559-0300 or 888/771-7171 US.

Honduras Plaza $$$
Five blocks from the Central Park, this hotel has more character than some, and some of the 40 rooms have nice mountain views. All rooms have AC, phone, TV, safe deposit boxes and hair dryers. Some have refrigerators and coffee makers. The restaurant serves local and international cuisine. Internet, fax and laundry services are available, and there's a private parking garage. *Info:* 4 Avenida, 6 Calle, NO Guamilito. www.hotelhondurasplaza.com; Tel. 553-2424 or 553-2255.

Tamarindo Hostel $$
SPS has plenty of budget lodgings, but most are located in neighborhoods that simply aren't safe to walk around after dark, and some are not very clean (said the master of understatement). The Tamarindo is an exception, and draws high praise from hip backpackers. Near **Mercado Guamilito**, a few blocks from the Hedman Alas bus station, the neighborhood is reasonably safe. Three dorm rooms with bunk beds and three double rooms with private bathrooms are clean and colorful, with quirky murals. The hostel has AC, free internet, lockers, a kitchen and a bit of garden. The hosts are friendly and helpful. *Info:* 10 and 11 Avenida, 9 Calle, NO. www.tamarindohostel.com; Tel. 557-0123.

BEST EATS IN SAN PEDRO SULA

SPS has a variety of restaurants serving specialties from various regions of the country, as well as international cuisine such as Italian, Swiss, Chinese, Mexican and American bar food.

Don Udo's, an upscale restaurant in the Los Andes neighborhood, serves Continental cuisine with a Honduran flair, including such specialties as lobster gratin and pepper steak. They have an air-conditioned dining room and an outdoor deck, a decent wine list, and live music on the weekends. *Info:* www.donudos.com; Tel. 557-7991. Another upscale place is **Pat's Steak House** (Tel. 553-0939), serving prime Honduran beef and seafood, also with a passable wine list.

The Zona Viva has lots of restaurants and bars. **Chef Mariano's** serves seafood in the Garífuna style of the North Coast. **Las Carnitas** grills up hearty skewers of beef, chicken and the namesake pork, and sometimes has live music.

The Central Park is lined with restaurants and small cafés. One of these, **Pamplona,** is a local institution that serves very good food cheap, if you can squeeze past the crowds of locals. Also on the square is **Antojitos Mexicanos**, a cheap Mexican joint that has live Mariachi bands in the evenings.

LA MOSKITIA

You've probably guessed that there are no five-star resorts in this remote region. In fact, only Puerto Lempira and Palacios have anything that you could even call a hotel. The villages where tourists go have some small *hospedajes*, which tend to be very cheap and very, very funky. Hot water and electricity are luxuries.

The lodgings that are associated with **La Ruta Moskitia** (see *Chapter 7*) are basic and rustic, but at least they are clean, and are run in a civilized fashion, which accounts for their comparatively high prices (mostly around $10 per person per night, plus $4 per meal).

Most visitors to La Moskitia come on package tours and fill up the better local lodgings. If you come here on your own, you may have trouble finding a decent place to stay if there's a tour group in town.

BEST LODGINGS ON LA RUTA MOSKITIA

Yamari Savannah Cabañas $$

On the shore of a small creek out in the Great Pine Savannah, each of these three little cabañas has four single beds with mosquito nets, and solar-powered lights, as well as a small restaurant. *Info:* Contact Dorkas or Macoy Wood in Brus. Tel. 433-8009; Radio: Brus Laguna (Channel 68).

Pawanka Beach Cabañas $$

On the beach in Belen, this is the nicest of the Ruta Moskitia lodgings. A cooling breeze blows through the three thatched huts (each with room for four guests), and the little restaurant serves lobster and other local seafood. *Info:* Contact Mario Miller in Belen. Tel. 433-8220; Radio: Alcon (Channel 68).

Raista Ecolodge $$

This basic but friendly place is right by the docks in Raista. The eight rooms have private decks and nice views of the lagoon. The proprietors, the **Bodden Family**, were some of the first to welcome visitors to Raista, and are fascinating to talk to about the area. Doña Elma Bodden serves home-cooked meals that some call the best in Honduras. They can help you book tours in the area, including boat trips up the river to Las Marias. *Info:* Call Melissa Bodden, Tel. 433-8216; Radio: Raista (Channel 68).

Hospedajes in Las Marias $

Up the Platano in the middle of the jungle, the tiny village of Las Marias has five small *hospedajes*. They are very basic, with no luxuries, but the local people are quite friendly, and these places are cheap, only about $5 per person.

LODGING IN PALACIOS

Formerly the main travel hub for La Moskitia, Palacios has gone to seed since the airstrip shut down. It's a pretty grungy town.

Hotel Moskitia $$

This is the best lodging in town, a civilized little place with electricity, purified water and 24-hour security. The five rooms have private bath with hot water, ceiling fans and TV. There's a restaurant and bar, laundry service and a gift shop. *Info:* www.hotelmoskitia.com; Tel. 440-1863, 443-8012 or 978-7397.

Other half-decent hotels are **Hotel Río Tinto** and **Hotel de Joselina**.

LODGING IN PUERTO LEMPIRA

The largest town in La Moskitia, Puerto Lempira has a selection of hotels and restaurants, but most are dilapidated and mildewy.

Yu Baiwan View $$
The nicest place in town is next to the dock. The name means "sunrise" in the Miskito language, and there is indeed a splendid view of the sunrise over the lagoon. The nine rooms each have private bath and TV. Most have AC. The hotel is clean, the décor pleasant, and the owners friendly and helpful. There's a restaurant and bar that also offers room service. *Info:* Tel. 898-7653.

Hotel Flores (Tel. 433-6421) is only slightly cheaper, and is a drab and cheerless concrete-block affair.

TEGUCIGALPA & THE SOUTH

BEST SLEEPS IN TEGUCIGALPA

As in San Pedro, most of the top hotels cater for business travelers: large, centrally located and lavishly appointed. All of these have rooms with AC, private bath, phone and cable TV, and all accept credit cards. Most of the hotels are in the Colonia Palmira neighborhood.

Real InterContinental $$$$$
In the center, across from the Multiplaza Mall. 157 rooms and suites have business-friendly amenities such as desks, double phone lines, voicemail and safes. Every room has a desktop PC with internet access. Some have kitchenettes. There's a 24-hour business center, a restaurant and bar (with live music!), spa, outdoor pool and Jacuzzi, gym, laundry, shops, tour and car rental desks, a complimentary airport shuttle and secure parking. *Info:* Avenida Roble. www.ictegucigalpa.gruporeal.com; Tel. 231-2727.

Plaza San Martin Hotels $$$$$
Three hotel towers make up the Plaza San Martín Hotel District, across from the Plaza San Martín in Colonia Palmira. They share a range of facilities, including business center, pool, gym, laundry, free parking and a set of restaurants and bars. The rooms have balconies, kitchenettes and every business amenity, including desks and internet connections. The interiors are quite el-

egant, decorated with paintings by local artists and Mayan artifacts. *Info:* **Plaza San Martin**, Tel. 237-2928 or 232-8268; **Hotel Plaza del General**, www.hotelplazadelgeneral.com; Tel. 220-7272; Hotel **Plaza del Libertador**, www.hotelplazadellibertador.com; Tel. 220-4141.

Portal del Angel $$$$$

What a contrast from the big business towers! This is an elegant little boutique hotel (14 rooms) in classic colonial style - colonnaded arcades around a central courtyard with a lush tropical patio and pool. The rooms have lovely wood floors and nice contemporary furniture. Every amenity is here: business center, gym, internet connections, a restaurant and bar. *Info:* 2115 Avenida Republica del Peru, Colonia Palmira. www.portaldelangel.com; Tel. 239-6538.

Humuya Inn $$$$

Located in a quiet residential neighborhood a short way from downtown, this is another exquisite small hotel. Beautiful wood, tile and wrought iron offer a classic example of the colonial style. There are 14 rooms and five apartments with kitchens. The rooms have vaulted ceilings, tile floors and large and elegant bathrooms, as well as every first-class amenity. Business people will be well looked after - each room has a work desk, there's a business center and the entire hotel is covered by wireless internet. The sumptuous free breakfast is served on a pleasant terrace overlooking the courtyard. *Info:* Colonia Humuya 1150. www.humuyainn.com; Tel. 239-2206, 239-8962 or 235-7275.

Leslie's Bed and Breakfast $$$$

Another small lodging near the center, Leslie's is less elegant but more affordable than the Portal or the Humuya, and has a more homelike feel. The 28 rooms are well-appointed, and the lush tropical gardens give it a peaceful vibe. *Info:* Colonia Palmira San Martín 452. www.dormir.com; Tel. 239-0641.

Hedman Alas Hotel $$

This budget lodging is run by the Hedman Alas bus company. It's six blocks from their bus terminal, just on the edge of downtown Tegucigalpa. The 19 rooms and two suites have private bath, TV, phone and ceiling fans. *Info:* www.hedmanalas.com/hoteleng.htm; Tel. 237-9333 or 237-1479.

There are plenty of cheap hotels in town, but most are dirty and dangerous. One exception is the well-run and welcoming **Tobacco Road Inn** (Tel. 222-4081), which offers inexpensive dorm beds a couple of blocks from the Central Park. American owner Tom knows all about the local scene, and the bar is a hangout for local expats, with live music on weekends.

BEST EATS IN TEGUCIGALPA

Like San Pedro, Tegus has a selection of international restaurants, as well as the usual offerings of *comida típica,* grilled meats, seafood, Mexican places and American chains. Most restaurants are closed on Sunday. Some of the upscale hotels have fine Continental restaurants, notably **Azulejos** in the Hotel Real InterContinental, **La Veranda** at the Hotel Honduras Maya (Tel. 232-3191) and the gourmet restaurant at the **Portal del Angel**.

Casa Maria

One of Tegucigalpa's finest restaurants, with classic colonial architecture and fine artworks. The cuisine is international, with an emphasis on fish and seafood and a fair wine list. Reservations recommended. *Info:* Tel. 239-4984.

La Cumbre

High above the city in the suburb of El Hatillo, there's a panoramic view of Tegucigalpa, and some of the best food in town. The menu offers Germanic dishes and other international cuisine, and the atmosphere is elegant and romantic. There's an indoor dining room and an outdoor deck. Reservations recommended. *Info:* Tel. 211-9000.

El Quijote

This venerable Spanish restaurant sits on a hill a few blocks from the Central Park, with nice views over the downtown area. The specialty of the house is *paella,* a massive skillet of yellow rice studded with a wealth of seafood. There are many other fish and seafood dishes, and a good selection of Spanish wines. *Info:* Tel. 237-0070.

Cocina Creativa
Not far from the Central Park, this place offers some of the capital's most interesting fare. Inventive combinations of typical Honduran dishes and trendy creations including many vegetarian dishes will tempt the jaded palate.

El Patio
This large patio with fountains, tiles and tropical plants is one of the best spots for typical Honduran fare. Specialties such as *tamales, anafre* and *pinchos* are very well done. There are oodles of atmosphere, including live Mariachi bands. This local institution now has several locations throughout the country. There are two locations in Tegucigalpa, both on the Blvd Morazán.

Be Safe, Take a Taxi

I've said this before, and I'll probably say it again before we get to the end of this book, because it's important. **It is *not safe* to walk around anywhere in Tegucigalpa at night**, and many areas are sticky even during the day. If you're going out at night, call a taxi from your hotel, and call another to bring you home. Unaccompanied ladies should think twice (at the very least) before venturing out to the bars.

Vinalia Wine Café
Just off the Blvd Morazán, this peaceful place serves light Mediterranean cuisine on a nice patio. There's a selection of wines and occasional live music. *Info:* Tel. 221-1002.

Tegucigalpa has lots of good Mexican restaurants. Two of the most famous are **La Posada de Don Chema** and the 24-hour **Plaza Garibaldi**. There are dozens of Chinese eateries, of which the most notable is the huge and bustling **Furiwa** (Tel. 239-1349 or 239-1396).

BEST SLEEPS IN VALLE DE ÁNGELES

If you'd prefer to stay in a pleasant little village, Valle de Ángeles would make a fine base for trips in the region. It has a perfect climate, awesome views and the biggest handicraft scene in the area. There are two nice little hotels and, thanks to all the day-trippers, several pleasant restaurants.

Posada del Angel $$

This clean and attractive hotel is right in the middle of town. The 25 rooms have private bath and TV. The swimming pool is very nice, and so are the restaurant and bar. *Info:* Tel. 766-2233.

Villas del Valle $$

This new hotel is just outside of town. Owned by a US expat and his Honduran wife, it's a spotlessly clean and well-run establishment on large landscaped grounds. There are 20 rooms, all with private bath. The pricier ones have porches with hammocks, and the "luxury suites" have nice bathtubs, small refrigerators and a dining area. There's a restaurant and bar, pool, laundry room, internet service, parking and a kids' play area. *Info:* www.villasdelvalle.com; Tel. 766-2534 or 996-0053.

BEST EATS IN VALLE DE ÁNGELES

La Casa de las Abuelas

This homestyle restaurant is famous all over Honduras. The restored colonial house belonged to the great-grandmother of the current hosts, who are a great source of information about attractions in the region. Steaks and grilled meats are on the menu, and a pretty good selection of wine is on the list. Open daily.

El Anafre

This is another venerable and well-known local eatery. The namesake bean dish and other *típico* specialties are very well done here. Closed Mon-Tue.

There are several other cutesy restaurants in town, including **Epocas** with its adjacent antique shop, **Restaurante Turistico**, just out of town with a nice view, and **Don Quijote**, a branch of the Tegucigalpa restaurant that serves excellent Spanish food and wines.

BEST SLEEPS IN SANTA LUCIA

There are only two options:

Hotel Santa Lucía $$$

Up on a hill just outside of town, this nice old colonial-style edifice has rooms with private bath, a nice restaurant and splendid views.

Posada las Nubes $$
This pleasant little B&B-style lodging is in the middle of town. The four rooms have private bath, TV and ceiling fans. There's an okay restaurant, a gift shop selling local crafts, and a wonderful patio with a nice view of the mountains. *Info:* Tel. 779-0441.

BEST SLEEPS & EATS IN COMAYAGUA

Hotel Casa Grande Bed and Breakfast $$$
This renovated colonial house has 10 rooms with private bath, AC, ceiling fans, TV and phone. The courtyard with its fountain, columns and tropical flowers is *muy español*. There's no restaurant, but rates include a nice Continental breakfast. Amenities include laundry service, internet access, safes and free parking. *Info:* www.casagrande-hotel.com; Tel. 772-0772 or 772-0512.

Hotel Villa Real $$
This is also a nice little colonial building, and it also has 10 rooms with private bath, AC, ceiling fans, TV and phone. This one has a pool, tennis courts, a restaurant and bar. *Info:* Tel. 772-1751.

There are several moderate and budget lodgings in town, of which the nicest is **Hotel Quan** (Tel. 772-0070), which has 30 rooms in several price ranges, with or without private bath.

The finest restaurant in the city is **Villa Real** (Tel. 772-0101), a beautiful old colonial building next to the Central Park, with a pleasant Spanish-style courtyard and excellent Honduran cuisine. There are lots of gringos in Comayagua, many of them military personnel from the nearby US air base. There are a couple of cool spots run by US expats, both with American-style cuisine and sports on the big-screen TVs. **Hannemann's**, on the main street, serves a bit of Cajun cuisine; **J&G Country Bar and Grill** serves seafood and big burgers.

BEST SLEEPS & EATS IN ISLA DEL TIGRE

Mirador de Amapala $$$

This is a new hotel just a short way from the dock in Amapala. The 30 rooms have private bath, AC and TV. There's a nice pool and a restaurant with an outdoor terrace and a panoramic view of the gulf. Laundry and internet service are available. *Info:* www.miradordeamapala.com; Tel. 795-8407 or 795-8592.

There are two budget lodgings in the village with double rooms under $10, **Hotel Internacional** and the whimsically-named **Hotel Ritz**. Neither is much more than a couple of small rooms attached to a local family's home, and neither is terribly clean.

A better lodging option is to stay at one of several **private homes** that have recently set up as bed and breakfasts. The local people are famous for their hospitality, and this would be a good (and cheap) way to go far beyond the usual tourist experience. Information is available at the tourist office at the dock.

The island is famous for **fresh fried fish**, which you can have at a bargain price at one of a few small *comedores*.

BEST SLEEPS & EATS IN SAN LORENZO

A hot and dirty port town with some okay beaches nearby, San Lorenzo does have one redeeming quality: it's a major seafood packing center, and there are lots of restaurants serving great fresh seafood.

Hotel Miramar Inn Plaza $$

This is by far the best hotel in town, on the waterfront next to the restaurant district. The rooms have private bath, AC, phones and refrigerators. They have a swimming pool, private parking with 24-hour security, the Crazy Fish restaurant and the lively and loud Arenas disco. *Info:* www.hotelmiramarinnplaza.com; Tel. 781-2138, 781-2106 or 239-9726.

Other passable hotels with similar prices are **Villas Concha Mar** (Tel. 781-2083) and **Hotel Morazán** (Tel. 781-2400).

The **Zona Viva** section, along the water past the Hotel Miramar, has many small family restaurants serving great seafood. Fish, shrimp, crab and a variety of mollusks are fresh from the Gulf and cheap by international standards. Seafood soups and surf and turf are local specialties.

You'll have no problem finding a place to eat, but some notable ones are **Mariscos Celso, Bahía Azul, La Cabañita, Crazy Fish** at the Hotel Miramar, and **Gulf View** on top of the Villas Concha Mar, with splendid ocean views. You can also gorge on fresh seafood in one of several little *comedores* in the **Municipal Market**.

11. BEST ACTIVITIES

Honduras offers **good shopping**, especially wood carvings and crafts of various kinds; **great outdoor sports and recreation** possibilities, from sunning yourself on a beautiful beach to diving, snorkeling, swimming, fishing and other water sports; and (on occasion and in the right spot!) **fun nightlife**, particularly in the cities and Bay Islands but in a few other spots as well.

We steer you to the best activities in this chapter, with our focus on what Honduras does best: the great outdoors. Enjoy!

SHOPPING

Honduras produces some very nice handicrafts, from wood carvings to leather to clothing and jewelry. You'll find crafts on sale throughout the country, especially tourist favorites such as hammocks and small Mayan-themed carvings. However, there are two areas where you'll find better quality, lower prices and a chance to see local artisans at work: the **Lenca Trail** in the Western highlands and the **villages around Tegucigalpa**.

Lenca Trail

Not far from Copán are the villages of the Lenca Trail, home to the indigenous **Lenca** people. These picturesque colonial villages, around **Santa Rosa de Copán** and **Gracias**, are wonderful places to shop for local crafts (see *Chapter 6*).

Tegucigalpa area

Near Tegucigalpa are several charming villages that are also fine places to shop for crafts. **Valle de Ángeles**, with its large **Municipal Craft Market**, is perhaps the best (but most touristed) place in the country for crafts. Here, in several large covered halls, you'll find a wide selection of locally-made items, and a school that teaches native crafts. If you're lucky, you may get to watch some of the local artisans making the famous mahogany boxes, furniture and animal carvings. You'll also find lovely pieces in silver, pewter, leather and ceramics, as well as paintings, tapestries, traditional clothing and hammocks.

Other crafty towns in the area are **Santa Lucia** and **Ojojona**, famous for its brightly-colored ceramic pieces (see *Chapter 8*).

In Tegucigalpa, you can visit the **San Isidro Market** for an authentic Central American shopping experience. This is not really a tourist market, but rather a place where locals go to buy their daily necessities. It's a bustling, noisy scene that will raise the pulse rate of any dedicated shopper, but keep a firm hand on your wallet!

San Pedro Sula

Guamilito Market, in **San Pedro Sula**, is probably the country's largest handicraft market. Here is a wide variety of ceramics, wood carvings, hammocks, woven clothing, baskets, rugs and wall hangings, as well as fresh vegetables and flowers, rum, cigars and the usual tourist junk. This is also a place to watch your pockets carefully.

Coffee and **rum** make good gifts for the folks back home. Both are best purchased in a local grocery store. The duty-free shop at the airport is not any cheaper. Prices in tourist shops around the country are usually higher.

NIGHTLIFE & ENTERTAINMENT

The most hopping locales are in the **Bay Islands**, the cities of **La Ceiba** and **Tela** on the North Coast, and the capital, **Tegucigalpa**.

Bay Islands Nightlife

As you might expect, the scene on **Roatan** is touristy and Spring-breakish, similar to the scene in most Caribbean resort areas. **Foster's**, in West End, is a good bet in the evenings for live music and, sometimes, rowdy crowds. The drinks are reasonable and the conch fritters are great.

Utila, the bargain destination, has more of a young and hip scene, with raves that have led some to speak of a "mini-Ibiza." Stop by the **Tranquila Bar** and scout out the scene for trance parties and drumming circles on the nearby beach.

La Ceiba Nightlife

La Ceiba is the unquestioned nightlife capital of Honduras. A rainbow mix of *catrachos, gringos* and *turistas* from all over the world slurp rum and dance to *punta* music in the clubs of the **Zona Viva** from midnight until dawn.

Punta is the traditional music of the indigenous Garífuna people who live all along the North Coast of Honduras. The current Punta Rock that you'll hear in the nightspots combines traditional rhythms played on the *garawon* drum, rattles, and turtle shells with modern instruments such as guitars and synthesizers, often with socially conscious lyrics. Pen Cayetano and the Turtle Shell Band were pioneers of Punta. Banda Blanca is another well-known artist.

If you're looking for a nice place to have a drink and meet English-speaking locals, head for **Expatriates Bar & Grill**, a thatched-roof spot in the Naranjal neighborhood featuring Anglo bar fare, ice-cold beer, sports on the TV, and Jimmy Buffett on the stereo. *Info:* On 12th Calle at Col. Naranjal. Open Thur-Mon from 4pm.

Restaurants and bars line 1st Street, which runs along the beach through the Zona Viva. The fanciest is the **Meson del Puerto**, a fine restaurant that becomes a lively bar after dark. Closed Monday. Across the street, **Mango Tango** has live music on weekends.

The most popular discos in town are **Cherry's, Alejandro's,** and **La Casona**. Other Zona Viva hotspots include the beachfront **Area 504**, the German-owned **Club 99** and the second-floor **Europub. Africa Dance** is a disco that sometimes has live Punta bands and dancers. The upscale **El Mussol** has a high-tech disco and an open-air beach bar.

La Ceiba's yearly **Festival of San Isidro** (*Feria Isidra*) is said to be the biggest Carnival celebration north of Brazil and south of New Orleans. It takes place the last two weeks in May, with street parties all over town, dozens of local bands and a parade down Avenida San Isidro for the grand finale.

Tela Nightlife

After La Ceiba, Tela is the nightlife capital of the North Coast. The beach area has a plethora of bars and discos. You can go from happy hour to dinner to drinks to disco till dawn.

The bar at the **Hotel Mango** is a favorite hangout of young travelers. **Sloppy Joe's** is the new local expat sports bar. The **Restaurant Garibaldi** sometimes has live music. Discos include **El Magnate** and **Enigma**.

Tegucigalpa Nightlife

There's a bit of live music going on, but the scene constantly changes, so ask around for the latest. The nightlife of the capital is pretty hopping, though it can't compare with the wild *punta* scene on the North Coast, or the spring-break atmosphere of the Bay Islands. The two best-known music venues couldn't be more different. **Bar Scenario** is located at the fanciest hotel in town, the Real InterContinental. The **Tobacco Road Tavern** is at the nicest low-budget hostel in town. The latter is a good place to ask around about what else is going on.

Discos include the over-the-top **El Nilo** (The Nile), which features faux Egyptian décor, including a miniature Nile running through the dance floor; the oh-so-hip **Bambú**; and the **Tropical Port**, where you'll hear the latest Salsa and Reggaeton.

SPORTS & RECREATION

Hiking

A day hike in one of Honduras's national parks or wilderness reserves is a fine thing – if that's all you have time for, then don't fail to take one. But to get the full experience, **spend at least one night in the rain forest**. The best time to see birds and other wildlife is always early in the morning, and you won't be there early in the morning if you have to spend a couple of hours getting to the park from the hotel in town. Plus, there's simply something magical about waking up to the sounds of water dripping, birds singing and maybe a troop of howler monkeys baying in the distance.

The North Coast has a few fine jungle lodges, where you can sleep in style right in the middle of the action (see *Chapter 5*). Elsewhere, overnighting in the forest means roughing it a bit. **Cusuco** and **Celaque National Parks** both have basic cabins placed at convenient locations along the trail, where you can overnight. It's a lot closer to camping than it is to staying at a luxury resort - you'll bring your own bedding and your own food.

A typical wilderness cabin has a roof and some semblance of walls to keep out the rain. Some have rudimentary bunks, but you'll need to bring a sleeping bag. There may be an outhouse and a place to make a fire, and that's probably about it. If you go with a local guide, they'll bring necessaries such as food and water. If you go on your own, you'll need to inquire with the locals before setting out, to make sure you know exactly what to expect.

In either case, you need to be prepared - a hike in the rain forest isn't like a walk in Central Park. Good hiking boots and some sort of rain jacket are a must. A change of clothes in a waterproof bag is a must for any sort of extended hike - you're almost certain to get rained on at some point, and you may get muddy.

Scuba Diving & Snorkeling

The **Bay Islands** have **some of the finest coral reefs** for diving and snorkeling in the world. You'll probably be told that Honduras has a barrier reef that is second in size only to the Great Barrier Reef in Australia, but this is not actually true. The world's second-largest barrier reef is off nearby Belize, but it is separated from the Bay Islands by the 9,000-foot Caiman Trench. Also, the reefs in Honduras are fringing reefs, not true barrier reefs. Of course, no one actually cares about this distinction except smartass dive-boat captains, as the reefs in the Bay Islands are as extensive and wonderful as any diver could wish.

Visibility is almost always superb. Most of the reefs are in good shape, with plenty of live coral and lots of fish. You'll see coral in all the colors of the rainbow – brain coral, staghorn, elkhorn, and the stinging fire coral – to say nothing of gigantic barrel sponges.

Years ago, it was rare to see large fish on the reefs of the Bay Islands, as the locals tended to eat them. However, long-time residents say that, since the islands were protected as a National Marine Park, that trend has reversed. You'll see plenty of fish large and small. **Colorful reef fish** include gobies, blennies, sergeant-majors, tangs, angelfish and parrotfish, which crunch coral with their strong beaks, digest the animal matter and poop out sand. Larger predators include barracuda (fearsome to look at, but not dangerous), snapper and grouper. If you're lucky, you may see snook, tarpon or sharks. Sea turtles and stingrays are frequent reef visitors.

The reefs are accessible to everyone, not just scuba divers. Snorkeling is very easy to learn, and this is one of the easiest places in the world to do it. Some of the most beautiful reef structure is quite shallow, and you can snorkel to wonderful reefs only a few feet from many Bay Island beaches.

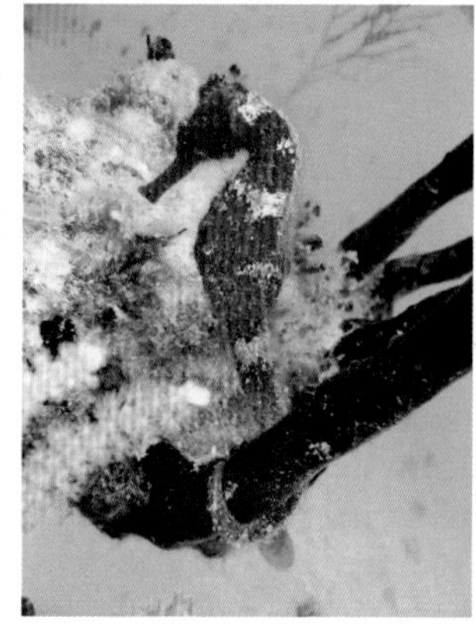

The Bay Islands are famous for being **the cheapest place in the world to dive**. There are dozens of dive operators competing with each other so the prices tend to stay low. It's possible to become certified for $100 including instruction, equipment and dive trips. What a deal!

Remember, never touch any coral, ever. In fact it's wise not to touch anything out on the reef. Bright orange fire coral can cause a nasty burn, and there are sharp sea urchins and other little nasties awaiting unwary fingers. But the pain that fire coral might cause to your little pinky is nothing compared to what you'll do to the coral. Touching coral tends to kill the little organisms. It's even worse with gloves, which is why some dive shops discourage wearing them.

Coral Reefs

Coral is a communal organism. The colorful formations you see are actually colonies of thousands of tiny animals, which filter food from the water. They secrete calcium as a base for themselves which, over hundreds of years, builds a coral reef.

The coral attracts tiny fish, shrimp and other organisms, which in turn attract larger predators, and so on up the scale. A living coral reef is an incredibly complex ecosystem, which provides habitat for many important fish species.

Coral reefs occur throughout the tropics. Like the rain forests, reefs worldwide are slowly but steadily disappearing. Pollution, sedimentation and overfishing chip away at the reefs. Slowly rising sea temperatures are killing reefs in some areas (coral needs a stable water temperature and chemical environment). Worse yet, some scientists now fear that, as absorbed carbon dioxide changes the chemical composition of the sea water, the corals' very ability to produce calcium could be impaired.

Whatever the future holds, Honduras's reefs are beautiful now, so get out and enjoy them now!

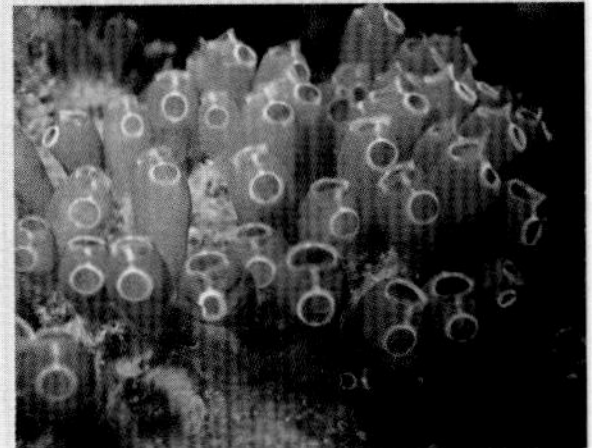

There are a variety of resorts that cater almost exclusively to divers. All of the hotels and resorts work with the dive operators and can put together a dive package for you. The lodging and food side of the dive resorts is covered in the *Best Sleeps and Eats* chapter.

Roatan Dive Operators

Roatan has over a hundred named dive sites, with walls, tongue-and-groove reefs, shark dives, wrecks, caves, etc. Excellent diving is available all around the island – most resorts have multiple great dive sites no more than a 15-minute boat ride away. At times, one side of the island or the other may experience windy weather kicking up waves and lowering visibility. When this happens the other side of the island always seems to be calm and clear. Many of the better dive resorts maintain boats on both sides of the island so that when windy conditions mess things up on one side of the island, they can drive guests to their boats docked on the calmer side.

Anthony's Key Resort

At last count, Anthony's had 14 dive boats, taking up to 20 punters each on dives usually no farther than 45 minutes away from the dock in Sandy Bay. They also have a large snorkel boat herding 30 snorkelers. Their PADI Gold Palm 5-Star Instructor Development Center offers more types of training than you can shake a snorkel at, from Discover Scuba to instructor level. Seven-night packages with all the goodies except for booze start around $1,100. *Info:* Sandy Bay. www.anthonyskey.com; Tel. 445-3003.

Bananarama Dive Beach Resort

Their dive operation has an excellent reputation and they have all the usual water sports equipment handy. *Info:* www.bananaramadive.com; Tel. 445-5005 or 727/564-9058 US.

Bay Island Beach Resort

Week-long diving package: $695, including three daily boat dives and one night dive, plus meals and transfers. *Info:* www.bibr.com; Tel. 445-3020 or 800/227-3483 US.

CoCo View Resort

With a variety of rooms and flexible dive plans, this is an all-around good resort choice, and the dive operation is considered to be one of the best in the area. Their list of PADI instructional courses goes on and on. Specialty courses include such exotics as Underwater Naturalist and Underwater Digital Photographer. Their dive shop is comprehensive. There is excellent diving directly in front of the resort, including a monumental wall and the wreck Prince Albert. *Info:* French Cay. www.cocoviewresort.com; Tel. 455-7502 or 800/510-8164 US.

Fantasy Island

A seven-night all-inclusive package with almost too much diving goes for a little over $1,000, depending on room selection and time of year. Their dive program is extensive with PADI training at all levels including children's classes all the way up to Fish Identification certification. *Info:* www.fantasyislandresort.com; Tel. 455-7499 or 800/676-2826 US.

Utila Dive Operators

The reefs around **Utila** rival those anywhere in the world. Larger Roatan has more reef acreage, but Utila is visited less and doesn't have cattle boats of divers churning things up and scaring away the big fish. In my opinion, the diving in general around Utila and Guanaja is better than Roatan for the simple reason that there are fewer divers in the water.

Utila has more than 50 buoyed sites, representing a variety of wall dives, caves, wrecks, stingrays, sharks, deep, shallow – something for all diving levels and interests. The web site at **www.utiladivebuoys.com** lists all the buoyed sites, with excellent interactive maps. Awesome steep walls line the north side of the island. You could spend a week just diving different walls.

Top dive sites around Utila include Stingray Point, Jack Neil Point,

Pretty Bush, Black Coral Wall, the Halliburton wreck, Sturch Bank, Airport Caves, Black Hills, Blackish Point, Willie's Hole and Ragged Cay.

Utila is famous for offering the cheapest diving and dive courses in the entire Caribbean, perhaps anywhere. There are no fancy places on the island but there are plenty of comfortable places to stay, eat and recreate. Both **Coral View Beach Resort,** in Sandy Bay (Tel. 425-3783), and **Deep Blue Resort** (Tel. 425-2015), are dedicated dive resorts with nice lodging, restaurant, bar and complete dive operations.

Utila Aggressor

This live-aboard dive boat leaves from La Ceiba (www.aggressor.com; Tel. 800/348-2628 US). $2,000 gets you seven days and six nights with accommodations, all food and drinks including beer and wine, tanks and weights. The 100-foot Utila Aggressor was built in 1999 and refitted in 2005. It's modern and comfortable. There are six staterooms sleeping 14 guests, who binge on over 27 dives during the trip, including night dives.

The diving includes wrecks, walls, shallow gardens of coral, visits to remote seamounts, cavorting with whale sharks and visits to rarely explored spots known only to the divemaster and captain.

All sorts of courses are offered, from beginner to Master Diver with Rescue and a selection of other interesting courses such as U/W photography, videography and wreck diving. All the equipment you need is available for rent on board, including digital underwater cameras.

Guanaja Dive Operators

The best dive sites in the **Guanaja** area include the wrecks around Pond Cay, Jado Trader, Jim's Silver Lode, Vertigo, Final Wall, Pinnacle, Volcano Caves, and Siberia Eel Garden.

There are a couple of dedicated, all-inclusive dive resorts. **End of The World Resort** (www.guanaja.com; Tel 991-1257) charges $900 for seven-night diving packages with all the goodies. Divers are catered to carefully with a full line of rental equipment and the usual panoply of courses. The dive boat is roomy and takes only 7 divers.

You can't get to **Nautilus Resort,** near Bonacca Town (Tel. 453-4389), by car. You'll need to hop a ride on one of the resort's boats to even get to the 60 acres on a hill overlooking the long, white sand beach that are the setting for Nautilus's 7 rooms, some with AC. Of course, diving is the thing here and all the usual rental equipment and certification courses are available.

Dolphin Encounters

Wild dolphin encounters can be the highlight of anyone's trip. Snorkeling around in the open ocean with frisky wild dolphins zooming around to check you out is an unforgettable cross-species communication experience.

Please reject any of the options for interacting with dolphins that are captive. Some of the resorts maintain rather large steel enclosures, covering several acres, for penning up dolphins. Their promotional materials sometimes do not make it clear that your "beach" or "reef" encounter will be with captive dolphins. Wild dolphins will usually come near swimmers just to check out what they are up to, though not close enough to touch.

The most famous place in the Bay Islands to interact with frisky dolphins is at **Anthony's Key Resort** (www.anthonyskey.com; Tel. 800/227-3483 US), where they have several of them penned up for your enjoyment. You can swim with them, touch them, attempt to communicate and otherwise "interact." Perhaps there is some therapeutic value in this ridiculous attempt to legitimize enslaving intelligent wild animals for profit.

A much better alternative is to take one of the snorkeling trips that go just offshore looking for schools of wild dolphins willing to swim around nearby while tourists snorkel. The dolphins are not usually harmed or coerced in the process. My experience is that wild dolphins will zoom around delightfully close enough to enjoy while snorkeling. Anthony's Key Resort arranges these types of trips as well as the other, more exploitive types of dolphin worship.

Paradise Beach Club (www.paradisebeach.com; Tel. 403-8062) in West Bay offers pretty much the same dolphin options for slightly less money.

Whale Shark Encounters

Whale sharks are the largest fish on the planet. They are members of the shark family but, unlike their more rapacious relatives, they are filter feeders, eating a variety of tiny fish and other sea life, and therefore not dangerous to humans (unless you get too close).

At most times of the year the giant fish migrate through the waters around Utila. They're **especially common in early Spring**. No one knows why for sure, but the locals will tell you they are mating. Sounds like fun to me but, as far as I know, no displays of mating between whale sharks have been observed in the area. Whale shark encounters are much like dolphin encounters – your boat cruises around in likely-looking areas while your eagle-eyed skipper looks for the tell-tale boil in the water that indicate the presence of whale sharks and the small fish that accompany them. When they are located, snorkelers and scuba divers plop over the side and, hopefully, swim quietly while the giant fish lurk around.

Whale sharks are usually **slow swimmers**, but may not show much interest in visitors. Sometimes they'll circle around a little but often they will just keep on swimming in the straight line they were swimming in when first spotted. The trick is to observe the whale sharks from the boat to determine which direction they are swimming in and then drop the tourists in the water a little ahead of their path. Be sure to take an underwater camera along on this outing.

All of the dive operators on Utila are in on this action, so you should have no trouble setting up an excursion. Some Roatan operators will also take you to see the whale sharks, about an hour's boat ride each way.

Fishing

The Bay Islands are an angler's dream come true. Bonefish and permit on the flats, tarpon in the channels, billfish and dorado (aka mahi-mahi or dolphin) offshore, and snapper and grouper over the reefs are all wonderfully plentiful. With luck, an elusive Grand Slam could be achieved here. The lagoons of La Moskitia are an almost-untouched paradise for tarpon and snook.

Fishing charters may cost up to double what dive trips cost, because they take fewer people and use a lot more gas. However, fishing in Honduras is generally a little cheaper than in other Central American countries. Expect to pay in the neighborhood of $300 for a half day or $600 for a full day, for a boat that can take two to four anglers.

You don't need a fishing license for sport fishing in Honduras, so if you're really hard-core you can bring your own tackle and fish from the beach for tarpon and snook.

Roatan Fishing

Fishing around Roatan is a well-kept secret, with some of the best fishing in the world for bonefish, tarpon, dorado, grouper, sails and even marlin. There are several charter captains and a few small operators, most of them in Sandy Bay and West End, who can take you out for half or full days, providing beer, bait and tackle.

On the sand and turtlegrass flats, you can stalk bonefish

that average 5-12 pounds. Permit, tarpon and barracuda are added bonuses. If you are a hard-core fly angler, you already know you should bring your own rods, reels, tippets and a few favorite flies.

On the reefs, you can bottom-fish for snapper, grouper and jacks. Yellowtail snapper are a favorite to take back to the lodge and throw on the grill.

Splendid deep-sea fishing grounds are only a few minutes' boat ride from the shore. Depending on the time of year, you may target blue or white marlin, sailfish, wahoo, dorado, blackfin tuna or yellowfin tuna, bonita, kingfish or shark.

Crystal Beach Cabins
Cap'n Sam knows the local waters and how to catch the fish – he was 2003 Bay Islands Billfish Tournament champ. All-inclusive packages (no booze included) run about $2,600 per person for a full week. Fly fishermen are encouraged to bring their own equipment. Otherwise, all tackle is provided. *Info:* West End. Tel. 403-8847.

Early Bird Fishing Charters
Capt. Loren Monterroso has a fully-equipped 24-foot Grady White explorer with full electronics and all the tackle you might need for offshore pursuits. Offshore trips run $600 for all day. Fly and live-bait flats fishing are done from a proper flats skiff with poling platform. Spinning, bait casting and fly equipment is provided. Flats fishing runs about $500 per day for two people. *Info:* Sandy Bay. Tel. 955-0001 or 445-3019.

Captain O
Captain O knows where the big 'uns are, and focuses on taking clients to the areas where the fishing is best. At certain times of the year he may focus on tarpon, and billfish at other times. His equipment is modern and newish. He has 27- and 25-foot sport fishers. You can hire the large boat and a full day of Captain O's expertise with all the trimmings for a mere $350. If you've always dreamed of catching a marlin, sailfish or wahoo, the Captain knows all the trolling tricks. *Info:* Tel. 403-8887.

Mango Creek Lodge

This is a seven-room lodge for serious anglers, concentrating on fly fishing. Extensive flats close to the lodge support schools of bones of up to 30 or 40 fish. Although they have adequate tackle on site, hard-core fly fishermen are encouraged to bring their favorite rods, reels and flies. Mango Creek has a great fishing guide you can download from their web site that goes into detail about tackle and the habits and habitats of the different local species. Check it to help make your fly selections.

A week of fishing including meals and lodging runs about $2,200 per person. The lodging and food are nice but not luxurious. The resort is very privately situated, on its own small island about 15 minutes (by boat) from Oak Ridge. Hot water is available in the evenings. *Info:* Near Oak Ridge. www.mangocreeklodge.com; Tel. 435-2576.

Marco & Carlos

With two boats and top-notch tackle, Marco & Carlos are a solid choice for a fishing adventure. They'll take you trolling for dorado, marlin and wahoo, or bottom fishing for jacks, grouper, snapper and barracuda. They will send a boat around to your hotel and pick you up, supply everything you need for a full day of fishing including food and drinks. They know how to find 'em, chum 'em up, hook 'em, and catch 'em! A full-day trip runs about $550. *Info:* West End. Tel. 445-4171.

Subway Watersports

This is the fishing operator for Palmetto Bay Plantation, Barefoot Cay, and Turquoise Bay Resorts. They offer the usual flats and offshore fishing trips with all equipment included. The best thing about them is their light trolling along the reef trips. These are a real bargain at only $290 for a full day. Trolling or bottom fishing along the edge of the reef is probably the most productive fishing method in the area. You are just about guaranteed to haul in your dinner. Cruise ship visitors can go for a half-day trip for only $200. *Info:* www.subwaywatersports.com; Tel. 387-0579 or 359-4190.

Utila Fishing

Fishing around Utila is nothing less than spectacular. The deep trough directly offshore funnels migrating pelagics past Utila, just a little out from the plunging reefs. Currents around the island form gigantic eddies off the southwest end of the island past Diamond Cay and Stingray Point. The eddies pull together baitfish and plankton in huge schools which attract passing billfish, tuna, whale sharks, dolphins and other interesting, free-swimming fish. The reefs in the same area hold another trove of baitfish and their predators: grouper, snapper, sharks, barracuda and a myriad of vivid reef fish.

There are also large areas of flats, which serve as hatcheries for an enormous variety of sea life. Poking about on the flats in a small skiff looking for bonefish (or whatever) is a great way to spend a day, a week, or a lifetime. There are always interesting things to see out on the flats: stingrays, sharks, lobsters, crabs and gringo snorkelers.

Deep Blue Resort

Although they cater mostly to divers, this all-inclusive resort, accessible only by boat, is a splendid spot for fishing. It's located on a quiet beach with nice reefs just offshore. The 10 rooms are not five-star, but the fishing and diving surely are. *Info:* www.deepblueutila.com; Tel. 425-2015.

Laguna Beach Resort

This spot is very close to the best fishing action. They operate their own fishing boats and cater to offshore and flats anglers. *Info:* www.utila.com; Tel. 378-1895.

Coral View Beach Resort

Also very close to world-class fishing, Coral View offers flats and reef fishing excursions. The restaurant focuses on seafood and they have a small bar. All you need, really. *Info:* Sandy Bay, next to Blue Bayou. Tel. 425-3783.

Guanaja Fishing

Some of the best bonefish and permit fishing in the world is found on the miles of sand and turtlegrass flats around Guanaja. Wading or poling small skiffs gets you within fly-casting distance of schools of up to 50, three-to-seven-pound bone fish. 10-25-pound permit and tarpon up to 90 pounds lurk nearby, making an elusive grand slam a distinct possibility. Reportedly, the **world record bonefish** was caught recently in front of the **Nautilus Resort** on Guanaja. Good luck!

Almost any of the resorts or hotel on the island can set you up with a fishing trip to the flats or trolling offshore. Both **End of the World** and **Coral Bay** do all-inclusive fishing packages. Call or email for specials.

End of the World Resort

This laid-back resort has no TV, no phones and no cars. Owner Captain Brian Rowland runs a very comfortable operation, with the emphasis on personal service. He meets guests at the airport with a smile, proffering a cold beer, and arranges flats, reef and offshore trips with most tackle provided. $1,800 gets you a seven-night fishing package with all the goodies. *Info:* www.guanaja.com; Tel 991-1257 or 888-447-4197 US.

Coral Bay Dive Resort

Most visitors here are divers, but anglers are also well taken care of. Charters to the flats, reefs or offshore provide all the spinning and deep-sea tackle you'll need. If you prefer fly-fishing, you will need to be self-sufficient with most tackle. *Info:* www.coralbay.ca; Tel. 877-682-9054.

La Moskitia Fishing

If you can get to it, you'll find the fishing in this remote region to be fantastic. Endless **lagoons, streams and canals** harbor four different species of snook as well as tarpon and exotic tropical species, almost undisturbed by gringo anglers. In a few areas, local gill-netters have decimated the fish stocks, but other regions are more or less pristine. **Brus Laguna** and **Laguna de Caratasca** (by Puerto Lempira) are both chock-full of tarpon and snookums. If you visit La Ruta Moskitia, or take a river trip down the Río Platano (see *Chapter 7*), you'll be able to do some low-key fishing along the way, but opportunities for immersive fishing trips comparable to the ones in the Bay Islands are few.

It's not hard to arrange a fishing trip with a local guide in Puerto Lempira. However, to the best of our knowledge, the only US-style fishing tour operator in the region is Team Marin Honduras Fishing. Team Marin offers complete fishing tours from two to eight days, sleeping at the basic Hotel Paradise in Brus Laguna. *Info:* www.teammarinhondurasfishing.com; Tel. 434-3261, 434-3421 or 987-0875.

The Moskitia would seem to be the ideal place for a fishing lodge, and several have tried to make a go of it. Alas, Cannon Island, Warunta Lagoon and Sika Lanka fishing lodges have all closed, done in by the logistical nightmares and high costs of getting supplies into the region.

Kayaking

Kayakers will find three very different ways to utilize their favorite watercraft. Sea kayaking is possible almost anywhere there's a coast. Most beachfront resorts in the Bay Islands and on the North Coast have kayaks available for rent or even free for guests. **Subway Watersports**, with several locations on Roatan, has kayaks and other boats for rent.

In the coastal parks of the North Coast and La Moskitia, a kayak may be the very best way to navigate the winding mangrove waterways and silently sneak up on shy wildlife. The kayak tours of Punta Izopo offered by Garífuna Tours are a perfect example (see *Chapter 5*).

The Cangrejal and other whitewater rivers along the North Coast are exciting territory for kayakers. All the rafting outfitters offers kayaks (see below).

Rafting

The **Cangrejal River**, on the eastern border of Pico Bonito National Park, offers some of the best whitewater river rafting in the world. In addition to thrills and spills, a rafting trip gives you another perspective on the rain forest, it's a chance to stay cool in the tropical heat, and it's just jolly good fun all around.

The river has class III and IV rapids, and is runnable year-round (the high water season is September through January). It's a double adventure to navigate the rapids while racing through the extravagant vegetation of the rain forest.

If you've never rafted before, don't worry – it's not as dangerous as it sounds (or perhaps it would be more accurate to say that it's only as dangerous as you choose to make it). You'll be riding in an inflatable rubber raft with an English-speaking guide, and wearing a helmet and life jacket. Your guide will give you a short training course before you plunge into the whitewater. After you've shot the rapids, you can relax with a peaceful swim in the river.

The two main rafting tour operators are **Omega Tours** and **Jungle River Lodge**. Both have basic but comfortable lodges right on the river. Our trip begins with a short warm-up, floating through some very mild rapids, and an instruction session with our bilingual guides. Now that we're clued in, we're ready to run the class III and IV rapids, with steep drops, long wave-trains, waterfalls, and passages through narrow gorges with rocks towering hundreds of feet overhead.

A half-day rafting trip takes around four hours, and will cost you $50-70 per person, including transportation and a light picnic lunch. Experienced rafters (and kayakers) can take a full-day trip, starting further up the river, with more intense rapids and technical whitewater.

If you'd like to get off the beaten path, line up a trip to the **Río San Juan**. About 45 minutes west of La Ceiba, this rushing jungle river has class III-V rapids for experienced rafters and kayakers.

Golf

Honduras is not known as a major golf destination. There are two 9-hole golf courses **near San Pedro Sula**. The Lomas Golf & Country Club and the Lima Country Club are both open to the public, and equipment rental is available.

Tegucigalpa also has a pair of 9-hole courses, the Tegucigalpa Country Club and the Villa Elena Country Club, located in a beautiful forested area.

Another 9-hole course is located **just outside of Tela**.

12. PRACTICAL MATTERS

GETTING AROUND

AIRPORTS/ARRIVALS

Honduras has two main international airports, at **Tegucigalpa** (TGU) and **San Pedro Sula** (SAP). Several US carriers fly to both airports. **Roatan** (RTB) and **La Ceiba** (LCE) also have well-appointed airports. Roatan has a few flights direct from the US, and many of the diving crowd fly in and out of there without ever setting foot on the mainland. Central America's airline group TACA (www.taca.com; Tel. 800/400-TACA), flies to Tegucigalpa, San Pedro Sula and Roatan from several North American cities.

Web-based travel search engines such as **Expedia** (www.expedia.com), **Orbitz** (www.orbitz.com) and **Travelocity** (www.travelocity.com) are useful for researching flight schedules and prices. Personally, I never actually book travel through these third-party sites, because it's just as easy to book directly with the airlines, and the third-party sites impose extra fees and more restrictive change policies.

If you can find a knowledgeable travel agent, she or he may be able to find you a better deal than you'd get directly from the airlines. It's also well worth considering buying your airfare as part of a package tour (see below). **Exito Travel** (www.exitotravel.com; Tel. 800/655-4053) and **Tico Travel** (www.ticotravel.com; Tel. 800/493-8426) are two companies that specialize in the region.

Tegucigalpa's **Toncontín International Airport** is quite small (only four gates). Facilities include a post office, a bank, restaurants and shops and a selection of car rental agencies. You can get into town by taxi or, if you're staying at one of the upscale hotels, via their courtesy van. If you're a real cheapskate, you can try to figure out how to catch a local bus.

Ramón Villeda Morales International Airport in San Pedro Sula (also known as La Mesa) is about the same size, and has similar facilities, although a major expansion is in the works.

There is a departure tax of about $32 that all departing air passengers must pay.

CRUISES

At least ten cruise ships stop at Roatan, disgorging a flood of wide-eyed tourists who have a quick snorkel and buy a t-shirt, or fly off on hurried excursions as far afield as La Ceiba or Copán, to be herded back on board in time for the evening feeding. Below are some cruise lines that offer stops in Roatan, most of them as part of a "Panama Canal" itinerary.

- **Carnival Cruise Lines**, www.carnival.com; Tel. 888/CARNIVAL
- **Celebrity Cruises**, www.celebritycruises.com; Tel. 800/647-2251
- **Regent Seven Seas Cruises**, www.theregentexperience.com; Tel. 877/505-5370
- **Seabourn Cruise Line**, www.seabourn.com; Tel. 800/351-9595
- **Princess Cruises**, www.princess.com; Tel. 800/774-6237
- **Holland America**, www.hollandamerica.com; Tel. 800/426-0327
- **Silversea Cruises**, www.silversea.com; Tel. 877/760-9052
- **MSC Cruises**, www.msccruisesusa.com; Tel. 954/772-6262
- **Norwegian Cruise Line**, www.ncl.com; Tel. 866/234-0292
- **Costa Cruise Lines**, www.costacruises.com; Tel. 800/445-8020
- **Oceania Cruises**, www.oceaniacruises.com; Tel. 800/531-5619

TOUR OPERATORS

Guided tours are a big part of the scene in Honduras. Tours to the national parks, the Copán ruins, and whitewater rafting are the main itineraries, but diving, fishing, horseback riding, city tours and all kinds of other activities are on offer.

The tour business is a complex web of larger and smaller operators. Wholesale tour companies subcontract with local tour guides, hotels, van drivers, etc. A tour can mean anything from a kid showing you the way to the local *balneario* to a door-to-door package with airfare, hotels, ground transport ... and a visit to that *balneario* with the local kid to show you the way.

Travel in Honduras is **adventure travel** – a lot of travelers like the convenience and safety of a package tour. Even if you travel independently in the States and Europe, you should at least have your ground transportation and hotels lined up before you leave home. Most hotels and tour operators are happy to arrange a van from the airport to your destination, avoiding the hurly-burly of the bus stations.

If you're the independent type however, you can get around perfectly well (and very cheaply) on your own by bus, pickup truck and boat. Even so, I highly recommend visiting the forest in the company of a local guide. You'll see much more, and learn more about the area, than you would on your own.

There are several other reasons why **using a local guide** is a good idea. For one thing, it's safer. Most rural areas of Honduras are safe enough, but some of the more popular parks are well-known hunting grounds for thieves, and hikers have been robbed.

A more common danger is the unreliability of local transport. Getting to where the jaguars roam may involve a complex itinerary of planes, buses, vans and even boats, any of which may be late, break down or not show up where your guide book tells you they're supposed to show up! A good tour operator can meet you at the plane with a nice new air-conditioned van, and take you where you want to go in safety and comfort. Finally, hiring local guides is a good way to help the local economy.

Here are **some of the most reputable** tour companies:

Omega Tours has a jungle lodge on the Cangrejal, and also runs tours to North Coast Parks and the Moskitia. www.omegatours.hn; Tel. 440-0334 or 965-5815.

Garífuna Tours, with offices in Tela and La Ceiba, is one of the top operators on the North Coast (Punta Sal, Punta Izopo, Pico Bonito) and they also do trips to the Moskitia. www.garifunatours.com; Tel. 448-1069 or 440-3252.

Maya Tropic Tours has been in business 30 years, offering trips to Cusuco, Punta Sal, Cuero Salado, Celaque and Azul Meambar, as well as whitewater rafting on the Cangrejal. www.mtthonduras.com; Tel. 557-7071.

La Moskitia Eco-Aventuras specializes in tours to the Moskitia region, as well as Cangrejal rafting and the North Coast parks. www.honduras.com/moskitia; Tel. 440-2124 or 965-7742.

Turtle Tours, run by two Germans and based in La Ceiba: North Coast, Copán, Moskitia. www.turtletours.de; Tel. 414-5368.

Coco Tours does one-day trips to the parks of the North Coast, as well as longer package tours all over the country. www.hondurascoco.com; Tel. 374-3663.

Arrecife Tours is a wholesale tour operator based in Tegucigalpa. www.arrecifetours.com; Tel. 207-4081.

Explore Honduras, wholesaler based in San Pedro. www.explorehonduras.com; Tel. 552-6242.

MC Tours specializes in shore excursions for cruise ships. www.mctours-honduras.com; Tel. 651-4453.

Destinos de Éxito is a wholesaler in Tegucigalpa. www.destinosdeexito.com; Tel. 236-9651.

Gray Line does one-day city tours of all the larger cities, and longer tours to the usual tourist routes (Copán, Pico Bonito, Lancetilla, Punta Sal). www.graylinehonduras.com; Tel. 220-1552 or 220-7257.

Mesoamerican Ecotourism Alliance offers tours throughout the country. www.travelwithmea.org; Tel. 800/682-0584 or 303/440-3362 US.

Yaragua Tours, in Copán Ruinas. www.yaragua.com; Tel. 651-4147.

Go Native Tours, at the Tunkul Restaurant in Copán Ruinas. Tel. 651-4410.

Lenca Land Trails, based in Santa Rosa de Copán, guides trips to the picturesque villages of the Lenca Trail and other sights in the region. Tel. 662-1375 or 662-0805.

GETTING AROUND BY AIR

Roads in most of Honduras are crummy, and in some areas they are non-existent, so travel by small plane is a popular option. For travel to some remote areas, such as the Moskitia, it's about the only option. You can get to the Bay Islands either by air or by ferry, both from La Ceiba. Flying is faster and a little more convenient, but costs a bit more.

Several small domestic airlines fly to small airfields all over the country. They tend to change their schedules, and even go in and out of business from time to time, so be sure to call for the latest schedule information. *Do not* rely on information on web sites, which may not have been updated in years. Reasonably-priced charters are another option, and are often included as part of package tours.

Other than the four main airports at Tegus, San Pedro, Roatan and La Ceiba, the rest are little more than landing strips with few or no facilities. Some of the smallest are nothing but a reasonably level field of grass. Little boys with sticks drive the cows off before each landing.

Atlantic Airlines (www.atlanticairlines.com.ni; Tel. 440-2343 or 440-2346) offers service to Tegucigalpa, San Pedro Sula, La Ceiba, all three of the Bay Islands and several other towns in Honduras, as well as to other Central American countries (note that there are a couple of other, unrelated, airlines with the same name elsewhere in the world).

Sosa Airlines (www.laceibaonline.net/aerososa/sosaingl.htm; Tel. 443-1894 or 443-2519) is based in La Ceiba, and serves Tegucigalpa, San Pedro Sula, all three Bay Islands and several other small airports, including Brus Laguna and Puerto Lempira in the Moskitia.

Isleña Airlines (www.flyislena.com; Tel. 441-3190) has service to Tegucigalpa, San Pedro Sula, La Ceiba, Roatan and Guanaja.

SAMI Airlines (Tel. 442-2565) offers flights from La Ceiba to Brus Laguna and Belen, with connecting flights to other airstrips in the Moskitia region.

CAR RENTAL

Renting a car offers the maximum in flexibility, but the poor state of the roads puts some people off. Anything that doesn't have 4-wheel drive is likely to be inadequate once you get off the major highways (and if you don't plan to drive off the major highways, there's little reason to rent a car). Fortunately, most rental agencies have a good selection of 4WD vehicles, from cute little Subarus to hulking SUVs.

Car rental agencies cluster around the airports - San Pedro, Tegus, La Ceiba, Roatan. You have a selection of both international chains and small local rental agencies. If you plan to rent from a chain, it's more convenient, and much cheaper, to reserve a car online before leaving home. A small local outfit may just give you a better price however, especially if you want to rent for a longer period, or if you want to hire a car and driver.

- **Toyota Rent a Car**, www.hondurasrentacar.com
- **Budget**, www.budget.com.ni
- **Hertz**, Tel. 668-3156 or 668-3157
- **Avis**, Tel. 668-3164

La Ceiba
- **Molinari Rent a Car**, Tel. 443-0055
- **Tropical Rent a Car**, Tel. 443-3071

Roatan
- **Coral Reef Rent a Car**, Tel. 445-1990
- **Caribbean Rent a Car**, www.caribbeanroatan.com; Tel. 455 6730
- **Island Rent a Car**, Tel. 455-7740, 455-7213 or 978-5347

San Pedro Sula
- **Maya Rent a Car**, Tel. 668-3168
- **Molinari Rent a Car**, Tel. 553-2639
- **Omega Rent a Car**, Tel. 557-0820 or 552-7626
- **Thrifty Rent a Car**, Tel. 668-3152 or 668-3153

Tegucigalpa
- **Econo Rent a Car**, Tel. 236-7244
- **Maya Rent a Car**, Tel. 232-0682
- **Thrifty Rent a Car**, Tel. 233-0922

Driving in Honduras can be very dangerous. **Roads are badly maintained**, and signage is poor, so it's easy to get lost. Many locals are terrible drivers, and are especially fond of passing on blind curves. Because of unlit vehicles and animals on the roads, driving after dark is simply not recommended.

And that's just on the major roads! Once you get on the little dirt country tracks, things really start to get interesting. Some of these roads are really bad – breaking the oil pan and being stranded in the middle of the jungle is a real danger. If you're going to drive, **carry a cell phone** (which you can rent from some car rental agencies). Many smaller roads are impassable during the rainy season.

Crime is also a concern for drivers (see *Emergencies & Safety*, below), both in the country and in cities. Keep windows rolled up and doors locked.

TAXIS

Taxis are reasonably priced and convenient. In most towns, four or five bucks will take you anywhere you want to go. After dark in Tegucigalpa and other cities, a taxi is the only safe way to get around. In larger cities, drivers are theoretically required to charge by the meter (called a *maría*), but elsewhere fares are usually negotiable. A word to the wise: any time you take a taxi in the developing world, be sure to agree on a fare *before* riding anywhere.

A taxi can also be an affordable way to get to rural destinations, or just to take a tour around the countryside, especially if you're with a group.

COLLECTIVOS

Throughout the developing world, **collective taxis** (called *collectivos* in Honduras) are an important way to get around. *Collectivos*, usually passenger vans but sometimes pickup trucks (*pailas*) or even boats, wait at certain designated spots until they have a full load going to a particular destination.

Traveling by *collectivo* is cheap, but it requires patience. First you have to figure out where the cars for your desired destination leave from (usually a square or market near the center of town), then you must sit and wait until the car fills up before you leave. The driver will instantly realize that you're a rich and impatient *norteamericano*, and will try to talk you into paying the fare for the entire vehicle, so that you can leave right away. If you're in a hurry, do so (even locals sometimes do). If not, politely decline and continue to wait patiently.

The price to each particular destination is fixed. Some (not all) drivers will try to get you to pay more than the locals do, so try to ascertain what the going rate is before you travel, perhaps by asking a fellow passenger.

BUSES

There are several different types of intercity bus in Honduras, from luxurious and pricey air-conditioned express buses to very cheap Central American torture buses (some are old school buses

from the US). All are reasonably punctual and reasonably safe (but do try to keep your eye on your luggage).

The best of the buses are those of the **Hedman Alas** line (www.hedmanalas.com; Tel. 557-3477 or 237-7143). Their buses are modern and air-conditioned, and most have bathrooms. They have a regular schedule that includes San Pedro Sula, SPS Airport, La Ceiba, Tegucigalpa, Tela, Guatemala City and San Salvador. A couple of sample fares: a round-trip from San Pedro Sula to Copán Ruinas runs about $27; San Pedro Sula to Tegucigalpa is around $29. Hedman Alas also runs a hotel in Tegucigalpa, which is low-priced and convenient to their bus terminal (see *Best Sleeps*).

There are several other "express" bus lines in various parts of the country, with varying prices and levels of quality. And of course, regular old Latin American bus service, crowded and slow but very cheap, goes almost everywhere.

In some cities, the buses for different destinations leave from different bus stations, which may require you to take a taxi ride across town, or to wander around looking for the right station in a seedy and dangerous neighborhood. In the latter situation, it may be well worth retaining one of the little blackguard boys who are usually to be found hanging about. For a Dollar or so, they'll carry your bags and guide you safely to the correct bus stop.

There's a very detailed guide to various bus routes and schedules at: hondurastips.honduras.com/english/transportation_guide.htm.

BASIC INFORMATION

BANKING & CHANGING MONEY

Honduras's monetary unit is the *Lempira*, named for a Lenca chief who fought valiantly against the Spaniards. At press time, the interbank exchange rate was about 20 to the Dollar (one Dollar = 20 Lempira). See www.oanda.com for current rates.

Many travelers don't really understand how currency exchange works, and this ignorance can cost you money. Here's the straight scoop. *Every time* you change currencies, you pay a fee in the form of the *spread* between the buy and sell exchange rates. The *interbank rate*, the rate at which banks exchange money among themselves, lies midway between the buy and sell rates, so the bank earns a fee on *every transaction*. Some currency-exchange places also charge a small fixed commission, the purpose of which is to prevent you from comparing rates between different exchange outlets. Even if a place trumpets "No Commission!" you're still paying a fee. To see if you're getting a good deal or a bad deal, look at the spread.

Credit cards and ATM cards offer the best spreads (about 2% from the interbank rate for credit cards, 3-4% for ATMs), and using them in Honduras has gotten much easier in recent years. **ATMs** are reasonably common in urban and tourist areas, and nowadays most cities have an ATM that will accept US cards belonging to one of the major ATM networks (Honor, Cirrus, etc). In the past, most Honduran ATMs accepted local bank cards only.

Large tourist-oriented businesses accept **credit cards** (Visa is far more widely accepted than MasterCard or American Express), but smaller places do not. Some businesses tack on an extra fee for using plastic (this is against the credit card companies' rules, but places do it anyway).

Changing money at banks is a bureaucratic nightmare, but they may offer the best exchange rates for cash. Most hotels will gladly change money for you, but will offer an unfavorable rate. Changing money at the change booths in the airport is a *big* rip-off.

Unofficial money-changers do business in major city squares. Unlike in some other developing countries, this is not a back-alley prelude to a mugging, but an accepted and partially respectable business. You'll see them strolling about with big rolls of cash, advertising the latest rates. You may get a slightly better rate from them, and they can be quite convenient, but exchanging cash in such a public setting may not be so safe.

Whether you get your cash from an ATM or from a street vendor, be very aware of your surroundings as you leave, on the alert for suspicious characters following you.

Most banks will accept only US Dollars (UK Pounds or Euros *maybe*, but anything else, forget it). Travelers' checks are not widely accepted, and are subject to extra fees.

In tourist areas, many businesses will accept US Dollars (and give your change in Lempiras), but you'll get a worse price than you would if you paid in local currency. Interbank exchange rates change daily, but smaller businesses will round up to a rough-and-ready rate, which will not be in your favor.

Honduran Lempiras are not convertible outside the country, so remember to change any leftover cash back to Dollars before leaving, or squander it in the duty-free shop at the airport.

BUSINESS HOURS

Most businesses are open from **around 9am to 5 or 6pm Monday through Friday**, and perhaps Saturday morning. Hours tend to be longer in larger cities and tourist areas. Many businesses and offices close for two hours at lunchtime. Most banks are open Mon-Fri 9am-4pm, but banks in small towns may have more limited hours. Most non-tourist-oriented businesses are closed on Sunday.

CLIMATE & WEATHER

Honduras has quite **a variety of climates** for such a small country. Generally speaking, the coastal areas are what you'd expect in the tropics: hot and humid, with plenty of rain. Up in the highlands, things are much cooler. Some of the highland areas have an amazingly pleasant climate, mostly between 75-80° F. year-round. Up in the high mountains, it can actually get quite cold, and very wet. If you plan to do some high-altitude hiking at Celaque or Pico Pijol, bring warm clothing and rain gear.

There are two main seasons. The **dry season** lasts from November through April, and is the main tourist season. The **rainy season** (which locals call *invierno*, or Winter) lasts from May through October, and sees far fewer tourists. Most areas of the country do get a lot of rain during this season, and some remote regions can become almost inaccessible by road. However, prices can be lower, and the crowds are gone.

CONSULATES & EMBASSIES

The following are in Tegucigalpa:

- **US embassy**, Av. La Paz. Tel. 236-9320 or 238-5114
- **Canadian embassy**, Col. Payaqui, Centro Financiero Banexpo. Tel. 232-4551
- **UK embassy**, Col. Payaqui, Centro Financiero Banexpo. Tel. 232-0612 or 232-0618

ELECTRICITY

Honduras uses 110-volt AC, **the same as in the US**, and the plugs are the same. Grounded (three-prong) plugs are not common, and the general level of electrical safety is low. Cheaper lodgings may feature "suicide showers," little electric heaters attached to the showerhead, sometimes with poorly insulated connectors (we've heard no reports of anyone actually being killed by one of these contraptions, which are also known as "widow makers," but *do not touch them*). Remote lodges get their power from generators, which may be turned off at night, and may deliver dodgy voltage.

EMERGENCIES & SAFETY

Crime

Let's tackle this issue head-on. Honduras has a reputation as a violent and dangerous place, and this reputation is to some extent justified, although not for the reasons you may think. Many Americans think of Honduras as a war zone, probably because the only time they ever heard of the country was in connection with the Nicaraguan war and ensuing US political scandal, which happened during the 1980s. However, all that ended over a decade ago, and the region is peaceful enough nowadays.

No, the main danger in Honduras is much more mundane: **common crime**. Honduras is a desperately poor country, the second-poorest in the Western Hemisphere. There are huge numbers of unemployed young men, and plentiful supplies of firearms.

Is it safe to visit Honduras? Yes, I believe you can travel perfectly safely there, or I wouldn't be writing this book. However, it certainly can be dangerous. Many a tourist has been robbed, and a few have been murdered (just to keep things in perspective, a dozen tourists have been murdered in Florida over the years, too).

Certain locales are much more dangerous than others, and I'll alert you to many of these throughout the book. Cities are more dangerous than the countryside, and the kind of crime to watch out for differs depending on where you are (pickpockets and con artists in tourist zones, muggers in isolated areas). Hotspots include **San Pedro Sula**, which has the country's highest crime rate, and parts of **rural Olancho Province**, where locals walk around with guns strapped to their hips, Old West-style. But please don't forget that crooks target tourists, and be on your toes wherever you are.

If you're thinking of traveling to Honduras, chances are you're an experienced traveler who doesn't mind a bit of adventure, and who is accustomed to taking precautions, rather than acting like a typical clueless tourist. Follow these rules and you should be fine:

- It is absolutely, positively not safe to walk around the streets of Tegucigalpa, San Pedro Sula or any other cities at night. Using the public bus system after dark may be risky as well. *Always take a taxi*. Some areas are dodgy during the day as well, so don't wander aimlessly.

- Never, ever leave any valuables in parked cars. In fact, it's probably unwise to park anywhere other than a watched hotel parking lot.

- Be on the alert for pickpockets in any crowded situation, especially at airports, bus stations and such places. Not only cities, but heavily-touristed parks and attractions such as Copán have their share of thieves.

- In some parks, walking alone on isolated trails is not recommended. Always check in at the ranger station, and hike in groups, preferably with a local guide.

- Walking on isolated beaches away from the crowds sounds like a wonderful thing to do, but it isn't always safe. In some locales, such as Tela, there are special Tourist Police who will accompany you if you wish to take a stroll on the beach. They aren't there for the sunshine.

- Driving is a dicey proposition. Thieves have been known to set up roadblocks on the highways and hold up passing vehicles. Certain areas are notorious for this, but it's a slight possibility almost anywhere. Highway robbers may also employ other time-honored ploys, such as staging a traffic accident, or pretending to be in need of assistance. Hitchhiking is a very common way to get around, but I really can't recommend doing so, or picking up hitchhikers.

- In crowded tourist areas, be on the alert for common scams: the "fellow American" who's been robbed and needs some money to get home, the fake fight or other disturbance, the "accidentally" spilled drink, the friendly stranger who offers you food (which may be drugged), the crowd of cute little kids who mob you and lighten your pocket, etc etc *ad infinitum*.

- Petty theft is not the only type of crime to watch out for. **Con men** run various investment scams on tourists and retirees. If you're doing any kind of business, buying real estate or investing in the country, be extra careful to deal only with reputable firms, and, most definitely, seek advice from a local third party such as a lawyer or accountant before signing anything or parting with any dough.

One of the saddest things about crime is that it can discourage you from making friends with locals. So remember, not every Honduran who approaches you is out to rip you off. They're friendly people in general, and many are simply eager to speak with a foreigner.

I highly recommend a **money belt**. *Not* the external "fanny-pack," but a small flat belt that goes around your waist (there are similar things that go around your neck) *under your clothes*. With your passport, plane ticket and main cash stash zipped up out of sight, you can relax and enjoy your trip (keep a small roll of walking-around money in a pocket, so you never have to pull out your money belt in public). Money belts are available at any good luggage shop or (much cheaper) at discount stores.

As for those fanny-packs, they're famous around the world as magnets for thieves and con artists. Even if you don't plan to keep any valuables in it, I strongly urge you to leave it at home. A fanny pack shouts "opportunity!" to people whom you'd rather not meet. The sight of a fanny pack to a street hustler is like the sound of a can opener to a hungry cat.

In many Latin American countries the police are famous for demanding informal "fines," to be paid in cash on the spot, for real or imagined traffic violations. This behavior is rare in Honduras, but we have heard reports that it does occur. If you do get cited, don't give the cops any cash, but make sure they give you a paper traffic ticket, which you will have to pay at a bank.

Unlike some tropical vacation destinations, Honduras is not particularly tolerant of **marijuana** or **drugs**. Laws are just as strict as those in the US, or more so. You may be offered *mota* or *ganja*, especially in party-hearty centers such as La Ceiba and the Bay Islands, but buying on the street exposes you to many dangers, including being ripped off or turned over to the authorities.

Police can ask for ID at any time, so keep yours with you. On the roads, you may occasionally pass through a police checkpoint. Have your passport and the car's papers available.

Prostitution is legal in Honduras, and "sex tourism" is big business. Theoretically, the government regulates the trade, but Honduras is not Amsterdam. There is in fact very little control at all, and the whole business is quite sleazy, with muggings and druggings a regular part of the scene. Another thing you may want to keep in mind is that Honduras has the highest rate of AIDS in the Western Hemisphere. Abuse of minors is a sore point with the authorities. Having sex with anyone under 18 is strictly illegal.

You can check the latest Consular Information Sheets and Travel Warnings from the US State Department at www.travel.state.gov.

HEALTH

Honduras's health care system is not so great. Larger cities have public hospitals and clinics, but you'll get better and quicker service from a private doctor or clinic, which you can find in the phone book (the Spanish for "doctor" is *médico*).

In an emergency, dial 199 for the police.

The health hazards here are the same ones you'll encounter in any tropical country. Be very careful about exposure to the sun: it can hurt you even on cloudy days.

Tap water is not safe to drink. Drink only bottled water, and use it to rinse any fruits or vegetables that you don't either peel or cook. Try to stay away from ice, and from raw vegetables like lettuce, that may be rinsed with impure water. Upscale hotels generally have a water purification system, so you needn't worry about any of that.

No matter how careful you are, it's not unlikely that a bit of Montezuma's revenge will be part of your Honduran adventure. Experienced travelers swear by Imodium AD, so bring some with you.

Malaria is a problem in low-lying areas on both coasts. It's especially prevalent in the Moskitia region, and is also present in the Bay Islands. Malaria is an extremely serious disease that's spread by mosquitoes, and it can be fatal. If you're going to one of these areas, consider taking a chloroquine drug as a preventive, which you start taking before your trip.

Take stringent precautions against mosquitoes. Cover up with socks and long-sleeved pants and shirts (mosquitoes' favorite place to bite is your ankles). Light long pants such as linens or khakis really are the best choice for tropical travel. Skeeters, fleas and other insects are most active right around dawn and dusk. Some ecolodges have mosquito nets to drape over the beds at night – use them! If you do get sick, chloroquine drugs are also available at pharmacies in Honduras.

Tiny little insects called sand fleas are a major problem in the Bay Islands, and you may encounter them in any beach area. Different people have different reactions to the little buggers: some people aren't bothered at all, some are mercilessly bitten, and some have dangerous allergic reactions. Most travelers agree that a liberal coating of Avon's Skin-So-Soft is effective against the sand fleas. It won't impress the mosquitoes however, so pack *plenty* of maximum-strength insect repellent, with DEET, for them. A tube or two of cortisone-based anti-itch cream is also a good thing to have.

Dysentery, cholera and other diseases caused by poor sanitation are present. You can check with the **CDC** (www.cdc.gov/travel/index.htm; Tel. 877/394-8747) for the most recent health advisories and immunization recommendations.

AIDs is epidemic in Honduras. If you choose to have sex with a prostitute or anyone else, be absolutely sure to use a condom.

Poisonous snakes are common throughout the country, but snakebites are rare. When hiking in the forest, watch your step at all times, and don't stick your hand in anywhere it doesn't belong. A stout pair of hiking boots is a very good idea for several reasons. Slipping in the mud and spraining your ankle is more likely than getting bit by a *terciópelo*, and it could ruin your holiday.

Travelers with special health concerns should note that remote jungle lodges have limited ability to evacuate you in a medical emergency: if something happens to you, it could be hours or days before you get to a hospital.

ETIQUETTE

Latins are great ones for politeness – when they meet, there's a great deal of handshaking, "How's the family?" and so forth, before any business gets discussed. The word *buenas* serves as an all-purpose greeting, short for the more formal *buenas mañanas/ tardes/noches* (good night/afternoon/evening). See the *Essential Spanish* section for more pleasantries.

Catracho? Gringo?

Hondurans call themselves *catrachos* (if they are male) or *catrachas* (if female). The nickname comes from the name of a Honduran general who fought against William Walker.

You should also realize that it is not the least impolite for Hondurans to refer to us as *gringos* (or *gringas*).

Most Latin Americans consider themselves to be "Americans" but realize that the word is usually reserved for people from the USA. In Spanish, the word *estadounidense* means someone from the United States. *norteamericano* has a similar meaning, encompassing Canadians as well.

Peoples' concept of time is different in Latin America than it is in the US and Northern Europe. If you have an appointment at three, then three is when you start thinking about heading that way (even if it's a half-hour trip). Businesses and public transport generally make a reasonable effort to be on time, but individuals do not. Don't get too upset when people show up fashionably late. You may hear the phrase *hora americana*, which means that something is (atypically) supposed to happen more or less on time.

Even though you're in the tropics, please don't dress as if the whole country is a beach. At beach resorts and tourist towns, beach bum attire is fine, but in places like banks and stores, you'll notice that the locals wear long pants, shirts, and even jackets and ties, just as we do at home (some older men wear the traditional *guayabera* shirt in lieu of a tie). Walking around in shorts, flip-flops and a baseball cap marks you instantly as a tourist.

LAND & PEOPLE

Honduras is located in Central America, between the Caribbean Sea and the Pacific Ocean. The country is roughly triangular, so the northern (Caribbean) coast is quite long, and the southern (Pacific) coast is quite short. Her neighbors are Guatemala to the northwest, El Salvador to the west and Nicaragua to the south. Eighty percent of the country is mountainous, but there are narrow plains along both coasts. The northeastern part of the country consists of the vast, sparsely-populated lowlands of the Moskitia.

Honduras is one of the poorest countries in the Western Hemisphere, with a per-capita Gross Domestic Product of $2,900 (compared with $41,600 for the US). The distribution of wealth is very unequal, unemployment is 28%, and 53% of the people live below the poverty line. Rates of literacy (76%) and life expectancy (69 years) are poor.

Most of the people (90%) are **Mestizos** (of mixed Spanish and Native American descent). The **Garífuna**, descendents of indigenous Caribs and freed African slaves, live on the North Coast and in the Bay Islands. Indigenous groups include the **Chortí Maya** and **Lenca** in the west; and the **Miskito**, **Pech** and **Tawahka** in the east. African-Americans are about 2% of the population, many of them descendents of Cayman Islanders. 97% of Hondurans are Roman Catholic.

Agriculture is an important and highly

highly visible part of the economy (14% of GDP), especially coffee in the highlands and bananas the North Coast. Other activities include cattle ranching, logging and increasingly, fish and shrimp farming. **Industry** makes up 31% of GDP, and mostly consists of textile and clothing factories around San Pedro Sula and the surrounding valley. **Tourism** is a growing earner, with Honduras rapidly gearing up to get a slice of the ecotourism business enjoyed by neighbors Costa Rica and Belize.

INTERNET ACCESS

Honduras is getting wired up slowly but surely. Internet cafés are common in large cities and tourist areas. Many larger hotels offer internet service (with the exception of the more remote wilderness lodges, which may be out of reach of the telephone network). See the list of Honduras-oriented internet directories and search engines at the end of this chapter.

LANGUAGE

The language of Honduras is **Spanish**, in its Latin American variant, which differs slightly from the Castilian Spanish spoken in Spain. It's not difficult to travel in Honduras without knowing much Spanish, as English is widely spoken in tourist areas (in fact, you'll find that the owners of hotels and other tourist-oriented businesses are often from the US or Europe). However, any experienced traveler will tell you that knowing a few key words will greatly enhance your trip. *Por favor* (please) and *gracias* (thank you) are the most useful, and using them liberally will smooth your way to a remarkable extent.

If you do want to learn Spanish, Honduras is a fine place to do so. Several **language schools** cater for beginners and experts, dabbling vacationers or long-term residents. Some offer accommodations in wonderful rain forest or beachside locations.

Copán Ruinas has a couple of schools, including **Ixbalanque Spanish School**. www.ixbalanque.com.

Centro Internacional de Idiomas is in La Ceiba. www.hondurasspanish.com; Tel. 441-6448.

CASS Language School has campuses in La Ceiba, Roatan and Utila. www.spanish-language.org; Tel. 440-1707.

NEWSPAPERS

Honduras This Week (www.marrder.com/htw) is an English-language weekly.

The monthly English-language **Bay Islands Voice** (www.bayislandsvoice.com) covers the islands of Roatan, Utila and Guanaja.

National papers include Tegucigalpa's **La Tribuna** (www.latribuna.hn) and San Pedro Sula's **La Prensa** (www.laprensahn.com).

PASSPORT REGULATIONS

Passports are required for entry. Citizens of the US, Canada and the UK are permitted to stay in Honduras for up to 90 days without a visa. Citizens of Australia, New Zealand, South Africa and Ireland may stay for 30 days without a visa.

If you want to stay for more than 90 days, the best thing to do is simply leave the country overnight and come back for another 90 days. It is possible to get an extension (*prórroga de turismo*) from the immigration office (*migración*), but it's a bureaucratic nightmare.

POSTAL SERVICES

Honduras's postal service (*correos*) is notoriously slow and inefficient. You can expect mail from Honduras to the States or Europe to take at least two weeks, if it arrives at all. When contacting hotels or tour operators in Honduras, use email or fax if at all possible.

TELEPHONES

The telephone system is also a little on the crummy side, but serviceable. Cell phones are common, and you can even rent one for your visit.

The country code is 504. To call Honduras from the US, dial: 011 504 [local number].

Most phone booths use **phone cards**, which you can buy at grocery stores and newsstands. Phone cards are a bargain, and offer the cheapest way to call North America. Try to avoid making calls from hotels, which love to add a hefty markup to the price.

Another good way to call home is by calling the direct access number for your long-distance company, and using your calling card:

- **AT&T**: Tel. 800-0123
- **MCI**: Tel. 800-0122
- **Sprint**: Tel. 800-0121

Many remote lodges are far from phone lines or cellular coverage, so the only option may be to use a satellite phone, which is quite expensive.

To call the US or Canada from Honduras, dial: 001 [area code and number].

You can send faxes at most post offices and hotels.

TIME

The time in Honduras is equal to US Central Standard Time (six hours behind Greenwich Mean Time, one hour behind Eastern Time). However, they do not recognize Daylight Savings Time. The length of the days and nights doesn't vary much here in the tropics. It gets dark about 6pm every day, year round.

TIPPING

Restaurants often add a *propina* (tip) automatically, so examine your bill. If a service charge has been included, there's no need to do more than round up to the next even amount, unless service is exceptional. Taxi drivers don't usually expect tips. Porters should receive a little something. Many tour guides have come to expect tips, especially in tourist-swamped regions such as Copán, but you really needn't give them anything extra unless they go above and beyond the call of duty.

When checking out of a hotel, I always leave a buck or two in the room for the housekeeping staff. Remember, that loose change that seems like a nuisance to you is a substantial amount of money to them!

You may occasionally be approached by freelance porters, usually young kids (in a former age, they would have been called "blackguard boys") who hang around tourist areas and offer to carry your bags, guard your car while you're away, help you through the intricacies of buying a bus ticket, or other small services. Use your discretion as to whether they are to be trusted. If your tip is too small, they'll let you know.

TOURIST INFORMATION

The **Honduras Tourist Board** has a lot of information at www.letsgohonduras.com. Most cities and other tourist destinations have a local tourism office - see the regional chapters for contact information.

WATER

Tap water is not safe to drink, unless you're staying at one of the nicest hotels, which have their own large-scale filters. Stick to bottled water, and pass on the ice cubes. Be wary of any fruits or vegetables that aren't either peeled or cooked. Cheap lodgings may have dodgy water supplies, with low pressure and little or no hot water.

WEIGHTS & MEASURES

All measurements in Honduras use the metric system. Liquids are sold by the liter, which is a tiny bit more than a quart. Food is often sold by the gram. One kilogram is 2.2 pounds, and 100 grams of meat or cheese is about enough for a sandwich. Distance is measured in meters (about 39 inches) or kilometers (1.6 kilometers equals 1 mile).

Temperature is measured in Celsius: 0° Celsius is freezing, or 32° Fahrenheit. 100° Celsius equals the boiling point of water, or 212° F.

100 kilometers is 60 miles. If the posted speed limit is 80 km/hr, that means 48 mph.

WEB SITES

Be very wary of information you find on the web. Many companies never update their sites. You'll find sites for hotels and tour operators that closed years ago. Always call for the latest schedules and prices.

- **www.letsgohonduras.com**. The official site of the Honduras Tourist Board has some good general information.
- **www.marrder.com/htw**. Honduras This Week is an English-language newspaper with all kinds of interesting local information.
- **www.garinet.com** is a hub for all things Garífuna.
- **www.roatanet.com** has lots of information about Roatan.
- **www.ecotourism.org** is the site of the International Ecotourism Society, and includes lists of environmentally friendly lodges and tour operators.
- **www.planeta.com** has lots of information about ecotourism in Honduras and the world.
- **www.tripadvisor.com** and **www.virtualtourist.com** have comments from fellow tourists about various attractions, lodgings and restaurants.
- **www.projecthonduras.com** is "an online portal for information on ways to help Honduras."
- **www.lib.utexas.edu/maps/americas/honduras.jpg** is a nice big map.

Honduras-based search engines

- **www.terra.com.hn**
- **www.in-honduras.com**
- **www1.lanic.utexas.edu/la/ca/honduras/**
- **www.hondirectorio.com**
- **www.cibercentro.com/honduras** has links to local search engines, internet providers and other useful sites.

Private sites with varying amounts of useful information

- **www.honduras.com**
- **www.hondurastips.honduras.com**
- **www.sidewalkmystic.com**
- **www.travel-to-honduras.com**
- **www.enjoyhonduras.com**

A SHORT HISTORY

Honduras has a highly colorful history. The fascinating lost civilization of the Maya built advanced cities deep in the jungle. Ruthless Spanish conquistadors decimated the locals, sparred with one another and battled it out with bold British pirates. North American adventurers carved out personal empires. Evil banana barons ran the country as a personal fiefdom, supported by US military might. Shady CIA types assembled a ragtag army in the jungles, and their antics almost brought down a US president. What fun!

Honduras has been home to a variety of indigenous peoples since prehistoric times. The ancestors of some of today's ethnic groups have been around since 2,000 BC or so, including the **Pech** and **Tawahka** in the east, and the **Tolupan** or **Jicaque** in the west.

The best-known of Central America's indigenous groups are the **Maya**, whose Classic Period lasted from around 300-900 AD. They built an advanced civilization, with a highly organized political system built around independent city-states. Their knowledge of astronomy, their calendar and their written language were unparalleled among ancient peoples. Honduras has several ancient Mayan sites, of which by far the largest and best-known is **Copán**.

Copán was an important city and ceremonial center, the capital of an ancient kingdom called Xukpi. Around the 9th century AD, Copán was abandoned, although people of Mayan descent continued to live in the area, and still do today. The Mayans' advanced civilization collapsed long before the Spanish came. The exact reasons for their demise are a mystery, but some scientists believe that poor stewardship of their environment played a role. You can read a fascinating discussion of the topic in the book *Collapse*, by Jared Diamond, which examines the decline and fall of various historical civilizations around the world. Could the same thing happen to us?

Copán came to the attention of the modern world thanks to a book called *Incidents of Travel in Central America, Chiapas and*

Yucatan, which was published in 1841. In the 1880s, archaeologists began excavation and research at the site, which continues to the present day. See *Chapter 6* for more on the history of Copán.

Christopher Columbus (Cristóbal Colón in Spanish) "discovered" Honduras in 1502 during his last voyage to the New World, landing first on Guanaja, and later in the vicinity of Trujillo. He gave the country the name Honduras, which means "depths," because of the steepness of the coastline.

In the years after Columbus brought his news back to Spain of a new world ripe for the taking, bold adventurers began heading over to make their fame and fortune. One of these was **Gil Gonzales Dávila**, who "discovered" the Gulf of Fonseca. Another was **Cristóbal de Olid**, a subordinate of **Hernán Cortés**, who founded the town of Triunfo de la Cruz, near present-day Tela. Olid proved a little too independent for Cortés, who had to show up personally and take off a few heads to restore his authority.

The Spaniards established a colony at **Trujillo** and set about killing, enslaving and exploiting the local inhabitants, as one did in those days. As in many of their colonies, the Spanish ruled through *encomiendas*, which were sort of like a franchise to conquer. As the grantee of an *encomienda* for a certain region, you had the right to exploit the land and its inhabitants as you saw fit, subject to the crown getting a slice of the profits, of course. Not that the Indians got nothing out of the deal - holders of *encomiendas* were expected to convert them to Christianity.

European diseases devastated the locals. By some estimates, within 50 years after the Spanish arrived, 90% of the indigenous inhabitants were dead. This left the conquistadors with a labor shortage, so they imported a small number of slaves from Africa. Some of the Indians put up a valiant resistance. A chief called **Lempira** was able to unify several tribes of the Lenca family in the West of the country and fought many battles against the Spanish until they finally did him in. Today Lempira is a national hero. A province of Honduras and the national currency are named for him.

The Spaniards mined for gold and silver in several parts of the country. The cities of **Comayagua** and **Tegucigalpa** began to develop as mining centers. However, the pay dirt soon ran out, and poor soil and rugged landscapes made farming a difficult venture, so Honduras was one of the poorest colonies on the Spanish Main.

The Spanish didn't have a monopoly on the region for long. Soon **French and British privateers** ("pirates" to the Spanish) were preying on the treasure galleons as they headed for Spain full of bullion. The Bay Islands and the mangrove coast of La Moskitia had thousands of perfect hiding places for shallow-draft vessels. The British made allies of the indigenous Miskitos, and almost succeeded in driving the Spanish out of the entire North Coast. The Spanish built forts at **Omoa** and **Trujillo** to protect their colonies from the constant pillaging.

The famous buccaneer **Henry Morgan** made Port Royal on Roatan his base, and it became a regular pirate town, where the scourge of the seas squandered their ill-gotten gains on rum and debauchery. The islands are rich in pirate legends – sunken treasure is said to lie among the reefs.

The British controlled the Bay Islands from 1643 until 1872, and they had a large impact on the cultural makeup of the region. At one point, they brought a group of Black Caribs from St. Vincent to the Bay Islands. These unique people, whose ancestry included

Amerindians and African maroons (former slaves), spread out along the north coast of Central America from Belize to Nicaragua, and evolved into today's **Garífuna** culture. Later the British brought a large group of former slaves from the Cayman Islands, and these were the ancestors of today's English-speaking Bay Islanders.

In 1821, the **United Provinces of Central America** declared their independence from Spain. The loose federation never worked out, and in 1838 Honduras withdrew and became a sovereign country. The short-lived union produced one of the region's heroes, **Francisco Morazán**. A dashing military leader, Morazán was elected President of Central America, and enacted liberal reforms such as freedom of speech, trial by jury and separation of church and state. Francisco Morazán Department is named after him, as is Tegucigalpa's Central Park, which also bears his statue.

In the 1850s, a scoundrel (or "grey-eyed man of destiny") named **William Walker** came into the Central American picture. In those days, if you had a small band of bloodthirsty and ruthless pals, and some guns and powder, you could march into a small country, declare yourself in charge, and begin to live the good life on the backs of whomever you could find in the area to oppress. *Filibuster* was the word used to describe this activity.

With financing from Wall Street tycoon Cornelius Vanderbilt (who had shipping interests in the region) and the tacit support of the US government, Walker was able to take control of Nicaragua. He planned the conquest of the other four nations in the region, but when he crossed Vanderbilt, granting use of the trans-isthmus trade route to a rival company, the US withdrew its support, and helped the locals to develop a military force to resist Walker. Eventually Walker was captured and executed by the British at Trujillo, where he is buried.

The late nineteenth century was another age of imperialism - this time by US and European companies that carved out economic empires in the young Central American nations. US mining interests extracted sweetheart deals to build huge mines, dug up big profits and left holes in the ground. British banks loaned the

Honduran government huge amounts for railroads that never got built. But the biggest exploiters of all were the **banana companies**.

Three large US fruit companies gained control of enormous areas along the North Coast, much of it given to the companies for a song by corrupt local officials. For decades the banana companies ran much of Honduras as if it were their own private country, using bribery and/or violence to keep the freebies flowing and labor organization down. On several occasions, the US military intervened when the Hondurans got uppity. Banana workers staged a major strike in 1954, which ended with them being granted some basic labor protections.

In 1969, Honduras fought the so-called **Soccer War** with neighboring El Salvador. For many years, farmers had been spilling over the border between poor Honduras and even-poorer El Salvador. In 1969, the government said they had to go, and thousands were thrown out of the country.

As fate would have it, the two countries were scheduled to play a series of three soccer matches for the World Cup. The games led to riots in which several people were killed. The Salvadoran air force and army attacked Honduras. However, the Hondurans counterattacked, and the war became a stalemate. Finally, the Organization of American States negotiated a cease-fire. The border dispute was only settled in 1980.

In 1979, a party called the **Sandinistas** overthrew Nicaraguan dictator Anastasio Somoza and established a left-leaning socialist government. The US government, fearing the establishment of a Communist state on our doorstep, sent aid to various groups opposed to the Sandinistas, which were collectively referred to as the **Contras**.

By and by, human rights groups began reporting that the Contras were indulging in attacks on civilians, torture, rape and other typical guerilla behavior, as well as destroying schools, health clinics and power stations. A report by Congress confirmed many of the accusations, and the US State Department declared the Contras to be a terrorist group. In 1982, the US Congress passed the **Boland Amendment**, which forbade any further aid to the Contras.

The administration of **Ronald Reagan** searched for creative ways to secretly continue to funnel support to the Contras, spearheaded by a shady character called **Oliver North**, an old Central America hand with ties to drug-smuggling Panamanian strongman Manuel Noriega. In the roadless and lawless expanses of La Moskitia and Olancho on the Honduras/Nicaragua border, guerilla armies, loyal only to their *comandantes*, mingled with drug smugglers and colorful soldiers of fortune from around the globe, witnessed only by the monkeys and the birds.

The shady doings culminated in the so-called **Iran-Contra Affair** of 1986-1987, in which high-ranking officials of the Reagan administration were found guilty of selling weapons to the US's enemies in Iran, and funneling the profits to the Contras.

During the "Lost Decade," the US poured vast amounts of military aid into Honduras. The government, led by **President Roberto Suazo Cordova** and military commander-in-chief **General Gustavo Alvarez Martinez**, began a campaign of repression against their own leftists. Political dissidents, labor leaders and priests were imprisoned, threatened and tortured. If that didn't shut you up, the infamous **Battalion 3-16** might come for you in the middle of the night, and you would never be heard from again.

As bad as it was, the repression here was small-scale compared to what went on in El Salvador and Guatemala, and most of the Honduran military was appalled by the nasty tactics. General Alvarez was eventually overthrown and exiled by fellow officers.

The decades of civil war in the region finally came to an end with an agreement mediated by Costa Rican president **Óscar Arias**.

In 1998, **Hurricane Mitch** dealt a severe blow to Honduras. 5,000 people were killed and 1.5 million made homeless. Not only the coasts were devastated – landslides killed many in the shantytowns around Tegucigalpa. Crops were destroyed and bridges and highways were washed away. An alphabet soup of aid agencies from around the world came to help with the recovery. Many remain in the country today.

Honduras's political system is reasonably stable. The current president, **Manuel Zelaya** of the Liberal Party, took office in January 2006. Honduras has five official political parties, but the most powerful are the **PNH** and **PLH**, or the Nationalist and Liberal parties for short. The two parties have traded power back and forth for the past 20 years or so, rewarding their supporters with jobs and government contracts in a cyclical fashion. Most observers of Honduran politics see little difference between the policies of the two parties: both tend to serve the interests of the wealthy elite. Sound familiar?

ESSENTIAL SPANISH

PLEASANTRIES

Please - *por favor*
Thank you - *gracias*
You're welcome - *de nada*
Excuse me - *perdóneme, permiso* or *discúlpame*
Good day - *buenos días*
Good night - *buenas noches*
Goodbye - *adiós*
Hello - *hola*
How are you? - *¿Como está Usted?*
Fine - *muy bien*
Pleased to meet you - *mucho gusto*

EVERYDAY PHRASES

Yes - *sí*
No - *no*
I don't know. - *No sé.*
Do you speak English? - *¿Habla Usted inglés?*
I don't speak Spanish. - *Yo no hablo español.*
Where? - *¿Donde?*
When? - *¿Cuando?*

Why? – *¿Por que?*
Because – *porque*
How much? – *¿Cuanto?*
How do you say… – *¿Como se dice…?*
Today – *hoy*
Tomorrow – *mañana*
I would like – *quisiera*
Here – *aquí*
There – *allá*
More – *mas*
Less – *menos*
Much – *mucho*
Little – *poco*
Large – *grande*
Small – *pequeño*
Good – *bueno*
Bad – *malo*

TRAVEL TERMS
Hotel – *(el) hotel*
Bank – *(el) banco*
Money – *(el) dinero*
Airport – *(el) aeropuerto*
Taxi – *(el) taxi*
Bus – *(el) autobús*
Car – *(el) coche, carro*
Bathrooms – *(los) baños*
Gas station – *(la) bomba, gasolinera*
How far is . . . – *¿Que distancia es . . . ?*
Road, highway – *(la) carretera*
Street – *(la) calle*
Avenue – *(la) avenida*

EATING & DRINKING (*comer y tomar*)
Meat – *(la) carne*
Beef – *(el) bistéc*
Pork – *(el) cerdo*
Chicken – *(el) pollo*
Fish – *(el) pescado*
Seafood – *(los) mariscos*

Shrimp – *(los) camarones*
Vegetables – *(los) legumbres*
Fruits – *(las) frutas*
Pineapple – *(la) piña*
Banana – *(el) plátano, banano*
Orange – *(la) naranja*
Apple – *(la) manzana*
Guava – *(la) guayaba*
Water – *(el) agua*
Milk – *(la) leche*
Coffee – *(el) café*
Tea – *(el) té*
Beer – *(la) cerveza*
Red Wine/White Wine – *vino tinto/vino blanco*
Glass of water – *(la) taza de agua*
Glass of wine – *(la) copa de vino*
Soft drink – *(el) refresco*
Smoothie – *(el) batido, licuado*
Juice – *(el) jugo*

HONDURAN TERMS

Balneario – swimming place, hot springs
Beneficio – coffee factory
Bomba – gas station
Catracho(a) – Honduran person
Champa – thatched hut, usually a small beachfront restaurant
Collectivo – a collective taxi, van or boat
Comedor – inexpensive local restaurant or diner
Fauna silvestre – wildlife
Ganja – marijuana (actually Jamaican slang)
Guaro – local cane liquor
Hora americana – more or less on time
Hospedaje – cheap lodging place
Máquila – factory, usually refers to a plant producing textiles for export to the US
María – taxi meter
Milpa – cornfield, usually refers to a subsistence farm
Mota – marijuana
Paila – pickup truck, the only way to get to many remote destinations

Pipante – a dugout canoe, the way one gets around in the Moskitia region
Pulpería – small grocery store
Punta – the popular music of the Garífuna
Sendero – nature trail
Vigilante – caretaker or park ranger
Yabba ding-ding – term used in the Bay Islands for a native artifact

PRONUNCIATION

It's important to have a basic idea of pronunciation, so that you can at least pronounce place names correctly. Spanish is a phonetic language, meaning that words are almost always spelled just as they sound.

Vowels are pronounced roughly as follows:
a – as in *father*
e – between *e* in *get* and *a* in *same*
i – as in *magazine*
o – as in *phone*
u – as in *prune*

There are **no silent vowels**. For example, *coche* (car) is pronounced KO-chay.

A written accent on a vowel means that it is stressed, as in Copán (ko-Pahn).

Consonants are pronounced roughly the same as in English, except:

c – like *k* before *a*, *o* or *u*; like *s* before *e* or *i*
h – always silent
j – like *h* in *home*
ll – like *y* in *yet*
ñ – like *ni* in *union*
z – like *s*

INDEX